M000085393

LUFTWAFFE
FIGHTER ACE

0 11557 03593 3

The Stackpole Military History Series

THE AMERICAN CIVIL WAR

Cavalry Raids of the Civil War
Ghost, Thunderbolt, and
  Wizard
Pickett's Charge
Witness to Gettysburg

WORLD WAR I

Doughboy War

WORLD WAR II

After D-Day
Armor Battles of the
  Waffen-SS, 1943–45
Armoured Guardsmen
Army of the West
Australian Commandos
The B-24 in China
Backwater War
The Battle of Sicily
Battle of the Bulge, Vol. 1
Battle of the Bulge, Vol. 2
Beyond the Beachhead
Beyond Stalingrad
The Brandenburger
  Commandos
The Brigade
Bringing the Thunder
The Canadian Army and the
  Normandy Campaign
Coast Watching in
  World War II
Colossal Cracks
A Dangerous Assignment
D-Day Deception
D-Day to Berlin
Destination Normandy
Dive Bomber!
A Drop Too Many
Eagles of the Third Reich
Eastern Front Combat
Exit Rommel
Fist from the Sky
Flying American Combat
  Aircraft of World War II
Forging the Thunderbolt
Fortress France
The German Defeat in the
  East, 1944–45
German Order of Battle, Vol. 1
German Order of Battle, Vol. 2
German Order of Battle, Vol. 3
The Germans in Normandy

Germany's Panzer Arm in
  World War II
GI Ingenuity
Goodwood
The Great Ships
Grenadiers
Hitler's Nemesis
Infantry Aces
Iron Arm
Iron Knights
Kampfgruppe Peiper at the
  Battle of the Bulge
The Key to the Bulge
Kursk
Luftwaffe Aces
Luftwaffe Fighter Ace
Massacre at Tobruk
Mechanized Juggernaut or
  Military Anachronism?
Messerschmitts over Sicily
Michael Wittmann, Vol. 1
Michael Wittmann, Vol. 2
Mountain Warriors
The Nazi Rocketeers
No Holding Back
On the Canal
Operation Mercury
Packs On!
Panzer Aces
Panzer Aces II
Panzer Commanders of the
  Western Front
Panzer Gunner
The Panzer Legions
Panzers in Normandy
Panzers in Winter
The Path to Blitzkrieg
Penalty Strike
Red Road from Stalingrad
Red Star under the Baltic
Retreat to the Reich
Rommel's Desert Commanders
Rommel's Desert War
Rommel's Lieutenants
The Savage Sky
The Siegfried Line
A Soldier in the Cockpit
Soviet Blitzkrieg
Stalin's Keys to Victory
Surviving Bataan and Beyond
T-34 in Action
Tank Tactics
Tigers in the Mud
Triumphant Fox

The 12th SS, Vol. 1
The 12th SS, Vol. 2
Twilight of the Gods
The War against Rommel's
  Supply Lines
War in the Aegean
Wolfpack Warriors
Zhukov at the Oder

THE COLD WAR / VIETNAM

Cyclops in the Jungle
Expendable Warriors
Flying American Combat
  Aircraft: The Cold War
Here There Are Tigers
Land with No Sun
Phantom Reflections
Street without Joy
Through the Valley

WARS OF THE MIDDLE EAST

Never-Ending Conflict

GENERAL MILITARY HISTORY

Carriers in Combat
Cavalry from Hoof to Track
Desert Battles
Guerrilla Warfare
Ranger Dawn
Sieges

LUFTWAFFE FIGHTER ACE

From the Eastern Front
to the Defense of the Homeland

Norbert Hannig

STACKPOLE
BOOKS

Published in paperback in 2009 by
STACKPOLE BOOKS
5067 Ritter Road
Mechanicsburg, PA 17055
www.stackpolebooks.com

LUFTWAFFE FIGHTER ACE, by Norbert Hannig, was originally published in
hard cover by Grub Street. Copyright © 2004 by Norbert Hannig and John Weal.
Paperback edition by arrangement with Grub Street. All rights reserved.

Cover design by Tracy Patterson

Printed in the United States of America

10 9 8 7 6 5 4 3 2 1

Library of Congress Cataloging-in-Publication Data

Hannig, Norbert.
  Luftwaffe fighter ace : from the Eastern Front to the defense of the homeland /
Norbert Hannig.
      p. cm. — (Stackpole military history series)
  Originally published: London : Grub Street, 2004.
  Includes index.
  ISBN 978-0-8117-3593-3 (pbk.)
  1. Hannig, Norbert. 2. World War, 1939–1945—Aerial operations, German. 3.
World War, 1939–1945—Campaigns—Eastern Front. 4. World War, 1939–1945—
Personal narratives, German. 5. Fighter pilots—Germany—Biography. I. Title.
  D787.H28 2009
  940.54'4943092—dc22
  [B]
                              2008048376

Contents

Foreword

Mine was the generation that was not granted the "mercy of a later birth", as ex-Chancellor Helmut Kohl so tellingly phrased it. Coming into the world in the aftermath of the First World War, I – and countless others like me – grew up fated to become embroiled in the Second.

In 1918 Germany was not the sea of ruins that she was in 1945. After the first great conflict her towns and cities had remained intact, her industries continued to produce and her infrastructure to function. The physical damage may have been minimal, but there was almost total internal, civil and economic collapse. The monarchy had been toppled, unemployment and inflation raged, and civil unrest became civil war.

Then an unknown corporal from the First World War took the decision to become a politician. His propaganda was simple but effective: he promised bread and work, the betterment of everyday life both morally and economically, the scrapping of the Treaty of Versailles, which had placed such a huge burden of debt on the country, and Germany's re-emergence as an equal among the nations of Europe.

When Adolf Hitler came to power in 1933 there were six million unemployed. "Give me four years", he urged. Few now remember that he kept those original promises. There was food and work for all. A sense of purpose and order was restored. And ambitious building programmes were begun.

But there was a hidden agenda. For every metre of autobahn laid, how many shells were produced? There were signs, of course; Hermann Göring's stated preference for guns rather than butter perhaps the most blatant of them. But the majority of the population – and as a teenager growing up in Silesia, I freely confess to being one of them – was unaware that they were being prepared for another conflict.

When it came the propaganda intensified. Ours was the age group it was aimed at, and we gladly answered the call. We also suffered the consequences. I lost my father, a brother and my homeland. Millions of others around the world paid a much higher price.

Prologue

Silesia, Summer 1944

"Achtung – am attacking!" I came in about 300 metres above the right-hand bomber of the high squadron. Matching my speed to his, I side-slipped down towards his tail, got in close behind him and aimed at his two starboard engines. Pieces flew off his wing as my shells struck home. Bright flames streamed from his engines... I continued to fire... an inferno erupted as his wing tanks went up. As I dived away I saw the bombs tumbling from his belly.

My fighter suddenly shuddered and I heard a loud rattling noise. I had been hit by return fire. I steepened my dive to get out of danger. All seemed in order, but as I began to pull out of my descent both undercarriage legs flopped down and locked. Try as I might I couldn't retract them again. The little 'wheels down and locked' indicator rods sticking up out of each wing refused to budge. Although there was still no sign of any enemy fighters, it was unhealthy to remain flying around for too long with my undercarriage on display for all to see. And to attempt a three-pointer on the uneven ground below would be tantamount to suicide; the risk of flipping over onto my back was too great. I had to find the nearest airfield, and quickly...

CHAPTER 1

Gliding as a Sport

My flying career began with a conversation I had with a school friend in the upper fifth shortly after Easter 1940. He belonged to the Flieger-Hitlerjugend, a branch of the general Hitler Youth movement, whose aim was to promote gliding as a sport among boys aged between 14 and 18. Its members were taught to fly gliders free of charge by instructors from the NSFK (National Socialist Flying Corps). This corps, itself a part of the political SA, was the umbrella organization responsible for furthering the cause of all things aeronautical among an already air-conscious German public. As such it had taken over, and now controlled, every aspect of sports flying in the country.

But when my classmate suggested that I team up with him and learn to fly too, I foresaw a slight problem. Five years earlier, at the age of eleven, I had joined the Jungvolk. Modelled along the lines of the scout movement, the Jungvolk was for youngsters not yet old enough to enter the Hitler Youth. When I reached my fourteenth birthday, however, I had decided not to transfer my allegiance, but rather to stay with the Jungvolk and become a senior leader. Since that time I had worked my way up through the ranks and was now a Fähnleinführer (troop leader), in charge of a troop of 150 lads.

Despite my 'advanced' years I therefore still belonged to the Jungvolk. And as a member of this junior organization I was not entitled, strictly speaking, to join the Flieger-Hitlerjugend. But if this difficulty could be overcome, I would grab the opportunity like a shot. To be able to fly had been my boyhood dream since the days of making paper aeroplanes. So my school friend made the necessary enquiries, I was accepted, and thus embarked upon my life of flying.

In the Whitsun holidays of 1940 the pair of us, both in uniform, set off by bike from Zobten, the village where we lived, for the nearby town of Bunzlau. This was the regional centre of what was then our part of Lower Silesia, but which is now in Poland. On arriving in Bunzlau we made our way to the NSFK workshops where we reported to the duty instructor. He in turn took us to the head of the establishment, an NSFK Sturmführer, who greeted us in a fatherly fashion with a smile and a friendly handshake. After asking a few questions, he briefly outlined for me the daily routine of a gliding school.

I was assigned to a group of fourteen Flieger-Hitlerjugend who were busy loading an SG-38 training glider on to a truck. This was in preparation for the drive out to the slopes next morning for a day's flying. Two other groups were similarly engaged. Once all three gliders had been securely stowed, there was an hour's lecture on the theory and practice of flight. Then the following day's programme and duties were read out before it was time for supper. Once this was over we spent a convivial evening getting to know one another.

These few hours were enough to make me feel completely at home in the company of my new friends. The next morning I woke, washed, dressed and breakfasted as usual. But then began a new routine: morning parade and roll-call, followed by the order to climb aboard the vehicles. Soon our small convoy – a van, three trucks each carrying a glider, and an ambulance (!) – were on the road and heading out to the practice slopes.

The weather was anything but good. Clouds chased each other across the sky and gusts of wind rattled the tree-tops. The practice slope turned out to be little more than a slight dip in the ground on the side of a gentle hill, at present covered with lush grass which would no doubt later be cut as hay for cattle-feed. Our convoy came to a halt on the path running along the crest of the hill. The gliders, which had been dismantled for the journey, wings removed and tied firmly alongside the fuselages, were unloaded and carefully re-assembled under the watchful eye of the instructors. First the wings were re-attached to the fuselages by means of socket bolts secured with split-pins. Then the braided steel bracing wires were connected up and tightened to bring the wings into proper alignment.

Special care had to be taken when connecting the control wires from the stick to the ailerons and elevators, and from the foot pedals to the rudder. Get these the wrong way round and it could spell disaster. A quick check proved that all was well. Pull back on the stick and the tailplane control surfaces moved upwards. This would cause the glider's nose to lift and the machine to climb. Push the stick forward and the opposite effect would be achieved: the elevators moved downwards and the glider went into a dive. Moving the stick to the left resulted in the simultaneous deployment of the two wing ailerons, the one on the left being raised and that on the right being lowered, to give a bank to port. Again, move the stick to the right and the reverse effect would be the result: left aileron down, right aileron up, and the glider would bank to starboard. The two foot pedals in front of the pilot's simple plank seat were connected to the rudder. Press down on the left-hand pedal and the rudder would move to the left causing the machine to turn to port. Depress the right-hand pedal and the glider turned to starboard.

What sounds so complicated on paper was, in reality, quite simple. The control stick allowed you to fly straight and level, bank to the left and right, or dive and climb. The rudder pedals enabled you to turn to left or right. Learn to co-ordinate these hand and foot movements and you had complete control of the glider in both the horizontal and vertical axes, which meant you could curve without losing height or even pull loops.

But there was one other factor which had to be taken into account at all times – at take-off, during flight and when landing – and that was airspeed. Sufficient speed had to be achieved, and maintained, to give the wings lift. At zero km/h the glider will remain firmly nailed to the ground. Only when a predetermined airflow speed is achieved will lift overcome the earth's gravitational pull and allow the glider, and its pilot, to take to the air. Once aloft, if this speed is reduced there is a corresponding decrease in lift and the glider will sink back towards the ground.

The landing itself posed problems of its own. In order to carry out a controlled return to earth a certain amount of airspeed had to be conserved. Once safely and smoothly down this excess speed was quickly lost through the braking effect of the landing skid and the glider was consequently brought to a halt. Only then could the pilot climb out on to terra firma. So much for the theory. . .

In practice it was much more straightforward. The SG-38 training glider was a very simple wooden affair. The pilot was provided with a small bench-like seat. In front of him were two pedals, between his knees the control stick, above his head a pair of wings each with its aileron control surface, behind his back the tail assembly complete with rudder and elevators, and beneath him the keel beam with its spring-mounted skid undercarriage. Held securely in place by belly and shoulder straps, the pilot perched on the aforementioned plank seat, his feet in the two pedals and the control stick clutched in either his right or left hand. There he sat at one with nature, completely exposed to the elements and without a single instrument to distract his attention. Airspeed had to be judged by the humming of the wind in the wires holding the glider together. The higher the pitch, the faster he was flying.

For most beginners the very fact of sitting out in the open high above the ground without any form of cockpit or fuselage covering they could hold on to, or hide behind, took a lot of getting used to, to say the very least.

This is why lessons began on the ground with so-called 'seat familiarisation'. The instructor stood at the end of one wing, usually the left, and moved it up and down. It was the pupil's job to try to keep the glider on an even keel by judicious use of the stick, moving it to the left or right to correct the balance. Once he had mastered this he progressed to the next step: a 'slide'.

The glider was launched by means of a rubber bungee cord fitted with a metal ring which was attached to a hook on the front of the aircraft. (On actual take-offs this ring automatically uncoupled itself from the hook as the glider flew past overhead and the released cord fell to the ground.) After being hooked up to the glider the rubber cord was laid out in front of it in a V-shape and the launch crew, some five to eight lads on each arm of the V, positioned themselves along its length ready to pick it up. At the same time other trainees sat in a line behind the tail of the glider, each digging his heels firmly into the ground and holding tightly to the man in front. The first in line gripped the retaining cord fastened to the back of the glider and all now awaited the instructor's command: "Pull...!"

The launch crew picked up the cord and started walking slowly forwards until the rubber was stretched tight, while those at the rear of the glider took up the strain. Then came the second order: "Ru-u-u-n!!"

Now the launch crew began to gallop down the hill. The rubber V became tauter until it was stretched to its limit and the crew, unable to pull it any tighter, were running on the spot.

The instructor directed his third command at those hanging on to the tail of the glider: "Release!!!"

With a jolt the glider began to move. As it gathered momentum it was now in the hands of the pilot. The less tension in the rubber cord, the shorter the distance of the slide or flight.

In this instance it was a slide, the glider remaining on the ground as it slithered and bumped down the hill, allowing the trainee pilot to get used to the feel of the controls and the sensation of sitting out in the open, buffeted by the slipstream. After the slide came the first few tentative hops. And only then would an actual glide be allowed – straight ahead and only for a second or two at first, but later for a full minute or more. The whole procedure reminded me strongly of the paper aeroplanes I used to make as a boy out of Kornfrank coffee packets.

As everybody took strict turns, there were at least fourteen launches before one could have another go. And after each and every take-off the glider had to be loaded on to the 'Bimbo', a two-wheeled cart fitted with a cradle and clamp into which the landing skid of the SG-38 was screwed, before the whole rig was manhandled back up to the starting point by sheer muscle power alone. It was healthy if somewhat sweaty work. But everybody set to with a will, knowing that the quicker the Bimbo was pushed back up the hill, the sooner it would be their turn to take the controls again.

Which was all very well on a nice sunny say with a steady breeze blowing, but not on this particular Saturday before Whitsun, with its gusting winds and fleecy white clouds scudding across the blue vault of the sky. We in our beginners' group contented ourselves with slides and the shortest of hops close to the ground. But the other two groups were practising for their A certificates, which demanded a full minute's free flight in a straight line.

They were taking off some 50 metres further along the hillside from us. The launch crew and the anchormen were waiting for the commands: pull – run – release! We watched as the training glider lifted off. But suddenly it went into a steep climb, and then seemed to stand still in mid-air before tipping forwards. Unable to recover, it slammed straight into the ground. There was a terrific noise, the wings snapped their bracing wires and were splintered into matchwood. This was the first total write-off I had ever seen – and I had not even got into the air yet! The pilot was hanging in his seat. The launch crew hurried to release him, carefully undoing his harness and loading him into the ambulance to be taken to hospital. He had sustained several broken ribs and was suffering from shock. On the whole it was considered that he had escaped lightly.

We and the other group carried on with our training and practice flying respectively. But two hours later came the unmistakeable sound of another crash. This time the pilot had landed too hard. His machine bounced back up into the air and came down again one wing low. The wingtip had dug in and the whole mainplane was damaged. Only we beginners still had a flyable aircraft. But it was now decided to call a halt to the day's activities. The wreckage of the two gliders was loaded onto the trucks and we set off back to the workshops. Thus ended my first glider lesson.

This experience ought to have cured me once and for all of any desire to pursue a career in flying. But, if anything, the opposite was the case.

Everybody was kept busy in the workshop for the next two days making good the damage suffered. I was no stranger to woodworking. I had my own set of carpenter's tools at home and had already built a canoe with the help and guidance of a boat builder who was employed in the carpentry shop on Count von Nostitz's estate.

My experience came in handy as we all sawed, planed, sanded and glued away, slowly putting the gliders back together again. Nobody seemed too disheartened by the two crashes – nobody was blamed or punished, and we all helped each other. It was this spirit of togetherness which made such an impression on me. Now, more than ever, I wanted to become one of this community – you might almost say brotherhood – of flyers.

As I had already arranged to take my Fähnlein of 150 Jungvolk youngsters to summer camp during the long school holidays, it was some time before I was again able to participate fully in glider training practice. The first opportunity came during the autumn holidays of 1940 when I attended the A certificate course, again at Bunzlau, and in the company of my by-now familiar group of Flieger-Hitlerjugend comrades.

In the meantime the year 1940 had brought a move of house for the Hannig family. My father had been teaching at the small Catholic school in Zobten. But when it was announced that this was to be combined with the village's bigger Protestant school, he decided it was time for a change. Preferring not to teach in a large mixed-religion establishment, he opted instead to take over the tiny single-class Catholic school at Hermannsdorf, a village less than 15 kilometres from Bunzlau. Our family lived in the schoolhouse itself.

Our leaving Zobten meant that I could no longer continue my duties as Fähnleinführer of the local Jungvolk group. I was, however, allowed to choose my successor. He was the son of the head gardener on the von Nostitz estate. I also bequeathed him the canoe which had given me so many hours of pleasure on the nearby River Bober.

Having resigned from my post with Zobten Jungvolk, I neglected to report or re-register with the local Hermannsdorf branch of the organization. Nobody noticed the omission. I continued to wear my uniform whenever the occasion demanded – such as on national holidays or Party days – at the high school I attended in Löwenberg, and also at weekends when taking part in glider-training sessions with the Flieger-Hitlerjugend in Bunzlau. I was paying no subscriptions anywhere, my name did not feature on any roll, and I was being taught to fly – what more could anybody ask?

In fact, as my uniform included the green-and-white corded shoulder lanyard of a Fähnleinführer (more commonly known as an Affenschaukel or monkey swing), I was constantly being appointed group leader by those in charge of our glider training at Bunzlau. This meant that I was held responsible for the behaviour of the group when not actually in the classroom or on the slopes. Although I was not a member of the Hitler Youth – nor even, technically, of the Jungvolk by this time – nobody seemed either to mind or to care. There were many such glaring holes in the supervision and organization of the Nationalist Socialist state, which was not the well-oiled and super-efficient machine as so often portrayed in the many post-war accounts of the period.

So the autumn holidays of 1940 saw me cycling yet again to Bunzlau. By now the beginner's rounds of seat familiarization, slides and hops were all well behind me. The SG-38 training glider had become a trusty friend, which I had learned to control with confidence. The sudden thrust in the small of the back, which came a split second after the command to release, was by now a familiar sensation. With my right hand holding the stick perfectly upright (I always used the left to grip the small bench seat just in case) and my feet jammed firmly on the pedals, I was all ready to go as the glider catapulted forwards and immediately began to climb.

The launch crew disappeared beneath me as I soared over their heads. The bracing wires sang like a finely tuned violin. The grass on the hillside, which at first had seemed to be racing past just beneath my wings, decelerated as I gained more height. I was flying! The wind in the wires took on a deeper, softer tone. Now it was a matter of holding the glider straight and level and trying to keep the same steady note thrumming in my ears.

All too soon I was sinking back towards the ground. The grass below began to pick up speed again. It was time to haul slowly back on the stick in order to reduce speed and prepare for the landing. When just above the ground the stick had to be pulled back slowly but steadily until the skid touched the earth and the machine began to slide across the grass. The skid then started to bite, acting as a brake. The machine jolted and slithered down the hill for a few more metres before finally coming to a standstill. The glider would then tip gently over to one side until the end of one wing was resting on the ground. One had to remain in this position while the launch crew came whooping and hollering down the hillside. Only when they had hold of the machine again were you allowed to undo your harness and climb off. Another free flight successfully accomplished.

The first flights of this kind only lasted for 20 to 30 seconds. But one's confidence and ability steadily grew until, at last, more hands were added to the launch crew and the full length of the rubber bungee cord was used to give the maximum possible thrust for take-off. This enabled you to stay aloft for a good minute or more.

My instructor professed himself satisfied with my progress. I was to be allowed to try for my A certificate. This required the candidate to maintain a straight and level course for a minimum of 60 seconds. A few last-minute words of instruction and advice and I was all set. I followed the familiar routine, but this time I was conscious of the fact that my flight was being measured by the stopwatch. The result: 1 minute and 25 seconds. I'd done it! I also knew what was coming as the launch crew streamed down the hill in my wake. True to custom, I was bundled across the plank seat and given a hefty slap on the backside by each and every one of them by way of congratulation.

The glider was then loaded on to the Bimbo and dragged back up the slope. At the top I reported to the instructor, who congratulated me in a decidedly more decorous manner with a hearty handshake. At the end of the course I was presented with my certificate. Happy and contented, I was now entitled to wear the badge of an A-rated glider pilot: a single pair of silver gull wings in a silver circle on a blue background.

While I had been taking my first faltering aerial steps in the quiet backwater that was Lower Silesia in the summer and early autumn of 1940, momentous events had been happening elsewhere. The Wehrmacht had fought and won the Battle of France. But after the British Army escaped from Dunkirk, the Führer's offer of a negotiated peace had been summarily rejected by Prime Minister Churchill. Now the Battle of Britain was in full swing. For us fifth formers, all sixteen or seventeen years old, it was clear that the war was going to last some little while yet. We knew that when we reached eighteen years of age and moved up into the sixth form we would be entitled to volunteer for military service. We could hardly wait. Full of the idealism of youth we regarded it as a matter of honour to serve one's country. But not only that. We were also fully aware of the fact that we were all rapidly approaching call-up age anyway, and that conscripts could not choose which branch of the armed forces they wished to serve in. And for me one thing was already certain: I wanted to become a fighter pilot.

But things hadn't got to that stage yet. I was still sitting at my desk in the Hindenburg High School for boys in Löwenberg where life was peaceful, if now somewhat regulated by the introduction of coupons and ration books. The only way we could follow the course of the war was by the weekly newsreels in the cinema, radio broadcasts and the newspapers.

The Battle of Britain was still in progress when I attended a second glider training course which was designed to take pupils to B certificate level. This demanded a flight of at least two minutes over a set route including an S-bend. As before, I applied to the NSFK officer in charge and was allotted a place on the course in Lauban, the neighbouring district to Löwenberg. I duly turned up in full Jungvolk uniform complete with the green-and-white monkey swing on my left shoulder. And once again I found myself being appointed group leader without the Hitler Youth members of the course having any say in the matter.

We were billeted in a country inn. The main hall was put at our disposal for lectures and as living quarters. We slept in the adjoining hay store, washed in the running water of the fountain in the yard, and were fed from a field kitchen. Everything was completely free and very well prepared. This time we were to fly SG-38 gliders which had a thin covering of plywood surrounding the pilot's seat. At long last we felt as if we were sitting in a real aircraft, not perching precariously on a narrow plank in the open air.

The course began as usual in the classroom or, more accurately, in the main hall of the inn. Everybody paid close attention as the instructor explained the control movements needed to execute a turn. Previously we had only flown in a straight line. But to get our B certificates we would have to make a 90° turn to the left, then a full 180° reversal of course to the right, before another 90° left put us back on the original heading ready for a smooth touch-down in the designated landing area.

The site itself was a large sloping meadow bordered by a turnip field on the left and a potato patch on the right. Way down towards the far end of the turnip field stood a large, solitary fruit tree. The instructor warned us against this tree, saying that it possessed "magical magnetic qualities" that attempted to lure every budding glider pilot towards it. We dismissed this absurd suggestion with loud laughter. But in the days to come, after starting the flying part of the course in perfect autumn weather, we began to wonder whether there wasn't an element of truth in the instructor's dire warning. Time and again pupils would come down, not on the wide expanse of meadow, but in the turnip field heading straight for the 'magic' tree.

Every time this happened the lower bracing wires, which connected the undersides of the glider's wings to the keel of the landing skid, would cut a swathe through the standing crops. First the leaves would be sent flying in all directions, and then the tops of the turnips themselves would be neatly sliced off before the skid dug into the loose earth and the machine came to a stop. This was a clear case of 'damage to public property', for which the farmer could justifiably have claimed compensation. But he was a wholehearted supporter of our activities and waived any rights to financial recompense.

Wherever we happened to land, whether on the meadow or among the turnips, the glider still had to be loaded aboard the Bimbo and hauled back up to the top of the hill. As our flights were now anything up to a full kilometre in length, this was hard physical work in the warm autumn weather and required a lot of effort, even for fit and active youngsters like ourselves. At the end of a day's flying training everybody was absolutely worn out. The evening meals served from the field kitchen, always of generous proportions and well cooked, were devoured with relish. After supper and the usual evening cleaning details, we were all ready for bed and a good night's sleep.

At seven o'clock the next morning we would be roused from our sleeping bags to begin another day: PT, ablutions, tidying up our sleeping quarters, cleaning the courtyard, and then breakfast before forming up to march out to the gliding slopes. Although we always had a medic with us, nobody fell ill or was seriously hurt. The minor cuts and abrasions we all acquired during the course of the day were cured with copious amounts of iodine (arrgh!).

After a fortnight I flew the required S-manoeuvre in the given time and thus qualified for the B certificate. This meant I could now display two sets of silver gull wings in the silver ring of my glider badge. I wanted to add the third and final set before the time came to volunteer for the Luftwaffe.

The winter of 1940/41 brought the usual seasonal conditions to our tiny corner of the world. The thermometer dropped to 15°C below zero and some 30 to 50 centimetres of snow covered the ground. The daily trip to and from the local station, which formed part of my journey to school in Löwenberg and which was made by bike throughout the rest of the year, was now done on skis. It was a thoroughly healthy lifestyle. But unfortunately exercise and sport alone are no absolute guarantee against illness – as I had discovered to my cost a couple of years earlier.

While in the upper fourth I had suddenly broken out in a rash and found myself covered in small red spots. The doctor's diagnosis: scarlet fever. I was rushed into the isolation ward of the nearby hospital where I was kept in quarantine for a month. Four weeks of doing absolutely nothing and with no contact whatsoever with the outside world. The days dragged by as I was feeling perfectly fit and had no pains at all. At the end of this time I was given a thorough examination. The scarlet fever had gone and I was no longer contagious. But now the doctor discovered that I was suffering from myocarditis, or inflammation of the heart muscles.

I was moved from the isolation unit into the men's general medical ward. Here, although forbidden to climb stairs or indulge in any other form of physical exercise, I was at least allowed to have visitors. But I still felt absolutely fit and well in myself. It was almost as if I was ill because the doctor said I was ill. There were no obvious symptoms to bring home to me the seriousness of my condition. In an effort to cheer me up the doctor had said, "There's one good thing about your illness, you'll never have to be a soldier." Needless to say, this statement didn't have the effect intended.

After three long months I was finally discharged from hospital – just in time to sit the end of year maths exam. But the lengthy disruption to my schooling, during which time the rest of the class had been introduced to the intricacies of trigonometry, meant that I was well behind. I flunked badly and scored the lowest marks of my entire educational career.

The bout of myocarditis was well in the past, however, and I thought no more about it. But, in the spring of 1941, I suddenly developed severe back pains. These grew steadily worse until they could no longer be ignored. Another visit to the family doctor established the fact that I had contracted a kidney disease. I was put on a strict, salt-free diet and ordered to bed for a fortnight. During the examination I had carefully noted the test that the doctor had carried out to confirm his diagnosis. He had heated a sample of my urine in a test-tube and then added a weak acid solution. The sample had immediately turned cloudy and tiny flakes of albumen had appeared.

My home chemistry set included a couple of test-tubes and I used these to carry out my own test. Producing a sample, I held it over a candle and then carefully poured in a little vinegar. The result was the same. I repeated this process daily and was thus able to monitor my progress. Slowly the cloudiness and flakes of albumen disappeared until, just before the two weeks were up, the sample remained crystal clear. Then it was time to return to the doctor's surgery for a second examination. Here too the test proved negative. The incipient nephritis had been stopped in its tracks and the pains had disappeared.

Not long afterwards I moved up into the sixth form. This heralded the premature ending of my formal education – or so I thought – for I now became eligible to volunteer for military service. With my mind set on joining the Luftwaffe and becoming a fighter pilot, I lost little time in applying to the personnel office of the regional area command in Bunzlau. My various illnesses were forgotten. And as for the doctor's remark about my myocarditis being "a good thing" as it would keep me out of the forces, I took exactly the opposite view. As far as I was concerned, all my ailments were behind me and I couldn't wait to join up.

Fortunately I didn't have to wait for too long. I was soon summoned to attend the obligatory medical examination. I set off quite happily by bike for Bunzlau, convinced in my own mind that I would be accepted. The examination itself was very thorough: heart, lungs, ears, weight and build – all passed with flying colours. But then the chief medical officer called me in and asked whether I had ever had any problems with my kidneys. I told him the truth, only to learn that I was considered unfit for military service as my kidneys were releasing too much albumen. My application was rejected.

My initial feeling was one of complete shock. I had been turned down for the forces on medical grounds. But after considering all my options, I became more determined than ever to get into the Luftwaffe. Somehow this decision would have to be reversed. First it was back to the family doctor to repeat the process that had cured me before, complete with my own tests at home to monitor my albumen levels. Within just a few days I was back to normal – no pains, my urine clear and without a single flake of albumen.

It was shortly after this – towards the end of June 1941, when the campaign against the Soviet Union was only days old – that I was offered the opportunity to take part in another glider course which, if successful, would earn me my C certificate. The course was to be held at Glogau, a town some 70 kilometres away on the River Oder, whose airfield was currently unused by either civilian traffic or military units.

As airfields are rarely built on the side of a hill, glider launches from the flat expanse of Glogau had to be carried out by means of a motorised winch and cable. From the winch situated on one side of the field, the cable was towed by a VW across to the waiting glider on the other side, to which it was then attached by a metal ring. Sitting strapped in the glider, the pilot had to pull back on the stick the moment the winch began to reel the cable back in, slowly at first, but then ever faster. As soon as sufficient speed had built up the glider would leap into the air and start to climb at a steep angle like a child's kite in a stiff breeze.

Just before over-flying the winch a flag would be waved from the ground to signal to the pilot, already high above, to release the cable.

The hook on the nose of the glider would open, allowing the ring to disengage and the cable to fall free. The glider was then in free flight. But if, for any reason, the cable was not released, the aircraft would be dragged down into a near vertical dive which invariably ended with the glider and its unfortunate occupant – for none of us wore parachutes – being smashed to pieces on the ground.

For the C course at Glogau we no longer flew the basic stick-and-string SG-38 training gliders. For the first time we were entrusted with more advanced, enclosed fuselage types such as the Grunau 'Baby' IIA and IIB models built by the firm of Edmund Schneider. The certificate itself demanded a complete circuit of the field, commencing at an altitude of approximately 300 metres and landing back at the point of take-off. Flight times lasted anything from five to ten minutes at an average cruising speed of 55 km/h.

Cable launchings, with the motorised winch reeling in at an ever-increasing rate and the glider being dragged faster and faster across the surface of the field, were very different from the gentle downhill lift-offs at the end of a rubber bungee cord being pulled by a bunch of galloping classmates. The pilot had to hold the stick firmly back in the pit of his stomach, while at the same time keeping a careful watch downwards in order not to miss the all-important wave of the flag signalling the moment to release. That was the great danger: not releasing in time.

The hook release mechanism was simplicity itself and absolutely reliable. You pulled on the release line, the hook opened and gravity did the rest. The metal ring attached to the end of the cable slipped free and the cable fell to the ground. The instructors stressed the importance of this simple action time and again. It was drummed into us that if anything went wrong during the initial climb we were immediately to push the stick forward and release the launch cable.

But what could possibly go wrong in the climb? Everything had worked perfectly so far. It was now my turn to strap myself in again for another practice circuit. After the usual commands from the launch crew off I went in anticipation of the initial hesitant bumps and hops across the grass as the winch took the strain, the quickly gathering speed, the stick back into the stomach, and her nose pointed upwards. The wind blew strongly in my face as I kept a careful eye over the side of the cockpit for the winch crew's signal. But there was still plenty of time yet; I was only halfway through the climb.

Suddenly the line slackened – the winch was not pulling any more. Hanging steeply from the cable and now almost motionless, I found myself reacting instinctively. The hours of tuition paid off. Without pausing to think for a moment, I automatically pushed the stick forward and released the limp cable. Then it was a case of building up sufficient speed in a shallow dive before I could assess my altitude and select a spot on the field for landing. All went well. Even before I had come to a stop the instructor's car was racing across the grass towards me. Climbing out he yelled, "Everything OK?" "Everything fine my end," I replied, "but what went wrong with the winch?"

The crew were already busy checking. It transpired that the motor had run out of petrol and the winch had simply stopped working. This was my first brush with the guardian angel who was to watch over me throughout my flying career.

After this minor drama the C certificate test flight was little more than a formality. I remember it mainly for the feeling of pure joy that engulfed me as I freed myself from the launch cable. I began to sing at the top of my voice, beating time with my right fist against the side of the cockpit. I let my eyes wander over the Silesian landscape as it unfolded beneath me, the fields and meadows, the trim villages, the silver ribbon of the Oder. My ears were filled with the soft sigh of the wind across the slender wings of my steed. I had never felt happier.

After landing came the usual round of congratulations, to which my instructor dryly added the fact that, as there was no engine noise to drown me out, they had heard every word of what I had been singing up there!

With the C certificate achieved and my third set of silver gull wings up, I re-applied three months later to become a volunteer officer candidate in the Luftwaffe. I felt fighting fit and this time was fully resolved to avoid any risks during the initial medical examination. Through my own tests at home I had discovered that a marked drop in my body temperature – say, for example, if my feet got cold – was enough to make my kidneys release that tell-tale albumen. I never felt any pain or ill-effects when they did, but a simple urine test could scupper my chances. Care would have to be taken. And I was determined to be *very* careful.

I knew from the earlier examination that, presumably in order to save time, a number of candidates were instructed to provide a sample in the same beaker. If the urine in the beaker remained clear, then the whole group was passed fit. But if the sample showed the slightest trace of cloudiness, or flakes of albumen, then all had to contribute a second, separate sample to find the 'guilty party'. This is how I had been caught out the first time round. On this occasion I simply handed the half-filled beaker to the man behind me without adding to its contents myself, and thus passed with flying colours. With that hurdle overcome I was now considered fit for military service. But I was not yet in the services.

As a potential officer candidate I still had to go before a selection board and pass yet another medical. At the end of August I was given a date to report to the reception centre in Berlin: 5 September 1941. The written and oral tests in front of a panel of officers did not hold too many terrors for me. But there was still that little matter of the medical examination. 5 September was set aside for travelling to Berlin and reporting there to the Duty NCO who checked the candidates' papers against a list before assigning each to a room and a bed which was to serve as accommodation for the four days' duration of the board examination.

Before supper on that first evening there was another roll-call. The Duty NCO read out each of our names, followed by the branch of the service we had volunteered for and details of the examination we would have to sit. I had put down for flying duties and wanted specifically to be a pilot. But when he called out my name, and then added "To flak" – in effect, assigning me not to flying personnel but to the anti-aircraft artillery arm – I was startled into momentary silence. It was only when he asked in a pleasant enough manner, "Hannig, understood?" that I managed to pull myself together and reply, "Jawohl, Herr Unteroffizier! To flak artillery."

My mind racing, I could only presume that I first had to be inducted and sworn in, irrespective of what it said on the NCO's piece of paper. Once accepted, I could then state my preference for flying duties. As the written, oral and physical examinations were the same for both flak and flying, and we all took them together as a group, this first part of the selection process went off without a hitch.

But then during the night of 7/8 September, the sirens suddenly sounded. RAF Bomber Command was mounting another attack on the capital. Jumping out of bed, we quickly got dressed and trooped down into the air-raid shelter. For the others, the coolness of the unheated shelter no doubt came as a pleasant relief after the day's late summer heat. For me the sudden loss of body warmth meant only one thing – kidney problems. But as flak candidates were not required to undergo any further medical examinations – whereas those volunteering for flight crew had yet to make the trip to Berlin's famous Charité hospital, where they had to face a more stringent medical before they could be passed fit for flying duties – I considered I had had a lucky escape.

At breakfast the next morning, however, I was called in to see the officer in charge of the course, a full colonel. "I see here you volunteered for flight crew. Why are you with the flak group?" he asked. He had my application papers on the desk in front of him and had obviously spotted the error. My explanation, that I had been detailed to join the flak candidates by the Duty NCO upon my arrival, was greeted with a resigned shake of the head. He went on, "The only item outstanding is the flight crew medical. Get yourself over to the Charité immediately and report to the gate. Somebody will take you from there and conduct you through the examination. I have already rung them up and everything has been arranged. Then report back to me here with the result."

Now I really did have a problem: my kidneys and the night spent in the cold air-raid shelter. And not only that – an individual examination upon which rested my entire future. I took the tram to the Charité with very mixed feelings. I was expected and a friendly nurse escorted me to the lift and accompanied me to an upper floor where a doctor was already waiting for me in one of the examination rooms.

I was subjected to the same routine as before: heart, lungs, eyes and ears – all perfectly normal. Then came the urine test. At that moment the doctor was called from the room. I was left alone with the nurse, who gave me a test-tube and turned to light a bunsen burner. The toilet was right next door to the examination room. There was no escape.

I returned to the room and handed the test-tube containing the sample to the nurse. As I did so, I said as casually as I could, "Sister, I'm something of a clairvoyant." She was clearly puzzled and asked, "What do you mean?" I quickly explained: "You will find traces of albumen in my urine sample. We had to spend the night in the air-raid shelter and my feet were like blocks of ice. My kidneys react immediately."

She studied me for a moment, and then looked at the untreated sample, still clear in the test-tube. "I understand you want to be a pilot? Do you have any pains?" "No," I was able to reply in all truthfulness, "I don't feel a thing." With that she went to the sink, poured out the sample and let the tap run to rinse away the evidence. Turning off the bunsen burner, she remarked, "That's all in order then." Just then the doctor re-entered the room and she repeated her words to him. He checked through the result one more time and filled in a lengthy form. Putting all my documents into one large envelope, he handed it to me saying, "All findings normal. Passed fit for flying duties."

12 September would be my eighteenth birthday. I could not have wished for a better present. I had been accepted for military service, had been declared fit for flying duties, and could reckon on being called up before the year was out.

With the benefit of hindsight, such enthusiasm may strike many in today's world as strange, perhaps even incomprehensible. But back then seventeen-year-old schoolboys – which I still was, just – had little or no knowledge of the horrors of war, or of the untold sufferings it had already visited upon countless thousands of people. Nor could any of us have visualised the barbarities and atrocities that were yet to come. In the summer of 1941 my circle of friends all hoped for a speedy and successful end to the war. But before that came about most of us were determined to do our bit by volunteering for active service rather than waiting to be called up.

Of one thing I was sure, however. My joining the Luftwaffe would bring about a fundamental change in my life. There would be long absences from home. We were a caring close-knit family and had been brought up surrounded by love and warmth, from our parents and for each other. I would be the third Hannig brother to join the forces. My two older brothers were already in uniform and had seen action; Kurt with an army signals unit, and Günter with the navy. My younger siblings were still at school. I would miss them all a great deal – especially mother and father. But they would remain with me in heart and mind wherever I was sent.

At the end of September I received my official call-up papers ordering me to report to the 4th Company of Air Training Regiment 33 (4/FlAusbRgt 33) at Detmold on 30 November 1941. I presented these papers as instructed to the school authorities at Löwenberg. As I had already completed my written school exams, I received in return my emergency Abitur certificate, giving my final grades, together with a note to the effect that my education was now completed as I had volunteered for military service.

I knew nothing of my destination except for the song, "Detmold, a beautiful town". But things had changed since those lines were penned. Detmold was now a garrison town dominated by a large barracks complex. I travelled there by train on 29 November and spent my last night as a civilian in a small guesthouse close to the barracks.

I had been instructed to report to the guard-house at the main gate at noon the next day. When I arrived there at 11.45 hours a number of youths of my own age were already standing around waiting. They were all volunteers like myself. One of them joked in a loud voice: "Five more minutes in civvy street and then it'll be nothing but spit and polish." The sentry on duty at the gate, impeccably turned out in full equipment and steel helmet, greeted this sally with a laugh: "Come on in then, lads. We've had the best rooms specially made up for you!"

And so we went. Surrendering our documents, we were formed into a loose column and marched to the admin office of the 4th Company, Air Training Regiment 33: company commander Hauptmann Müller-Gebühr.

My civilian life was over. I was about to embark upon the military career I had so long wanted.

CHAPTER 2

Wartime Training

The Luftwaffe's Air Training Regiments (Fliegerausbildungs-regimenter) had first been established in the spring of 1939. They were created by the simple, and sensible, expedient of amalgamating the existing basic training camps with elementary flying schools. Each Air Training Regiment generally consisted of a basic training battalion and a flying training wing and was thus able to fulfil both functions. All new recruits had first to undergo the three-month basic training course, which taught them the essential rudiments of military life, before they could progress to flight training.

By the time I arrived in Detmold late in 1941 most basic training battalions comprised five or more companies. My regiment was merely providing basic training; we received no flying training. Luckily, we volunteer candidates, all assigned to the 33rd Regiment's 4th Company, were no strangers to barracks life and the parade ground. Our years in the youth organizations meant that we were already familiar with drill movements. Each of us knew how to stand perfectly still to attention, how to about-turn, march in step and come to a halt in unison. As well as how to obey orders we were familiar with the concise and correct military manner of answering questions put by a superior. As a group we could sing on the march at whatever volume required – the louder the better – and on the sports field we could keep up with the best of them.

What we *didn't* know was how to handle weapons such as the Mauser 98k rifle and the MG 34 machine gun. Gas masks were an unknown quantity too, and we lacked all knowledge of infantry tactics and the proper use of terrain. The wording of the military oath, which we would all have to take, and the complexities of international military law were also subjects completely new to us. Despite our youth training we obviously still had an awful lot to learn. And although we had all heard the usual horror stories about instructors delighting in putting raw recruits through the mill, each and every one of us was determined to give of his best.

Our introduction to life in camp began with the customary paperwork, without which no self-respecting orderly room seems to be able to function. But once all the initial bumph was over it was out onto the parade ground to be divided up into individual groups and sections. This was followed by the assignment of rooms, beds and lockers. Then it was off to the clothing store to be fully kitted out, and to the armoury to be issued with weapons. The whole process went like clockwork, even down to the distribution of cold rations. Each of us received one-third of a loaf, a pat of butter, some sausage, cheese and jam, plus an apple or tomato. These were our provisions for breakfast and supper. The midday meal would be eaten in the other ranks' mess hall, which offered a varied menu.

Our first appearance as a company saw us assembled outside the barracks block in full uniform. The parade was taken by the senior warrant officer. Resplendent in his badges of rank, and with the yellow braided duty cord around his right shoulder, he left us in no doubt as to who ruled this particular roost. Like all 'Chiefies', he was proud of the volume of sound he could produce. His bellowed commands were further proof, if any were needed, that we were now part of the military machine. But as we had not yet taken the all-important oath, we could – in theory – still be rejected for one reason or the other. And that was something I wanted to avoid at all costs. So far everything had gone smoothly.

The purpose of the parade was to present the new recruits to their company commander. We were dressed in our blue service uniforms, complete with greatcoats and steel helmets. Bayonets hung at our belts, but we were not yet carrying rifles. Section leaders and instructors stood in front of their men and carried out the commands with them: attention, right dress, eyes front – and wait. When the CO appeared in the doorway 'Chiefy' let rip with his loudest roar yet: "Company… atten-shun!"

Boot heels crashed together, bodies froze, eyes stared straight ahead, fingers stretched in line with seams of trousers – utter silence. You could have heard a pin drop, but nobody had been foolhardy enough to bring anything so unmilitary on parade. Then the next order at full volume: "Eyes right! Reporting to the company commander – all present and correct!"

Our heads snapped to the right as one. The company CO acknowledged the report, thanked Chiefy and addressed us in an almost soft, but pleasantly masculine voice: "Good morning, recruits."

It was exactly ten o'clock. We replied in one voice, "Good morning, Herr Hauptmann!"

Then it was the SWO's turn again: "Eyes front. Stand at ease."

We relaxed our rigid stance and regarded our commanding officer with respectful interest. In a brief speech he bade us welcome and promised that we would be given a thorough training to prepare us for our future careers in the Luftwaffe. He closed with the flyer's traditional words of good luck: "Hals und Beinbruch!" – literally "Break your neck and leg" – and then disappeared back into his office.

Chiefy took charge of the parade again: "We need an orderly for each instructor. Any volunteers? Hands up."

Despite the old adage never to volunteer for anything, my hand was in the air almost before he had finished speaking. I knew that there were definite advantages in being an orderly. Not only was one excused parades when on cleaning duties, but closer personal contact with the NCOs could bring benefits to the whole room. You got to hear in advance, for example, when kit and locker inspections were to be carried out. I was soon on good terms with the corporal to whom I was assigned and he, realising I would never knowingly drop him in it, was able to warn us in good time of many unpleasant surprises which lay in store for us in the weeks ahead.

A second call for volunteers followed close on the heels of the first: "Who has had any experience of waiting at table? We also need five orderlies for the NCOs' canteen. Hands up!"

Whoosh, my hand shot up again. I was accepted and thus found myself both room orderly to our corporal, and a waiter in the NCOs' mess. The corporal shared a room in the barracks with our section leader, and I was now responsible for its upkeep. The benefits to be had from these two extra-curricular duties, both for my comrades and myself, would become apparent over the next three months.

But first there was one more obstacle to overcome: yet another medical examination in the station sick-bay. The urine test was again done collectively. Mindful of my condition, I followed the usual practice of simply passing the beaker to the next in line without actually contributing to its contents. This method had proved successful in the past and it worked again this time. I was confirmed fit for military service.

It was now time to take the oath which would officially transform us into fully-fledged members of the Wehrmacht. The whole battalion was drawn up on the parade ground. The individual companies formed an open square, into which marched the standard bearer and his escort accompanied by an additional honour guard of six recruits. The entire ceremony unfolded in the traditional manner, culminating in the report to the battalion commander, a full colonel, who was to conduct the oath.

We new recruits stood ramrod straight, in full equipment and steel helmets, but still without rifles. Then came the order: "Raise your right hands and repeat after me":

> "I swear by Almighty God this sacred oath, that I will yield
> unconditional obedience to the Führer of the German Reich
> and Volk, Adolf Hitler, the Supreme Commander of the
> Wehrmacht, and, as a courageous soldier, will be prepared
> at any time to lay down my life for this oath."

We all repeated the oath loudly and clearly; each and every one of us fully prepared to abide by its obligations to duty and obedience, and, if called upon, to sacrifice our lives. Our signatures were then required to make the oath legally binding, as well as to confirm that we had read, and would also adhere to, the "10 Commandments Governing the Conduct in War of the German Soldier". (These ten commandments, which were printed on the inside front cover of the pay-book we had each been issued with, still represent to my mind the most concise and precise declaration of the true meaning of international military law; see Appendix.)

The soldier's pay-book was, in effect, his own personal identity card. It had to be carried with him at all times, except when in action, and entries could only be made in it by the relevant authorities, not by the soldier himself. Included in its pages were full details of the holder's service career, his branch of the armed forces, his postings, appointments and promotions, current rates of pay and allowances, items of clothing and equipment issued, his state of health and details of his next of kin, the periods of leave granted – in short, everything that had a bearing on his military life.

Legally, every German citizen was subject to the National Defence Regulations of 21 May 1935. These stated that a man's liability for military service lasted from his nineteenth birthday until the time he reached the age of 45. They also laid down the rules governing reserve commitments and emergency mobilization orders for national and local service in times of war. The 1935 regulations began with the words:

> "Military service is a matter of honour for the German people. Every German man is liable for military service. In time of war every German man and every German woman is obliged – above and beyond recognized military service – to render his or her services for the good of the Fatherland."

The regulations then went on to list those not eligible or liable for military service. Among the categories was one which read, in part: "Anyone who has been pronounced unfit for military service by a medical officer, or by a doctor appointed by the Wehrmacht, will not be liable to conscription."

It was this latter clause that had nearly ruined my chances of joining up. It had not only meant my having to pull the wool over the doctors' eyes in the past, it also entailed keeping my guard up to ensure that they didn't discover their mistake in the future. Fortunately, I was successful on both counts.

The three months of basic training were hard in some respects. Several of the younger instructors pulled tricks deliberately designed to torment us, but we didn't take these too seriously. When something was in the wind 'my' corporal would often discuss it with his room-mate, ignoring my presence as I pottered about tidying up, but knowing full well that the gist of their conversation would be speedily relayed to all my comrades, giving us time to prepare for anything untoward.

The winter of 1941/42 was particularly cold, long and hard in northern and central Germany. But the conditions were as nothing compared to those being faced by our troops on the eastern front as they ground to a halt at the gates of Moscow in temperatures of 40° below zero. The events in Russia during that first winter of the campaign have since been picked over by the historians in minute detail. But we in our little nine-man barracks room world knew nothing of what was going on elsewhere; we had neither television nor radio to keep us informed.

What we did have was a bed, a locker and a stool each, and two tables to share between us. We used the lockers to divide the room into two. The bunk beds were arranged in the smaller half behind the lockers in tiers of three to provide our sleeping quarters. In the other half, onto which the lockers opened, were our stools and the two tables. This was our communal living area where we worked, ate and relaxed. But nobody complained about the lack of space. We all made allowances and helped each other. Our view of the outside world was framed by two large windows, beneath which were two smaller windows, covered by metal grilles, which let light into the cellar space below. Behind the barracks block was a patch of grass and a few bare trees which, by the middle of December, were covered by almost half a metre of snow as the thermometer dropped to minus 25°.

The first major benefit to be derived from my orderly duties was a purely personal one. The two NCOs let me use their room during their weekend absences. I was able to listen to their radio, and could write letters or read a book undisturbed. The same applied over the Christmas holidays, the first I had ever spent away from home. It was like having my 'own' room all to myself. What a luxury, especially as we were not allowed to leave camp for the first six weeks of our training. An additional advantage was that I was excused an hour's PT every Saturday morning in order to attend to my domestic duties and give the room a thorough clean.

Weapons training was carried out on the snow-covered parade ground. We had to throw ourselves to the ground with our rifles and belly-crawl through the deep snow. The corporal in charge, having tried unsuccessfully to get this training moved indoors, ordered us to put on an extra layer of underclothes and to wear fatigues over our uniforms, plus woollen balaclavas and gloves. It was not until a number of recruits had been sent to the sick-bay to have their gloves cut off and be treated for frostbite that these exercises out in the open were finally called off. Such was the daily lot of Luftwaffe recruits under training in the Homeland at that time. But with the bravado of youth we shrugged off minor problems of this nature: "If it doesn't kill us it can only make us harder", was the general attitude.

But one thing we couldn't take quite so lightly. And that was the growing pangs of hunger. Almost the entire stock of potatoes had been spoiled by frost in the camp's stores and there were no replacement supplies. Each man's midday ration was three carefully counted potatoes, but these had often been frozen solid before cooking, which made them taste unnaturally sweet and almost stink. If you were lucky, your three potatoes were edible; if not, you went away hungry. And this was on top of the strenuous daily exercise which our training demanded.

It was at this point that my volunteering to be an orderly in the NCOs' mess began to pay dividends. Their midday meals, like ours, had to be collected from the kitchens. But meals could only be obtained upon the production of a valid meal stamp. The procedure was to show the cook behind the serving counter your stamp before dropping it into an empty bowl next to the hatch. Only then would you receive your food. The system had obviously been designed to prevent anybody coming back for seconds.

I had discovered, however, that a tiny dab of spittle on the fingertip would make the paper meal stamp stick fast. This meant you could now hold out your hand, palm upwards, to show the cook the stamp, and then turn your hand over and make as if to drop the stamp into the bowl. By this time the cook was usually busy doling out the meal and did not bother to check whether the stamp actually fell. Then it was simply a matter of closing your fist and accepting the meal tray with the other hand. Of course, this only worked if you had just the one meal to collect.

As canteen orderly I usually had to carry two trays to the NCOs' table. But, even so, I was able to 'save' three or four stamps each day, which were quickly passed to my hungry room-mates waiting in the corridor outside the kitchen who immediately made use of them to claim a second lunch. I'm still not sure whether the cook was aware of what was going on or not. But he played along and always served the 'latecomers' with a full portion. Either way, the extra meals helped to fill a hole in our bellies and the harmless subterfuge drew us closer together as a group.

It was hunger which almost got us all into serious trouble on another occasion not long afterwards. The rations truck, a 4-tonner with a tarpaulin cover, which was used to fetch the loaves for our cold rations from the field bakery, had arrived back somewhat late. Training was over for the day and it was already pitch black outside. The quartermaster-sergeant needed volunteers to help unload the truck. We didn't hesitate, hoping there might be a little something extra in it for us

– although this was by no means certain, as the loaves had undoubtedly been carefully counted.

The truck drove across the barracks square and then backed up close to the small window of the quartermaster's stores in the cellar, leaving just enough room to lower the tail-gate. This meant undoing the rear flap of the tarpaulin, which left a small gap between the tarp and the body of the truck. Boards were then used to form a ramp from the bed of the truck, through the small window, down into the cellar.

Two of us had been ordered up on to the truck to place the loaves on the ramp, while two others were sent down into the cellar with the QM-sergeant to catch them as they came sliding down. The truck driver stood next to the 4-tonner to keep an eye on proceedings. But from his position he could not see the far side of the vehicle, nor the half-hidden doorway into the barracks block beyond.

It was in this doorway that others of us were waiting, each clutching an empty briefcase. As soon as a loaf came sailing through the gap in the tarpaulin it was scooped up and smuggled away in the briefcase. Altogether we managed to collect six loaves for the eighteen hungry occupants of our two rooms. No time was lost in cutting the loaves into slices and soon everybody was chewing furiously.

A little later I took a pot of tea into the NCOs' room and heard – quite by chance, of course – my corporal complaining to the section leader that his plans for the evening had had to be postponed as there was to be a snap inspection of the barracks. The quartermaster-sergeant had reported the theft of the loaves to the SWO and it was Chiefy who had ordered our rooms to be searched.

I immediately raised the alarm. All the bread not yet eaten was hurriedly flung out of the windows into the deep snow. Somebody leant out, wielding the barracks broom to cover up the telltale holes, and then the windows were slammed shut again just as the Duty NCO's whistle sounded and a loud voice shouted: "Doors open!!! Room inspection!! All stand by your lockers!" The instructors burst into the room. Our senior man reported all present. Everybody was standing stiffly to attention in front of their lockers. More orders: "Move! Lockers and rations cupboard open!"

We jumped to obey. A quick glance inside the room's rations cupboard revealed nothing untoward, but this did not satisfy the searchers. They began rummaging through the lockers. Everything went flying – neatly folded underclothes, shoes, socks, the entire contents of the lockers ended up on the floor. Even the pad-locked drawers containing our personal valuables had to be opened. The items were scrutinized but not touched. Otherwise every drawer in the room was emptied. As we slept on palliasses, these too were prodded and examined. After just a few minutes the room was a scene of utter chaos. Even we were impressed. But there was no sign of the missing loaves.

A good hour later the search was called off. We were ordered to tidy up and restore everything to its proper place as there would be another inspection in two hours' time. We did as we were told and, sure enough, two hours later the instructors returned – but this time they resisted the temptation to throw things around. The day finally ended with the sounding of taps and lights out.

At early roll-call the next morning Chiefy had still not given up. But when he demanded "Who took the six loaves yesterday?" nobody moved a muscle. For, in fact, nobody *had* taken all six loaves – each of the culprits had made off with only one or two at the most. In the end we escaped fairly lightly with just three hours punishment drill. And as we had crept out during the night, retrieved what remained of the loaves and had eaten our fill, this was no great hardship!

At long last the three months' basic training at Detmold was drawing to a close. For our little group this meant that we would soon be moving on. As volunteer officer candidates we would receive our elementary flying training at one of the Luftwaffe's Luftkriegsschulen (Air Warfare Colleges).

24 February 1942 thus saw us pulling into the station at Werder on the River Havel. Waiting for us on the platform was a brand-new Chiefy, who soon had us fallen in. At his command we were marched off singing at the tops of our voices to our new home: the 2nd Volunteer Officer Candidates' Company of Luftkriegschule 3.

The town of Werder is located to the south-west of Berlin. It is linked to the capital, via Potsdam, by metropolitan railway (S-Bahn). Conjuring up prospects of visits to the theatre and concert halls, or simply strolls around the big city, this suited us down to the ground. Werder itself is noted for its spring blossoms and its heady local fruit wines. These latter are very sweet, produce instant good cheer and high spirits if taken in moderation, but can dramatically impair the ability to walk straight – or even stand upright – of those who imbibe too freely. We would have ample opportunity to put these qualities to the test ourselves later on.

Werder airfield, with its grass surface, hangars, workshops and multitude of ancillary buildings, was idyllically situated on a peninsula where the River Havel broadens out into a succession of picturesque lakes. Most of the admin and school buildings were grouped around an oval ring road which enclosed a carefully manicured stretch of lawn and a stand of trees. This area was sacrosanct and it was strictly forbidden to walk on it. The whole place exuded an air more of an elegant spa resort than a military training establishment.

The commander of the Volunteer Officer Candidates' course was Oberstleutnant Schibilsky. He was in charge of all training staff, both those teaching in the classrooms on the ground and the flying instructors. The officer candidate trainees were split into two companies, each of four sections. Sections A-D made up the 1st Company. They had commenced their training several months before our arrival and were some way ahead of us. 2nd Company consisted of Sections E-H. We 'Detmolders' landed up in the 2nd Company, and I was assigned to F Section. 2nd Company was headed by Hauptmann Repenning and the CO of F Section was Oberleutnant Große. All these officers had had previous operational experience with front-line units. The military instructors were mainly NCOs chosen for their experience and suitability for the job.

Our military instructor was an older flight sergeant. He took charge of us, dividing us up alphabetically into groups of six and assigning us rooms on the lower floor of one of the school's three accommodation blocks, which formed an open square around an inner courtyard. On entering our room we saw that it contained three pairs of bunk beds. But what really caught our eye was that on each bed, upper and lower, lay a bulky straw palliasse.

This posed our first problem, for we couldn't help noticing that the beds in the rooms across the corridor – to be occupied by E Section, who had yet to arrive – were furnished with comfortable-looking mattresses. So as soon as the instructors went to lunch, we quickly exchanged our sacks of straw for E Section's mattresses and made up our beds to hide the evidence. When our fellow E Section trainees turned up towards evening, however, their instructor, a grizzled warrant officer, noticed the swap. Although he expressed sympathy for our situation, he requested that would we please return things to the way they were. In the face of such reasonableness, we had no option but to grit our teeth and comply with as much grace as we could muster. A few weeks later our palliasses were also exchanged for mattresses, much to our satisfaction.

As at Detmold, the daily routine at Werder was run by the clock and organized to the minute, from reveille at 06.00 hours until the end of the day's duties at 18.00 hours and lights out at 22.00 hours. In addition to our military activities and daily sports sessions, we were now not only spending more time in the classroom being taught tactics and the advanced theories of flight, but were also receiving practical tuition in the workshops and hangars. In contrast to the basic training to which we had been subjected at Detmold, our exercises at Werder were designed to include the formulation, giving and execution of orders. In short, we were being groomed to become officers. There were no calls for volunteers to act as room or mess orderlies.

For those of us who had served as section or troop leaders in one or other of the youth organizations it seemed something of a natural progression. Great store was set on comradeship to encourage the sense of unity which formed the moral and ethical foundations of the entire officer corps. Everybody turned to and helped each other to complete the exercises we were set and to solve any problems. There was never a moment's boredom. Every day was a contest to achieve peak performance in which all played a part: the instructing officers, the NCOs and we, the aspiring officer candidates.

Although the training regime was becoming more serious and focused, we still had our light-hearted moments. Every Sunday 2nd Company was responsible for camp guard duties. We decided to carry these out strictly by the book, and word soon got around. Nobody was permitted to pass the sentry on the gate, for example, without first showing their pay-book as proof of identity – not even the officers. Naturally, everybody wanted a spell on the gate, it was too good an opportunity to miss.

There were very few private cars in camp. Nearly everyone used the train to get into Berlin, and this meant leaving the gate on foot for the walk to the nearby S-Bahn station. If it was one of our own section officers who was on his way to town, the exchange would run something as follows: "May I request to see the Herr Hauptmann's pay-book?" the gate sentry would politely ask the officer, whom he knew perfectly well. "Don't you know who I am?" was the usual response. "I know who the Herr Hauptmann is. But I am only obeying standing orders."

There was no answer to this. Either the pay-book was produced as requested, or the officer had to return to his quarters to fetch it. A quick glance at the document in question and the sentry would snap to attention and present arms, which required a salute in turn. Only then could the officer continue on his way to the flesh-pots of the capital. If a crowd wanted to leave camp all at once, other members of the guard would lend the gate sentry a hand. It was almost like peacetime.

But we knew where to draw the line. If the station commander, Oberst Graf von Luckner, or any other senior officer was seen approaching the gate, the entire watch would turn out, fully armed and equipped, and be brought to attention by the guard commander.

It was different for those guards patrolling the camp. Weapons were loaded, but kept on safety. Patrols were always carried out by two men, day and night, and whatever the weather. If anything suspicious was seen, safety catches were released and weapons held ready to fire. If a suspicious person was spotted they had to be challenged: "Achtung! Halt!!! Stay where you are! Hands up or I will fire!!!"

But none of us was ever faced with this situation, thank God. On one occasion a patrol did find a parachute on the banks of Lake Havel, but nobody ever discovered how it had got there.

And so the first two months at Werder passed. And then the great day finally dawned: we were about to begin flying training. Paraded in front of the flight control centre, we were split into groups by the chief flying instructor, Hauptmann Mössinger. Names were checked against the inevitable lists and then we were issued with helmets, flying overalls and all the rest of the equipment we would need before we could be allowed into the air. Other essential items, such as the indispensable 'Knemeyer' course calculator and navigational aid, protractors, rulers and the like, we had already been using in the classroom during the previous weeks of theoretical training.

The instructor of the group I was assigned to was a flight sergeant old enough to be my father. He was a quiet, steady type without airs and graces and spoke with a faint Saxon dialect. An ex-bomber pilot wearing the Iron Cross, First Class, and the combat clasp, he gained our immediate trust. Noticing my C certificate glider-pilot's badge, which we were permitted to display on our Luftwaffe uniforms, he commented to me on it, saying that he too had begun flying on gliders. But now we were going to have to get to grips with powered flight.

Each group consisted of an instructor and six pupils, the same number as occupied a barracks room. First we were to be introduced to the A 2-class primary trainers used by all beginners. The most important of these were the:

- Heinkel He 72 'Kadett', a tandem two-seater biplane which was fully aerobatic;
- Bücker Bü 131 'Jungmann', a similar type capable of inverted flight;
- Klemm Kl 25 and Kl 35, both tandem two-seater low-wing monoplanes, but of different construction and with differing flying characteristics; and the
- Bücker Bü 181 'Bestmann', a low-wing monoplane with an enclosed cockpit and two side-by-side seats. This latter feature had the advantage of allowing direct communication between instructor and pupil but, as both occupants sat outside the longitudinal axis of the machine, it produced a somewhat uncomfortable feeling when rolled.

Once the A 2 primary trainers had been mastered, pupils would progress to the B 1-class Gotha Go 145, another tandem two-seater biplane but with a more powerful engine. After this came the heavier B 2-class of single-engined transport aircraft, such as the Junkers W 34, which could carry six passengers or a cargo of freight.

The course would end with conversion onto the so-called K types (K = Kampf, or combat). These included the Focke-Wulf Fw 56 'Stößer', a single-seat high-wing monoplane advanced trainer; the Arado Ar 68 single-seat biplane, which had equipped most of the Luftwaffe's fighter squadrons during the latter half of the thirties but was now used for fighter training; and the elegant Arado Ar 96 advanced trainer, a tandem two-seater low-wing monoplane with enclosed cockpit and retractable undercarriage.

Each of the above types possessed different flight characteristics and was used for specific training purposes. They varied widely in their equipment and engine power. A pilot had to take all these factors into consideration, together with the types' different performance envelopes – duration, speed, altitude and range. This was the task that now faced us if we wanted to learn to fly.

The flying training programme would begin with straightforward take-offs and landings. Then would come turns, banks and other manoeuvres until we had complete mastery of each type in all situations, including the stall and recovery from a spin. After this we would be taught aerobatics and instrument flying, at first in the company of an instructor, and then solo. The course was planned to provide every trainee with 125 hours of flying time.

And the reward for all the effort and sweat this was undoubtedly going to cost us would be the award of our military pilot's licence and the right to wear the pilot's badge on the left breast of our uniform tunics. But more than that, I wanted specifically and above all to be a fighter pilot. I was not interested in flying bombers, dive-bombers, reconnaissance or transport aircraft.

As Werder was too small to accommodate all four sections of 2nd Company, E and F Sections were to carry out their flying training from the satellite field of Beelitz. Also grass-surfaced, Beelitz lay to the left of the autobahn some 20 kilometres due south of Werder. The field was surrounded by a pine forest. To facilitate landings a 100 metre-long swathe had been cut immediately below the approach path. But although the trees had been felled, the stumps were left in the ground. The procedure was to come in over this avenue of stumps before touching down on the landing cross marked in the grass and taxiing to a stop close to the flight line.

We soon settled into a fixed routine. After we had breakfasted in our rooms, each instructor would fly down to Beelitz in the aircraft assigned to us for the day, taking one of the pupils with him. The rest of us would follow by bus. Midday meals were provided by the field kitchen set up at Beelitz. At the end of the day's flying programme we would return to Werder and eat supper there together in the mess. After a quick shower, we would change into our track-suits and settle down in our rooms for an evening of hard swotting over our text books.

On 1 April 1942 all trainees on the course were promoted to Gefreiten (lance corporals), the first lowly step on a very long ladder. Exactly one month later, on 1 May, we were elevated to Fahnenjunker-Gefreiten (flight cadet lance corporals).

Fortunately, I discovered that flying came naturally to me. I experienced no difficulties and found it a pure pleasure. The instructor expressed satisfaction with my progress and I was gratified to be among the first to master the A 2 primary trainers. It may not have been a huge achievement, but I really felt that I was at last on my way.

I shall never forget my first solo. To be aloft on my own in a powered aircraft, not dependent on winch or bungee cord, thermal or updraft, but with an engine that obeyed the slightest touch on the throttle and allowed me to climb and dive at will was wonderful. My dream had been fulfilled.

The first flying test was now looming, however. This required each pupil to carry out six measured landings, bringing the aircraft down from an altitude of 600 metres, its engine idling, to touch down between the landing cross and the first marker along the grass runway 50 metres beyond. The machine to be used was the Bü 181, which was equipped with landing flaps. This allowed the pilot to control his speed and angle of approach despite the lack of power from the windmilling propeller. With the instructor by my side my practice approaches and landings had gone without a hitch. Judging the time to be right, he reported to the section commander that I was ready to take the test.

During these tests there was a special rule which had to be observed by all other aircraft in the circuit. The test machine had a long thin red streamer attached to each wingtip. This made it highly visible in the air, the purpose being to warn other aircraft to keep well clear. They were not permitted to impede its progress for any reason. It had absolute right of way. This was a strict order and applied to every pilot in the immediate vicinity of the approach path, pupils and instructors alike.

The day's flying was already nearing its end when I was given the order to take off and carry out my six measured landings. It had been a warm May day, not a cloud in the sky, the sun shining brightly. The signs of spring were all around, the landscape of woods and lakes looking particularly attractive from the air.

I took off and climbed away to the required 600 metres before heading back towards the field. As I flew over the landing cross I eased the throttle back to idle and commenced a wide turn to the right. With the engine just ticking over and the propeller hardly moving, I glided out over the pines before making another turn and lining myself up for the approach. With the use of the flaps I carefully began to reduce speed and lose altitude, aiming for the landing cross. Pulling slowly back on the stick I put the Bücker safely down well within the stipulated 50-metre stretch. With a blip of the throttle I taxied across the field to the take-off point and repeated the process. I had just touched down for my fourth landing when I received the order to return to Werder. It was getting too late to complete my final two landings. Tomorrow was another day.

The following morning I was the first to fly back down to Beelitz with my instructor. I landed and taxied over to the take-off area. The instructor climbed out and the red pennants were attached to the machine's wingtips. I was ready to go. The starting flag was lowered to signal cleared for take-off, I gave her full throttle, and set off afresh to do my six measured landings.

While I was thus engaged other aircraft began to arrive from Werder. Each gave my beflagged Bücker a wide berth as ordered, and I continued the test undisturbed. The first four landings again passed uneventfully and to the apparent satisfaction of both my instructor and section commander. It was time to get on with the fifth.

All went well until the final glide-turn onto the approach. Concentrating on getting the nose lined up on the landing cross, I was suddenly aware of something off to my right. It was a 'Kadett' coming from Werder with an instructor and pupil aboard. The Heinkel was now close alongside, almost flying in formation, and slowly overhauling me.

I fully expected him to break off his approach and go round again. Surely the instructor had seen the red pennants streaming from my wingtips? He must realize I had right of way. By this time I was below the level of the tree-tops and fully committed to landing. With my motor idling I was slowly sinking towards the tree stumps, but my entire attention was focused on the biplane now just ahead of me.

All at once the trees to either side of me began to wobble wildly. The machine was yawing and on the point of stalling. I slammed the throttle forward, the engine coughed – but failed to catch. The next moment there was an almighty crash. I was pressed hard against my harness and shaken about violently for a moment of two before total and utter silence descended on the scene.

Crash landing!!! My Bü 181 lay in bits between the unyielding stumps – a total write-off.

"What a sh...!" I swore loudly into the stillness. It relieved my feelings, but didn't change matters. For it had suddenly dawned on me that this could spell the end of my flying career. If I put a foot wrong now I might very well be washed out. I was entirely to blame for the crash. After all, I could have opened up the throttle earlier – and more gently – and simply abandoned the test landing. True, the pilot of the 'Kadett' had disobeyed the rules, but maybe he had good reason to. An emergency, perhaps?

All these thoughts went racing through my mind. I had to decide what to do, and quickly. Then I saw a glimmer of a chance. Attack being the best method of defence, why not come straight out with it, admit responsibility, acknowledge that my actions alone were the cause of the crash, and request due punishment from my immediate superiors? They might be inclined to take a more lenient view of the incident than if it went before a board of enquiry. It was a slender enough hope, but it was the only one I had.

I unbuckled my harness and climbed slowly out of the wreckage.

Everybody who had been standing around on the flight line, including the section commander and my instructor, were running across the field towards me. I set off to meet them. I made straight for the section commander, drew myself to attention and made my report: "Fahnenjunker-Gefreiter Hannig crashed a Bü 181 among the tree stumps during the approach for a measured landing... I request due punishment."

I watched a range of expressions flit across my superior's face. His initial look of concern for my well-being was replaced by one of quizzical surprise. It was presumably rare for someone to ask for punishment without first making at least an attempt to explain their side of the situation. Maybe he thought I was suffering from shock?

"Your punishment is not a matter for me. I will have to submit a report to the chief instructor and your company commander. You will hear from them what action is to be taken. Have you yourself suffered any injuries?" That was obviously still his main worry.

"No, Herr Oberleutnant, I have not been hurt in any way", I was able to reply (with a mental nod of thanks in the direction of my guardian angel). But the final three metres of my descent into the tree stumps – which, according to the onlookers, had displayed all the grace, but none of the gentleness, of a falling autumn leaf – had left the Bücker a complete wreck.

We made our way back to flight control. The section commander went into his office to telephone details of the crash to Werder. In the meantime my instructor had been having a few words with me. I felt I could be completely honest with him and explained what had happened. He clapped me on the shoulder: "Don't worry, we'll get this sorted out!" I felt a slight glimmer of hope.

A little while later the section commander reappeared. He called me over and said: "Hannig, you are to fly back to Werder at once. Report immediately to chief instructor Hauptmann Mössinger's office. After that you will report in uniform, with full equipment and steel helmet, to your company commander. Any questions?" "No, Herr Oberleutnant!" "Take that machine over there," he said, pointing to another Bü 181 parked nearby, before quickly correcting himself: "Halt, as you were. You are not permitted to fly on your own now. Your instructor will accompany you."

We saluted and were dismissed. Climbing into the Bücker, my instructor indicated that I should take the left-hand pilot's seat while he settled into the right-hand one. Despite what had happened, he let me do the flying as usual. In fact, once in the air he took off his shoes, put his feet up on the instrument panel, and grabbed forty winks.

After landing back at Werder I taxied across to flying control as ordered and switched off the engine. Fully attired again, shoes back on, plus belt and cap, my instructor clambered out, saying to me as he did so: "Wait here until I call you." He knew Hauptmann Mössinger well, having served with him in a front-line bomber unit. It wasn't long before he returned: "Get in there and listen to the Herr Hauptmann's sermon."

I did as I was told. The next few minutes were impressive. I got to hear all about the man-hours and material that had been wasted by my carelessness. I was informed of the cost of the aircraft I had wrecked. This was followed by a discourse on my reckless action in the air. Finally I was dismissed.

Then came a quick change out of my flying overalls and into full uniform, equipment and helmet, before I presented myself to the company commander. He was more brief and to the point. By this time it was already late in the afternoon and he presumably had plans for the evening. "As you acknowledge your guilt, I hereby punish you with a strong reprimand. You will resume flying training in the morning, now get out of here!"

I could have hugged him – my superior officer! In less than sixty seconds he had dispelled all my fears and doubts: I could continue flying. What was said to the instructor who had cut in and landed in front of me was no doubt more serious, as were the consequences. He was relieved of his duties and posted away.

It wasn't until I got back to my room that I was really able to unwind. A lively discussion was soon underway. Everybody had seen what had happened and were unanimous in declaring the other pilot to have been at fault. He had not followed standing orders. But so what? I was the one who had pranged the Bücker, I said, nobody else. Let there be no doubt in anybody's mind about that. My only aim thereafter was to be allowed to continue flying. And that aim had been granted me. The 'strong reprimand' was no punishment at all. It was more for the record to show that my superiors had taken suitable disciplinary measures.

So it was back to normal the following day. I finally achieved my six measured landings at the third attempt. My room-mates had stood by me and, apparently, I was still in the instructor's good books. Another lucky escape.

Our proximity to Berlin had its advantages and its disadvantage. First the disadvantage: several of our number couldn't tear themselves away from the delights of the capital and didn't get back to camp until after lights out. The result was that the entire company was confined to barracks and was given three hours' punishment drill on the Sunday morning.

We were instructed to fall-in on the parade ground wearing fatigues and in full marching order. The commander took the parade himself, ordering us to sing as he marched us out of camp. What we were then put through over the course of the next three hours wasn't just a hard slog; it was sheer physical torture. Everything had to be done at the double. On the command "Air attack!!" we had to throw ourselves down on to our stomachs. Then it was "On your feet! March – at the double!" Moments later we would be flat on our faces again. To add to our discomfort we were periodically ordered to put on our gas masks. The sweat had been pouring off us from the word go. At the end of the three hours we were completely exhausted, but still had to find our voices and sing as we marched back to camp. The drill ended with our goose-stepping past the commander. As he took the salute his face was streaming with sweat too, for he had done everything that he had ordered us to do. We felt an enormous respect for the man.

Those who had been the cause of all our woes only stayed out late once again. After that we took matters into our own hands. None too gently we persuaded them to mend their ways and, once they had seen the light, there was no further trouble.

But the advantages of having Berlin on our doorstep far outweighed these relatively minor irritants. What the capital had to offer in the way of theatres, concerts, musicals and operettas was almost limitless. I can still recall many of the famous performers – actors, singers, musicians – that I saw during my time at Werder. I managed to take in at least one show every weekend I had free. Tickets could be got from the Wehrmacht welfare office in camp. And a tin of Schoka-Cola chocolate, which formed part of our special flight rations, always added to the enjoyment of the occasion.

I soon discovered a home away from home in Berlin. This was the infants' care home in the Alte Jakobsstraße where Margot was working as a student paediatric nurse. Margot, or 'Göttchen' as we called her, was the daughter of our chief-of-police back in Zobten. We had grown up together and she was like a sister to me and my brothers. We used to travel to school together each day: first the 3 kilometres by bike to the station at Siebeneichen, and then the 7-kilometre train journey to Löwenberg, where she attended the girls' secondary school, and we the Hindenburg school for boys.

Göttchen was a pleasant, open girl and was delighted to see a friendly face from home. She was sharing a room with another student nurse, which they had furnished very cosily and where I was always welcomed and made to feel at home. The porter, who normally exercised strict control over all visitors, and who would not allow anybody to enter the nurses' quarters unaccompanied, soon got to know me and would let me in at any time.

My cold rations from camp came as a welcome change for the girls, as rationing was becoming tighter and most foodstuffs could now only be bought on coupons. If they had been on night duty on a Saturday, they would still be fast asleep when I arrived from Werder on the Sunday morning. I would then lay the breakfast table as quietly as possible, put the coffee on and make myself comfortable in an armchair until they woke. They were always pleased to see me, but would bundle me out of the room while they got washed and dressed. Once they were presentable, I was allowed back in and we enjoyed breakfast together as we discussed our plans for the day.

Göttchen and her friends loved coming to the theatre and to concerts with me if their duties allowed. Such afternoons made a refreshing break in our otherwise busy and hectic schedules. In 1942 the centre of Berlin was not yet the target for massed bombing raids by the British and Americans. Now and again reconnaissance aircraft or small numbers of bombers would be reported approaching and the sirens would sound. When this happened all the young children and babies had to be taken from the wards and carried down into the air-raid shelters. I was able to offer my help on several such occasions, which the staff gratefully accepted. Once everybody was safely underground it was simply a matter of waiting for the all-clear.

During one air-raid alarm, however, I decided to go up and see what was happening. I sheltered in the doorway of the courtyard. It was already dark, but the gentle drone of aircraft engines could be clearly heard. Searchlight beams were probing the night sky. Then the flak opened up, the barking of the guns followed moments later by the crack and flash of the explosions high above. The shrapnel made a soft whirring sound as it fell back to earth. But where it landed on roofs, tiles would invariably be broken and the pieces clattered noisily into the streets below. Although not exactly a baptism of fire, this was my first experience of real warfare.

Berlin possessed another advantage as far as I was concerned. The capital was a major rail junction and leave trains passed through it from all points of the compass. I was thus able to meet up with all three of my brothers in turn as they travelled home on leave: my eldest brother Kurt, now promoted to Leutnant and transferred from signals to infantry, back from the eastern front; Günter, on his way down from his naval base in Norway; and the youngest, Joachim, also now in the infantry and fighting the Soviets on the Volkhov front to the east of Leningrad.

We met either at the Döhnhoff-Platz or at Göttchen's. I was able to spend a few hours with each of them as they broke their journeys in Berlin – a few hours in which to swap experiences and recall old times before parting again for who knew how long? But this was wartime. All four sons of the Hannig family were now serving in the armed forces: army, navy and air force. And all, with the exception of myself, had already seen action.

In the meantime I continued with my training. But there was to be one consequence of my writing-off the Bücker at Beelitz. On 1 September members of the course were scheduled for promotion to Fahnenjunker-Unteroffiziere (flight cadet corporals). This took place during a ceremonial parade on the barracks square. After the usual military formalities had been observed, the course commander began to read from a list the names of those to be promoted. As each name was called out the trainee took three paces forward. By the time the commander had finished almost the entire company had re-formed three paces ahead of its original position. Only myself and one or two others, whose names had not been read out, remained standing on the spot. We had not been promoted. I cannot deny that it was a bitter blow for me.

Nevertheless, training went ahead as usual, with me the only lance corporal in my group. But none of my comrades made me feel in any way different. They all knew the reason why I had been passed over.

We were now far enough advanced to be sent off on cross-country exercises. The basic essential for all such long-distance flights was an accurate set of navigational charts and maps. The map was marked beforehand with the course to be flown, from A to B, via a number of specific intermediate points in the terrain en route. It was then up to the pupil to work out the exact flight path, calculate the compass bearings of the individual legs, measure distances and estimate flight times. All this information was then transferred to the navigational map and entered in the flight plan. This meant that you would know in advance what features you could expect to see to left and right of you, and at what times they should appear, as you progressed along your set route – features such as towns and villages, lakes, rivers, distinctive rail and road junctions, and the like. You also had to establish heights above sea level of any obstacles in your path, the amount of fuel to be used, and determine the reserve remaining at the end of the flight.

These were all subjects we had been taught in the classroom and were now familiar with. But there was a much easier way of cross-country flying: you simply plotted your course along an existing railway line or autobahn which led in the direction you wanted to go. This practice was known as 'left-hand wheel, right-hand rail'.

The only thing to remember when using this method was to avoid overflying restricted military areas or large cities. Berlin already had a ring autobahn which passed close by our satellite field at Beelitz. And it was impossible to miss Werder, situated on its distinctive peninsula in the middle of the Havel lakes to the south-west of Berlin, even with your eyes closed.

But this method, although practically foolproof, could still throw up the odd nasty surprise, as I was soon about to discover. One Saturday morning in mid-September I was scheduled to fly a cross-country in a Go 145 from Werder to Sagan in Silesia. I already had tickets for the theatre in Berlin that evening. My brother Kurt, who was currently on an infantry course at Döberitz, was going to join me and we had arranged to meet outside the theatre at 8 o'clock, thirty minutes before the performance started. I would be back from my trip to Sagan hours before that. There was time and enough to spare.

Take-off was to be at 09.00 hours, estimated flight time one hour and twenty minutes each way; total two hours and forty minutes. It would not be necessary to refuel at Sagan. All I would have to do was report my arrival to flight control, hand in my flight plan for the return journey, and be off again.

I took off at 09.00 on the dot. In glorious weather I first headed south towards Beelitz, before banking to port to follow the ring autobahn eastwards. Just short of Königswusterhausen I turned right and settled on a heading of 170°, which would take me in an almost straight line, via Lübben, Cottbus, Forst and Sorau, to Sagan – left-hand wheel, right-hand rail. I hadn't a care in the world.

The town of Lübben and the Spree woods were just coming up on my left when the engine began to miss and started emitting bluish-white puffs of smoke from the port exhaust, a sure sign that the engine was about to seize up and the propeller come to a standstill. I had to get down on an airfield as fast as possible, or make an emergency landing on the nearest suitable patch of ground. Fortunately I had marked all the airfields along my route on the map and saw that the small, unoccupied field at Lübbenau lay off to my right just beyond the railway line.

The puffs of smoke had grown into a solid stream by now and the engine had lost all power. From an altitude of 500 metres I began to glide down straight towards the small grass field. I had a slight tailwind and crossed the railway line with plenty of height to spare. Then I put the left wing down and tramped hard on the right rudder pedal. Quickly losing all my excess height in an enormous sideslip, I touched down just over the perimeter of the field.

What I hadn't noticed from the air, however, was that Lübbenau's surface was not flat, but rose to a slight crest in the centre. The engine had now stopped completely and the twin-bladed prop had come to a halt in the vertical position, but the kite was still bumping along quite happily across the grass. When I reached the top of the crest I discovered to my horror that a tractor and trailer were trundling across the field directly in my path and not 50 metres in front of me!

I trod on the hydraulic brakes as hard as I could but realized at once that I was not going to be able to stop in time. Skidding straight towards the tractor I had no option but to try and point the nose of the Gotha between it and the trailer. There was a faint cracking noise as the lower blade of the wooden propeller snapped off. My aim had been good. The aircraft finally came to rest with its engine cowling slotted neatly in the space between tractor and trailer, and the upper wings projecting to left and right above them both to form a perfect, if rather expensive, sunshade.

Fortunately the tractor driver and his helper on the trailer had both jumped clear when they saw me approaching. Nobody was hurt. But neither vehicle was flying the obligatory red warning flag which all airfield traffic is supposed to display when crossing a runway. I might have spotted such a device as I came in to land and have been able to avoid the collision. In a way, though, it was lucky for me that the red flags were not being flown. Although Lübbenau was presently unoccupied by any flying units, the duty control officer had been present and had chanced to witness the entire incident. He was able to absolve me from all blame (my guardian angel was on the ground and in uniform this time). Towards midnight I thus found myself, parachute pack under my arm, travelling back by train to Berlin along the very tracks I had been intending to use to guide me to Sagan. In Berlin I changed on to the S-Bahn to make my way out to Werder to report. I never did get to the theatre that evening.

Again I had been lucky – unlike several of my comrades, whose flying careers were terminated after solo cross-countries and who ended up facing a court martial instead. They were charged with misconduct under Para. 75 of the rules governing military flying offences for deviating from an ordered flight plan.

Every cross-country had to be carried out above a certain height. The actual altitude flown was recorded on a barograph inside a small bakelite casing carried by every aircraft. The barograph itself was a straightforward enough device, consisting of a continuous roll of graph paper wrapped around a slowly revolving cylinder. As the flight progressed a spring-loaded nib would draw a line in blue ink on the graph paper. This line recorded both the flight time, along the horizontal axis, and the altitude flown, along the vertical axis.

Pupils were issued with a barograph before the start of each flight. Having signed for the equipment, they would take it out to their aircraft, secure it in the luggage locker and switch it on prior to take-off. After landing the barograph would be returned to stores and the strip of graph paper handed in to the instructor as proof that the exercise had been flown according to instructions.

Naturally, we all wanted to present our instructors with a nice 'clean' graph curve, which was perfectly achievable if one flew the cross-country strictly by the book. But, once again – like 'left-hand wheel, right-hand rail' – there was an easier way of doing things. As all details of the flight, including times and altitudes, had to be worked out in advance and were thus known to us beforehand, it was simple enough to get hold of an unused roll of graph paper and a bottle of blue ink, and draw in the curve of the coming flight by hand. It was this strip which would then be given to the instructor at the end of the exercise, rather than the one actually recorded by the barograph. And once the latter had been carefully disposed of, there was no proof that the pupil had not followed his flight plan exactly to the letter.

But the longer our cross-country training went on, the more phone calls the station commander was getting from irate citizens complaining that one or the other of his aircraft had been seen low-flying over village

X or lake Y. Nothing could be proved, of course, and training carried on as usual, albeit with several stern warnings from flight control about unauthorized low-flying.

After one particular exercise the instructors were waiting for us on the flight line. They accepted the preferred strips of graph paper from us with knowing smiles, then went to our machines, reached inside each one, and took out a second barograph which we had known nothing about. By comparing the strips it quickly became apparent that three of our number had deviated from the set flight plan. The unfortunate trio were immediately placed under arrest by the company commander and led away by the waiting guard to the cells in the detention block. A court martial was convened a few days later and all three were to be found guilty. They were demoted to the rank of airman and posted to other units. After this there were no more violations of Para. 75!

One of the miscreants was related to a Luftwaffe Generalfeldmarschall: a certain Freiherr von R. As this august individual happened to be in Berlin on official business at the time, he had been informed of the incident. At 09.00 hours the following Sunday morning a large staff car bearing a field marshal's flag drew up at the main gate.

We of the 2nd Company were on guard duty as usual. Luckily, the armed sentry on the gate recognized the imposing blue and gold standard on the vehicle's mudguard even before the occupant began to climb out. He was able to yell a quick "Fall in, the guard!", before hurrying to open the small side gate. Those of us off duty were lounging fully dressed on our cots in the guardroom. Despite being dozy with sleep, the urgency in our comrade's voice spurred us into action. In a matter of moments we were outside, fallen in, correctly-dressed, and presenting arms.

By now the field marshal had made his way through the gate. The guard commander submitted his report, which was acknowledged by the marshal raising his baton to the peak of his cap. He walked along our file, giving us the courtesy of a brief inspection, before saying, "Thank you, Luftwaffe soldiers. Stand at ease." We ordered arms and stood at ease. Our distinguished visitor turned back to the commander of the guard: "I understand you are holding Fahnenjunker-Unteroffizier von R. under arrest here?" The commander confirmed that this was indeed the case; the camp's detention block formed part of the guardroom complex. "Please open the cell door for me." The field marshal disappeared inside.

We couldn't hear what was said within the narrow confines of that cell. Nor did we ever find out. A few minutes later Generalfeldmarschall von R. reappeared, ordered us to fall out, returned to his car and was driven off. The prisoner subsequently received the same punishment as his two companions, despite belonging to the family of one of the highest-ranking officers of the Luftwaffe. It was another event during our training which made a huge impression on us.

But now that training – or, at least, that part of it provided by the instructors of LKS 3 at Werder – was nearing its end. There was no doubt that they had done their job well. We had all mastered the many types of training aircraft operated by the school. I, for one, had revelled in the rolls, loops, Immelmann turns and inverted flying that I had been taught and could now perform with ease. It made me all the more determined to become a fighter pilot.

And there was one more thing I could do to help ensure that I achieved that ambition. One of the last tests we had to sit at Werder was the sending and receiving of morse. The minimum pass rate was a transmission speed of 60. Those who could transmit at a faster rate would be destined for one of the B 2 schools; in other words, multi-engined training for service in bomber, Zerstörer, reconnaissance or transport units. I clocked up the required pass rate of 60, but was careful not to go any higher, and was thus considered unsuitable for B 2 training.

On 19 August 1942 I was awarded the Reich Sport Medal in bronze, the first metal decoration to adorn my tunic, and on 1 October I was made up to Fahnenjunker-Unteroffizier, thus bringing me in line with the other members of the course. The following month we sat the last tests of all at Werder and on 1 December everybody was promoted to the rank of Fähnrich (ensign). This meant that we were now entitled to wear the Unteroffizier flyer's dagger with its silver-aluminium port epee on our belts. Finally, we were informed of our next postings: the schools where we were to receive advanced training.

I would not have to travel far. My destination was to be 1 Staffel of Jagdfliegerschule 1 (1st Squadron, No 1 Fighter School). This was situated at Werneuchen, roughly the same distance to the north-east of Berlin as Werder was to the south-west, and likewise connected to the capital by a line of the S-Bahn railway.

It was at Werneuchen, on 10 December, that we were presented with our pilot's badges: the black eagle in a silver wreath of laurel and oak leaves. At the same time we were each issued with our military pilot's licences, which listed the types of aircraft we were qualified to fly. And, last but not least, we were now to receive flight pay.

It was the job of the fighter schools to convert newly-qualified trainees such as ourselves on to the Luftwaffe's then standard front-line single-engined fighter, the Me 109, and to teach us combat flying and tactics.

All the instructors at Werneuchen were experienced fighter pilots who had seen service with one or other of the operational Jagdgeschwader on either the western, eastern or southern fronts. We would now have to learn how to fly in Rotten and Schwärmen (sections of two and four aircraft). These were the basic tactical units, irrespective of whether one was flying as part of a larger formation, or in smaller individual combat groups. We would also be taught how to fight in these same sections of twos and fours, as well as how to survive one-on-one in the chaos and confusion of a dogfight.

While the basic tactical structure remained the same for each, there were three specific types of fighter mission: direct escort, indirect escort, and 'freie Jagd' (literally 'free hunting'). Escort duties entailed the protection of one's own aircraft – anything from large groups of bombers to single reconnaissance machines – from the attentions of enemy fighters. Direct escort required cover to be flown no further than 100 metres from the aircraft in one's charge. Indirect escort extended the range of air cover to anywhere between 100 and 500 metres. Freie Jagd gave the fighter pilot the freedom to attack any hostile aircraft in an assigned area at any altitude. This latter was naturally the most popular and sought-after type of combat mission.

There were two fundamental differences which characterized each of the three major fronts, west, east and south: the behaviour and tactics of the opposition, and the living conditions enjoyed – or endured – by the pilots in each of the respective theatres.

Every instructor at Werneuchen was full of praise for 'his' old Geschwader, wherever it had fought. Air operations in the west and south were generally comparable, as the enemy employed basically similar tactics and had been through the same training programmes. Off-duty conditions and facilities were markedly better in western Europe than they were in the Mediterranean, particularly in North Africa. On the eastern front it was a different matter entirely. The Soviet Air Force followed a strategy of its own. Living conditions for the vast majority of the population were primitive in the extreme. And the almost limitless, and featureless, expanse of the land itself posed problems in the east not encountered in either of the other theatres.

My instructor had previously served with Jagdgeschwader 54 in Russia. The unit emblem, a large green heart – symbolizing Thuringia, the 'green heart' of Germany – was proudly displayed on all its aircraft. The then Geschwaderkommodore, Major Hannes Trautloft, was not just a successful fighter pilot in his own right, he was a natural leader of men. His obvious care and concern for his subordinates made him liked and respected by all.

From the experiences recounted by my instructor of his time with JG 54 in the east, it was clear that a unique bond of comradeship held the whole unit together as one, pilots and ground crews alike. Every member of the Geschwader could rely implicitly on every other one of his fellows. Greatly impressed by these accounts of life in a front-line fighter unit, I now had my next goal: to serve with JG 54 'Grünherz' in Russia.

Training at Werneuchen concentrated solely on flying and preparing us for combat. We were four to a room and had much more space to call our own. As ensigns we now ate in the officers' mess, and guard duties were a thing of the past.

We were again divided into groups for the purposes of training. Every instructor had three pupils. This meant, in effect, that each group was the equivalent of a tactical Schwarm. The Me 109 was a new experience for us. The operational Geschwader were flying the F and new G variants of the famous Messerschmitt fighter by this stage of the war. We would get our hands on these models later in our training. The school's current equipment consisted in the main of earlier versions, most of which had previously seen front-line service before being retired and handed over to the training establishments.

The Me 109 was the first armed aircraft we had flown, although the various models on the school's strength meant that we were faced with a number of different gun arrangements. The major weakness of all Me 109s was the narrow-track undercarriage, which did not stand up well to any form of maltreatment. But there were two other specific things which could trap the unwary beginner.

On the early B, C and D models this was the canopy lock mechanism. To secure the light plexiglass canopy properly it was necessary to move a lever through 180° and then lock it by means of a spring-loaded catch. If the lever was simply moved into the forward position and not locked, or if the spring-loaded catch was not fully engaged, the canopy would fly open after take-off. This would then result in the loosely flapping canopy either becoming bent out of shape, or else breaking off completely. A further consequence was the automatic stopping of two-thirds of the unfortunate pilot's pay for a month. This punishment was felt keenly by all those who suffered it, as I recall only too well. I once flew a circuit without a canopy. The offending item came open during my first turn to port after take-off, worked itself loose and then tore off entirely.

The other thing one had to be careful of was the tendency of the E, F and G models to swing sharply to the left during the take-off run. This was caused by engine torque, and was something else of which I can claim personal experience.

The first snows of winter had already fallen as I taxied a Me 109F to the eastern end of the runway. Wind conditions dictated that I start from east to west on this occasion. But this placed the workshops and hangars some 100 metres to the left of my take-off run – an obvious hazard given the Me 109's known propensity to swing to port.

As the Me 109 had evolved and improved through its various models, so too had its engine power been increased. And the greater the engine power, the greater the torque effect. The F variant's DB 601 power plant was rated at 1,200 hp for take-off. If the throttle was opened too quickly, before the rudder became effective, the aircraft would begin to swing ever more sharply to the left. Ultimately, if this crabbing became too severe and wasn't checked, the narrow undercarriage would collapse altogether. Any pilot still attempting to take off would invariably plough in to the left. This usually resulted in the machine becoming a total write-off and could prove fatal for the pilot.

We were all aware of this fact. The instructors had drummed it into us time and again: advance the throttle slowly, stick forward, right full rudder, keep the machine straight, and fly – don't pull – it off the ground. Easy enough, you'd think ... wrong!

I was in too much of a hurry. Throttle forward – the Friedrich began to pick up speed, the engine howled, the variable-pitch propeller bit at the air. The torque effect kicked in almost immediately, dragging me inexorably to the left towards the hangars. I tramped down even harder on the right-hand rudder pedal, at the same time pressing the right wheel brake. I caught it just in time, arresting the swing and gathering sufficient speed to lift off. As the hangar wall flashed past my port wingtip I felt I could almost have reached out and touched it. From that day onwards I made sure I was in full control every time I took off in a Me 109.

When combat flying in a Rotte or Schwarm the aircraft were positioned in a loose line abreast, with the wingman – or men – slightly behind the leader. (The RAF had by this time also adopted the equivalent of a Schwarm formation, which they aptly described as a 'finger four' to illustrate the relative position of each machine as the fingertip on a spread hand.) Each aircraft was spaced about 50 metres away from the next. The formation leader was always referred to as the number 1. The wingmen were tactical numbers 2, 3 and 4. Every training Schwarm at Werneuchen had its own radio call sign, chosen from the fertile imagination of the instructor. One typical example was 'Edelweiß'.

Before take-off R/T communication always had to be checked. Once we were settled in our cockpits the instructor/Schwarmführer (leader) would ask: "Edelweiß 2, Frage Viktor?" Literally, the latter meant "Question: Victor?" Viktor was the phonetic for V, which in this case stood for Verständigung (reception). In other words, the leader was asking "Are your receiving me?"

The proper response if all was clear was "Edelweiß 1 from 2, Viktor, Viktor," with the V now indicating Verstanden (understood, or affirmative). If something was wrong, or the answer was "no", the correct reply over the R/T was "Negativ". Orders in the air always had to be acknowledged either by 'Viktor' or 'Negativ'.

But of course it was combat-flying training upon which we were now concentrating and towards which all our efforts were directed. We learned how to scramble, adopt close formation after take-off and then, upon a given order, open out into battle formation. Great emphasis was also placed upon formation turns, which we had to master in order not to become split up and separated in the air.

There were set manoeuvres which had to be followed. In 90° turns, if a leader announced that he was turning *across* his wingman's line of flight, the latter would lose a little height, follow into the turn behind and below his number 1, and then quickly add a little extra power to resume his position alongside. If the leader made a turn *away* from his number 2, the wingman would immediately slide into a sharper turn inside his leader and take station on the opposite side. It sounds simple enough, but it required just the right touch and a lot of practice was needed to get it absolutely right.

One day another Rotte took off with Fähnrich Abs, a young Berliner, in the number 2 position. Those of us not flying stood in the hangar doorway to watch their departure. The two Me 109s lifted off cleanly and we saw them open up into combat formation before becoming just two small dots in the distance. Suddenly, an angry red fireball blossomed in the blue vault of the sky and tiny black pieces could be made out tumbling through the air. One of the dots was still visible, trailing a long streamer of smoke as it slowly lost height.

"They've collided!" somebody yelled. Although it cast a pall and left us all feeling depressed, the accident was not allowed to interfere with the day's flying programme which continued as usual. It was not until we went into the mess for supper that we heard the news. The instructor, who had been forced to make an emergency landing in a ploughed field, had reported in by telephone. He explained that he had ordered a 90° change of course and had turned in towards his number 2.

Abs, however, instead of losing altitude and turning below and behind him as the manoeuvre required, had suddenly climbed. His machine was immediately above the leader's cockpit when the explosion occurred. The instructor reported seeing bits of aircraft falling to the ground but said there was no sign of a parachute. This meant that Fähnrich Abs must have been killed in the crash. The mood in the dining room became even more sombre. It was the first fatality we had experienced during the entire time of our training.

But then the door opened and in trudged Abs, his flying overalls none too clean and his parachute bundled together under his left arm. Everybody present stared at him as if they had seen a ghost. Abs looked around for the Kommandeur, spotted him, and made his way across to his table. Drawing himself up to attention, he saluted and delivered his report: "Fähnrich Abs returned from the mission. My aircraft exploded. I was able to save myself by parachute."

The entire room rang with relieved laughter and the hero of the hour was urged to explain what had happened: "I saw my instructor turning towards me, started to bank, and then he wasn't there any more. So I straightened out again and was suddenly in the middle of a fireball! The earth was spinning round me. I must have been thrown clear, for I was wearing the canopy frame around my neck like an enormous great ruff. I couldn't open my parachute until I got rid of the damned thing. And all the time the ground was getting closer and closer.

"At last I was able to free myself. I banged the release and the 'chute opened with an almighty crack. I was coming down over a farm. I just missed the roof and landed nice and softly in the manure heap," – hence the somewhat overripe overalls – "and then the farmer gave me a lift to the station."

We all congratulated Abs on his miraculous escape. There were no other serious incidents. And on 18 February 1943 the course came to a successful end, as attested to by the fresh entries in our pilot's licences: we were now qualified to fly all variants of the Me 109.

It was time for our first home leave. The passes tucked securely in our pockets granted us a whole sixteen days of freedom; from 19 February to 6 March. The family's joy when I appeared in the doorway of our home in Hermannsdorf was itself a sight to behold. And I must say it was wonderful to be able to sit and listen to father playing the piano, to be fussed over by mother, and to relax playing games with my young sisters. The days seemed to fly by, but I managed to visit a lot of old friends and acquaintances before, all too soon, the time came to depart. Father accompanied me to the station. Saying goodbye is always hard. A final hug on the platform, one last wave as the train drew out of the station, and I was on my way back to Werneuchen.

There my next posting awaited me. It was to Cazaux in southern France, a journey which took me and my six travelling companions two days to complete. Cazaux housed the Stab (HQ) of Jagdgruppe West. This was an Ergänzungsgruppe, or operational training unit, whose task it was to prepare newly-qualified fighter pilots such as ourselves for the realities of front-line service. The instructors were all highly experienced operational fighter pilots who were on temporary rotation back from their combat units for the sole purpose of imparting to us fledglings their expertise and knowledge of the latest conditions at the front. It was at Cazaux that the final decision was made as to where each new recruit was to be sent as a replacement: to the western or eastern theatre of war. As I had already expressed a preference for the east, I was assigned to Oberleutnant Clerico's 2 Staffel, which was based outside the well-known holiday resort of Biarritz on the French Biscay coast just north of the Spanish border.

Having spent our entire military careers to date in barracks, we discovered to our delight that we were now to be quartered in private houses which had been specially requisitioned for the purpose. The grass-surfaced airfield at Biarritz was located on high ground above the town. Because of the mildness of the climate, the aircraft were dispersed out in the open. The workshops were accommodated in large tents around the edge of the field.

The squadron mess was in a hotel down nearer to town on the shores of a small lake. It was idyllically situated and very comfortably appointed. It belonged to an American, who had left it intact upon his departure, complete with staff, and with his large limousine still sitting in the garage. The entire establishment had been taken over lock, stock and barrel by the Wehrmacht. The kitchen and dining room personnel continued to perform their duties. The Staffelkapitän used the vehicle as his staff car.

The whole building was decorated in an attractive Moorish style. The main room had sandstone walls and featured a huge open fireplace. Leading off it were three rooms, each in a different colour scheme: blue, red and green. All were furnished with silk tapestries and contained valuable antiques, which we were not permitted to touch. The green room, whose walls were covered, somewhat bizarrely, with a vast collection of door-knockers from all over the Mediterranean region, served as our dining room. The squadron's permanent staff occupied rooms in the hotel. As an ensign, I was given a single room in a villa nearby. Here too there were civilian personnel to look after our needs. We wanted for nothing and lived in the lap of absolute luxury.

Although not yet mid-March, the temperature when we arrived was already summer-like. We were issued with short-sleeved tropical shirts; a novelty for us. But there was to be little time for reflection or enjoyment. Training began the very next day, and we were constantly in the air; seven days a week. There was no such thing as weekends. The front urgently needed reinforcements. As far as our immediate surroundings were concerned – the town of Biarritz with its hotels and gambling casino, the beaches along the Biscay coast, the Pyrenees mountains marking the French-Spanish frontier – *all* we got was a bird's-eye view.

After three or four flights a day we wanted nothing more in the evenings than to fall into bed and get a good night's sleep. The instructors did not spare themselves, and they did not spare us. After our next move we would be flying operations in deadly earnest, weapons fully loaded, against the Red Air Force. And three weeks later my posting came through: to Jagdgeschwader 54, headquartered at Gatschina, south of Leningrad.

The rail journey from Biarritz to Gatschina – diagonally across almost the entire width of Europe from the south-western extremity to the north-eastern – was to last ten days, including planned stops in Paris and Berlin. The endless hours in jolting trains would transport us from the balmy warmth of the Biscay, through the burgeoning early spring in Germany, into a Russia still in the grip of winter. It was both an experience and something of an ordeal.

In Paris we stayed overnight in the Soldatenheim, the Wehrmacht leave centre set up in the Palais Rothchild. We were a group of twenty replacement pilots, all on our way to the front, but had 'organized' ourselves a few hours off to go sight-seeing in the French capital. We took in the Eiffel Tower and the Sacré Coeur, rummaged around in a flea-market, and paid a flying visit to the Louvre.

When we got to Berlin I managed to drop in to see Göttchen, who was still working as a nurse at the infants' home in the Alte Jakobsstraße. A trip on the Wannsee Lake also provided a brief but welcome relief from the constant rattling of railway carriages.

The final stages of the journey from Berlin to Gatschina were a real eye-opener. Before reaching the one-time Polish border we passed neat little communities, brick-built houses with red pantile roofs, cultivated fields, paved highways and well-tended woods. The change after crossing the frontier was startling: mainly wooden dwellings, often little more than huts, few roads and seemingly endless miles of forest. The towns were an exception, of course, but these were few and far between.

When the leave train we were travelling on, packed with soldiers returning to the front, eventually pulled into Gatschina it was two o'clock in the morning. We weren't expected and there was nobody to meet us, so we had to spend the rest of the night huddled together in the unheated waiting room. Outside all was still and quiet. Only far away to the north was there any sign of activity. Flak bursts twinkled fitfully in the night sky and the muffled rumble of artillery fire could be heard.

We had arrived at the front.

CHAPTER 3

With JG 54 on the Russian Front

As soon as the Gatschina RTO's office opened the following morning the transport officer phoned through to the Geschwader to inform them of our presence. Vehicles arrived to collect us at 07.00 hours. JG 54's headquarters were in one of the larger wooden buildings in the town. Here we were given a hearty breakfast and as much hot coffee as we wanted to take the chill of the hours spent in the freezing waiting room out of our bones.

By the spring of 1943 the Geschwader's strength in Russia had been reduced to just two Gruppen: I and II/JG 54. A few weeks earlier the third Gruppe had been transferred to the west. Initially, this had been intended as part of an experimental exchange scheme between eastern and western front fighter units. But, in fact, III/JG 54 was never to return to Russia. It remained in action against the western Allies right up to the end of the war.

So it was between I and II Gruppen that we newcomers were now divided. I was assigned to the latter's 5 Staffel: 5/JG 54. But before we went our separate ways, our little group was presented to the Kommodore of the Geschwader, Oberstleutnant Hannes Trautloft. He gave us a short address, welcoming us to the unit, before having a few brief words with each of us in turn. One by one we introduced ourselves in the regulation manner: "Fähnrich Hannig, transferred from Jagdgruppe West to Jagdgeschwader 54, effective 27 March."

"Hannig?" he queried. "Are you related to Leutnant Horst Hannig, our Knight's Cross winner serving with III Gruppe on the Channel front?"

"No, Herr Oberstleutnant," I was forced to confess, as I was neither related to – nor did I even know – this other Hannig.

"Regard him as a role model, then. Follow his example and you won't go far wrong," was the Kommodore's advice.

"Jawohl, Herr Oberstleutnant," I replied as he offered me his hand. Then we were dismissed and sent off to our new Staffeln.

It had begun to snow again, adding to the thick mantle already covering the ground. Fortunately, I did not have as far to travel as some of my comrades. 5 Staffel was also quartered in Gatschina, occupying several of the town's wooden houses. After the usual ritual of reporting in, handing over my travel orders and other documents, I was welcomed by the Staffelführer (acting CO) and introduced to the other pilots. The Staffelkapitän himself was away on leave. He was an Austrian, I learned, who had joined his country's air force back in 1935. He later became a member of the Austrian national aerobatic display team. When Austria was annexed into the Greater German Reich in March 1938 this entire team, pilots and ground crews, had been assimilated into the Luftwaffe and used to form the nucleus of the unit which had since become our II/JG 54. I was told, too, that he had been awarded the Oak Leaves to his Knight's Cross back in October for 100 victories, and that his score was now standing well above the 150 mark!

As an ensign I was to share a room with three Feldwebeln (sergeant pilots). Walter Heck was a wiry, sporting type, of medium build, who hailed from Hannover. Xaver Müller was a likeable, laconic native of Swabia. And Karl Brill, who was known to all as 'Ede', was a typical Rhinelander, always cheerful and ready for a joke. They immediately made me feel welcome. We addressed each other with the familiar "du", just like old friends. Walter had more than forty victories to his credit, and Xaver twenty-eight. Ede had arrived not long before me, but had already notched up two kills in his first thirty-odd missions.

I was number twenty-six on the pilot roster; the Staffel currently being well above its official complement of sixteen. But of that twenty-six, only five were officers, all of whom were fairly new.

Undoubtedly the most striking amongst them was a stocky, ex-Lufthansa pilot, who had a seemingly bottomless fund of anecdotes and stories that kept us all in fits of laughter. Because of his powerful, ox-like physique, Leutnant Emil Lang rejoiced in the nickname of 'Bully'. In contrast, another whose face I remembered from Werder – he had been ahead of me in the 1st Fahnenjunker-Kompanie – was a rather weedy type, who struck me as being a bit too boastful and arrogant. He tended to pull rank over the NCO pilots, one of the very few officers I ever encountered who did so, and consequently was not very well liked.

A number of NCOs and other ranks among the ground crews also sported decorations, including the Iron Cross, 1st and 2nd Class. These veterans of the front were equally welcoming and went out of their way to be helpful and make me feel at home. I could not have wished for a better group of comrades, both in the air and on the ground.

After the short-sleeved tropical shirts of Biarritz – was it really only a fortnight ago? – we were now issued with fur flying gear: two-piece sheepskin flying suits, with the fleece on the inside, fur-lined flying boots and gloves. The sheepskin jacket and trousers were worn over our normal uniforms and proved extremely effective in keeping the cold of the Russian winter at bay.

At night we slept in olive-green Soviet sleeping bags. Wool-filled and quilted, these bags were practical and very snug. They did not have a conventional hood, just an extension of the back section. But when this flap, which was about a metre in length, was pulled over the head and tucked into the front of the sack, it kept out both cold and light. The occupant was entirely hidden, giving every impression of a large and lumpy chrysalis waiting to hatch. White linen sheets from our normal bedclothes were used as lining and to preserve standards of hygiene. Lastly, if the side-toggles of the bag were unfastened it opened out into a very acceptable eiderdown.

The airfield at Gatschina had a paved runway which, if kept clear, permitted flying to carry on throughout the winter. Our Staffel, like the other two in the Gruppe, was equipped with the Me 109G, the take-off and landing foibles of which had been demonstrated to us during training so that we could now handle them with confidence. After a few days the weather cleared up and flying could be resumed. We newcomers were instructed to do a few circuits in order to familiarize ourselves with our surroundings.

During the night a couple of Pe-2s had flown over the field, one shortly after the other. Each had dropped its quartet of bombs, stirred our flak defences into activity, and then disappeared into the darkness again. One of the eight 250-kg bombs had failed to go off, however, and was still lying out on the field somewhere. At daybreak the seven craters were clearly visible in the snow, as was the spot where the dud must have landed.

As we set off by car around the perimeter track towards the take-off point to watch the first circuits being flown, we saw an armourer in black overalls making his way towards the position of the unexploded bomb. He must have found it, for he stopped, bent down and began to fiddle with something in the snow. Suddenly there was a huge explosion and we ducked instinctively. Once the smoke had cleared, and with the station fire brigade and ambulance already on their way, it was obvious to us what had happened: the bomb had exploded and the armourer had been blown to pieces. The medics carefully picked up the mangled body, but there were a number of small bloody spots in the surrounding snow which the ravens soon discovered and began to peck at.

As the ambulance drove off, my mind went back to that first day on the gliding slopes when the Hitler Youth pilot had nose-dived into the ground and had also been carted away. But he had been suffering from nothing more than a few broken ribs. This was real. This was war.

Nevertheless, the circuits were duly flown as ordered, although not entirely without excitement. As one of the Gustavs taxied in it dug a wheel into the soft earth of another freshly-filled crater and had to be towed back to dispersal by tractor.

On the aerial front all was quiet. The Soviet air force seemed reluctant to put in an appearance during the hours of daylight and missions were being flown without any sign of the enemy. The temperature began to climb and, even in Russia, the first unmistakable signs of spring were soon apparent.

II Gruppe was normally based at Siverskaya, a grass field situated some kilometres to the south of Gatschina (or Krasnogvardeisk, as the site of Geschwader HQ was alternatively, and somewhat confusingly, known). But, for the second year running, Siverskaya had been vacated by the flying units when the first snows of winter started to fall. The snow had then been left undisturbed ever since. It was not rolled flat, nor was anybody allowed either to drive or even walk upon it. Not having been compressed in any way, this snow was the first to melt. At the end of April, with the snow gone and the grass surface by now drained and firm enough to permit operations to resume, the Gruppe was thus able to move back to Siverskaya.

I found my new 'home' to be a large expanse of grass surrounded by a perimeter track. The flight control buildings and ops room were located on the northern side. In front of them stood three colourfully painted and larger than life-size plywood figures. These were caricatures of Roosevelt, Churchill and Stalin. A sign read, 'Comrades, leave them alone and don't get your fingers dirty!' Airmen's humour!

The dispersals of the Gruppe's three component Staffeln, 5, 6 and 7, were spaced around the edge of the field. Taxiways, take-off and landing strips were aligned on a west-east axis and indicated by red and white markers. At dawn an Alarmrotte (emergency section) of two aircraft would take up position behind the take-off area and be at instant readiness to scramble. The signal to do so was a green flare, fitted with a whistle or siren, fired from Gruppe ops.

5 Staffel's dispersals occupied a pleasant spot sheltered by a small birch wood on the south-western perimeter of the field. A collection of huts along the edge of the trees served as the ops and pilots' readiness rooms, and provided working facilities for the mechanics, armourers and signals personnel. If Gruppe gave the order, all twelve operational aircraft of a Staffel could take off together straight across the field from their dispersals. In dire emergencies, when all three Staffeln were to be scrambled in this way, green and red flares would be used to indicate the sequence of take-off.

Siverskaya's main barracks were three-storey buildings with running water and flush-toilets – luxurious by local standards. The first two floors accommodated the technical personnel, with the top floor being occupied by the pilots. The arrangement worked well and, with Russian civilians taking care of the quarters, everybody felt quite at home. Each Staffel's pilots also had the services of a cook, who looked after the cold rations and collected the warm midday meal from the field kitchen before bringing it out to the dispersal in a wagon drawn by one of the tough little Russian panje ponies.

In the meantime, we tyros had been poring over maps of the area, acquainting ourselves with the locations of the various emergency landing rounds and fixing in our minds the exact position of the front line. The northern sector had been the most stable part of the entire eastern front for many months past. Consequently, the front itself was clearly visible as a long – although not continuous – line of trench systems, earthworks and artillery emplacements scarring the landscape.

At this time the northern end of the line was anchored on the shores of the Gulf of Finland to the west of Leningrad. From here it looped around the southern outskirts of the city before following the course of the River Neva, which flowed north-eastwards into Lake Ladoga at Schlüsselburg. Some 10 kilometres short of the lake, however, the front turned due east, running in an almost straight line for 50 kilometres to the swampy region bordering the River Volkhov. Here it angled sharply southwards, again following the river line all the way to Lake Ilmen.

As the Soviet Union's second city, Leningrad was normally well served with road and rail communications. Three main railway lines radiated southwards from the city. The easternmost linked it to Novgorod on the northern shores of Lake Ilmen. The middle one connected up with the main east-west artery at Dno. And the westernmost line ran down through Gatschina to Pskov (Pleskau) and from there on into the Baltic States.

The whole region was one of vast forests and swamps. There was little agricultural land to be seen from the air. Minor roads, often little more than dirt tracks, connected an occasional village to its neighbour. Incongruously, the area was also dotted with the summer palaces and castles of the Tsars and one-time ruling nobility. Compared to the normal citizens' humble wooden dwellings, these flamboyant edifices, sitting in their own landscaped parklands, only served to emphasize the enormous gulf between the classes.

Along the coast of the Gulf of Finland to the west of Leningrad, and separated from the city by a corridor some 30 kilometres wide, was the isolated Soviet pocket of Oranienbaum. Of no strategic importance to the Wehrmacht, this had been left to wither on the vine.

On 12 January 1943 – before our little group had arrived at Gatschina, and while the world's attention was focused on the developing drama of Stalingrad to the far south – the Red Army had launched yet another offensive aimed at breaking the blockade of Leningrad. And this time they finally succeeded. In temperatures of 30° centigrade below zero, the German army had been dislodged from Schlüsselburg and pushed back 10 kilometres from Lake Ladoga.

The '900-day' siege of Leningrad had been lifted. The trickle of supplies into the beleaguered city, which had previously had to be transported laboriously across Lake Ladoga – by small ships during the summer, by truck along the famous 'ice-road' laid across its frozen surface during the winter – had now become a steady stream delivered directly by the newly laid field railway which snaked through the 10-kilometre gap opened up between the shores of the lake and the German front line.

Both Gruppen of JG 54 had been heavily involved during the fighting around Schlüsselburg, as they had been during operations over the Demyansk cauldron to the south of Lake Ilmen immediately thereafter. All this we had only learnt second-hand, of course, from the accounts of those who had taken part in these actions. We had not yet seen any fighting ourselves. But that was soon about to change. For the first few operations, however, we would have to be 'nursed' by one of the more experienced pilots.

The first priority after arriving at dispersal each morning was to divide the pilots scheduled to fly that day into Schwärme and Rotten. They would each be assigned one of the serviceable machines and it was then the ground crew's job to adjust the seat height and rudder pedals to suit the pilot's size. The older members of the Staffel had their 'own' machines that they flew regularly and which didn't need adjusting before every sortie.

On 1 April I had been made up to Oberfähnrich (senior ensign). For a moment or two I had wondered whether this was another of Ede Brill's April Fool jokes. But even though my promotion was official, I knew I still had a tremendous lot to learn. On this particular morning I was therefore delighted to be told that I was to fly as number 2 to Walter Heck. I could not be in safer or more capable hands for my first operational mission.

Take-off was to be at 09.00 hours. We synchronized our watches and Walter gave me a short briefing. It ended with the words: "... and always keep to the side of me *away* from the front line – stay at the same altitude and maintain position slightly behind me and 50 metres away. And keep a constant look-out at all times. When I waggle my wings on the way back, you close up to me. Our call signs are 'Dackel' [Dachshund] 1 and 2. Start engines at 08.55. Any questions?" "No. Everything's clear," I answered simply. I was eager and ready to go.

Then came the moment that sixteen months of training had been preparing me for. Start engines, R/T check, taxi out and line up for take-off. A quick glance across at my number 1, a nod of his head... throttle slowly forwards, foot hovering on the right brake – we start to roll. The rudder begins to respond, hold the nose down slightly, more speed, and then fly her off and keep close to the leader as we climb away. While climbing adjust the trim and then, at a hand signal from Walter, open up into combat formation and flick the weapons switch. The click is audible. The indicator panels show white: cannon and machine guns armed and ready to fire.

I am at the controls of a lethal fighting machine. But it is no time to be complacent. My head swivels constantly as my eyes search the skies around us: to the front, above, to the right, behind, to the left, above, to the front again. The movements soon become automatic.

Meanwhile, Walter had set course northwards, flying at an altitude of 1,000 metres. Below us to the right I could see the railway line from Siverskaya up to Gatschina, and beyond to Leningrad. As we overflew the junction at Krasnoye Selo the Gulf of Finland, the easternmost arm of the Baltic Sea, appeared ahead. Offshore, Kotlin Island, which housed the major Soviet naval base of Kronstadt, was clearly visible.

We were still over friendly territory, the 30-kilometre-wide strip of land separating Oranienbaum, the Russian-held enclave to our left, and the sprawling mass of Leningrad to our right. When we reached the coast near the ruins of Peterhof Castle, Walter signalled a turn to starboard. We flew along the front line around the southern edge of Leningrad and then followed it north-eastwards along the Neva. On the horizon another large body of water loomed up: Lake Ladoga. Shortly before Schlüsselburg we left the Neva and headed due east towards the Volkhov swamps. Here, one more right turn took us southwards again, across the tracks of the main Leningrad-Novgorod railway, towards home.

These tracks, by the way, played an important role in the Geschwader's operations. Cutting arrow-straight through mile upon mile of virgin forest – and flanked for much of their length by a major highway – they provided the one unmistakable reference point in an otherwise featureless landscape. If a formation was broken up and badly scattered during a dogfight over, or beyond, the front lines – or if a pilot became disorientated for any reason – the Leningrad-Novgorod railway line was the ideal re-assembly point and a sure signpost for the way back to base.

Although Walter had, in effect, taken me on a grand tour of almost the entire sector, we had not spotted a single enemy aircraft. My first operational flight had been about as exciting as a cross-country exercise. Admittedly, the landscape was new and unfamiliar. But the only indications that we were in a war zone were the occasional muzzle flash and explosion of an artillery exchange far below, and a few columns of smoke drifting lazily upwards.

Since February the pilots of I and II Gruppen had been rotating back to the Homeland in small batches for conversion on to the Fw 190A. The 'Forke', or 'Pitchfork', as we christened it, was a much more robust bruiser of a fighter than the Me 109G. It was powered by a 1,700 hp BMW radial engine and was armed with two 20-mm cannon in the wing-roots, plus two fuselage-mounted 12.7-mm machine guns. It possessed a sturdy, wide-track undercarriage and, despite its more powerful engine, displayed none of the Me 109's tendencies to swing on take-off. Set high on the fuselage, the cockpit offered excellent visibility to the rear. Unlike the Me 109, the canopy was not hinged at the side, but rearward-sliding. Normally operated by hand-crank, it could be jettisoned by explosive cartridge in cases of emergency.

The Fw 190's performance and flying characteristics were equally impressive. In a dive it could exceed 700 km/h. It was highly responsive around all axes, could be reefed into a tight turn, and gave its pilot ample warning of a stall by sharp, jerky aileron movements. If these were ignored, the machine would automatically go into a flick half roll, losing height and turning through 180° in less time than it takes to describe here. This manoeuvre was virtually impossible for another pilot to follow. If you were in a dogfight, and had sufficient altitude, it was a sure way of getting an opponent off your tail. This 'built-in' escape tactic was the saving of many a Forke pilot who found himself *in extremis*.

The conversion course took place at Heiligenbeil airfield in East Prussia, where the new fighters were delivered direct from a nearby factory. The Geschwader kept a rear party based at the field, who were responsible for conducting the conversion training.

A group of us left Siverskaya on 20 April 1943 in a Junkers W 34 transport. The driver of this venerable old bird, a firm believer in the 'left-hand wheel, right-hand rail' method of progress, conveyed us along the 850-kilometre route of the Pleskau-Riga-Tilsit railway line and deposited us safely at Heiligenbeil after 3 hours and 40 minutes in the air.

There were eight of us: Eckert, Hoffmann, Koller, Brill, Pomberger, Kuzel, Tangermann and myself; two Schwärme, in other words. First it was back into the classroom for lectures on the machine's technical systems and equipment. I never quite understood why I, as a pilot, needed to know which particular piece of plumbing delivered fuel to the engine and which distributed the oil; or how and whether the electric motors for the undercarriage and landing flaps derived their power from the generator or the battery.

All that interested me were the instruments on the panel in front of me that told me how the aircraft was behaving, the state of my weapons, the amount of fuel I had remaining, and other such incidentals. After all, when in the air you couldn't just get out and have a poke around under the bonnet to see what was wrong. Nor, if a serious fault developed, could you simply stay up there. You had to get back down on the ground again as quickly as possible. This is one of the basic laws of flying and combines the twin merits of simplicity and unalterable fact. And there were only three ways of doing it: on your wheels, on your belly, or by parachute.

Our heads stuffed with information, we were finally allowed into the cockpits of our new machines. And from the moment we flew our first circuits we were won over by the Fw 190's undoubted qualities. Very soon we were taking off in Rotten and heading across the lagoon-like Frische Haff and out over the open waters of the Baltic to indulge in some freie Jagd practice.

Although it was no Berlin, the picturesque little town of Heiligenbeil, which was the seat of the local rural district government, was a popular destination in our off-duty hours. Literally translated, the town's name meant 'holy hatchet' (now it is Mamonovo in Poland), but we quickly learned to refer to it as Saint Axe. In the market square the town hall was surrounded by shops and taverns. One of our favourite watering holes was Korn's Gesellschaftshaus, a café bar where the tables and upholstered benches were arranged in booths.

It was here one evening that we bumped into two I Gruppe pilots who were still awaiting delivery of their Fw 190A-4s. One of them was 'Schorsch'. He was a cheerful type from Vienna and, like Ede, always ready for a joke and a laugh. There were hardly any alcoholic drinks to be had. The so-called 'flyers' beer' that was on offer, a weak 1% brew, tasted like the proverbial gnat's pee and was to be avoided at all costs. Meals were only available on coupons, which none of us had.

Despite this, the conversation around the table soon grew animated. Naturally the subject was flying; the talk all about missions flown and dogfights fought. Hands drew curves in an imaginary sky, describing manoeuvres that any fighter pilot would have recognized instantly.

Sitting in the next booth were five young ladies. We had not been unaware of their presence. Schorsch seemed to be showing particular interest. But how to strike up an acquaintance? At about ten o'clock they got up and went to put on their hats and coats. One, a particularly attractive brunette who had not paid the slightest attention to us, took a wide-brimmed blue hat from one of the hooks. That was when Schorsch turned to me: "I dare you!" he challenged. "Dare me what?" I replied suspiciously. "Dare you to escort the young lady in the blue hat home."

"Just you watch," I countered, sliding quickly out of the booth and going over to the girls by the coat-rack. I could tell which coat the girl in the blue hat was about to reach for and just beat her to it. I took it off the hook and held it open for her, asking politely: "May I be of assistance?" She was a bit taken aback. But after studying me for a moment, she agreed.

I helped her on with the coat before summoning up the courage to chance my luck a little further: "Would you perhaps permit me to escort you home, it's already pitch black outside?" She considered for a moment and then gave her assent.

I grabbed my cap from the other hat-stand, waved to my companions still sitting open-mouthed in the booth, and left with the young lady in the blue hat.

She showed me the way through the darkened streets. As I was a good head taller than my companion, she suggested with a smile, "Why don't you walk in the road beside the pavement – that way I won't feel quite so short and we can chat more easily." I was more than happy to oblige. The remark had been typical of my new-found friend. I soon discovered that she was full of mischief and possessed an impish sense of humour. Her laughter rang out with a bell-like clarity. But she also had a serious side, displaying an enquiring mind and a wide range of knowledge. Her tone of voice perhaps expressed her true feelings more than the actual words spoken. I found myself very attracted to her.

We arranged to meet again and did so on a number of occasions. We took long walks together, and were soon on Christian name terms and using the familiar term of address to each other. I had learned that Fräulein Pultke, or Gisela as I now called her, lived with her grandparents – her parents being divorced – and that she worked in the personnel office at Heiligenbeil airfield. We exchanged addresses and she promised that she would write to me.

On 29 April we took off in our brand-new Fw 190s to fly – you've guessed it, left-hand wheel, right-hand track – back to Siverskaya where we all landed safely.

The northern sector had remained quiet in our absence. The Geschwader had by now exchanged all but six of its Me 109Gs for Focke-Wulfs. These last half-dozen Gustavs had been fitted with bomb racks and were to be employed on Jabo (fighter-bomber) missions. Each could carry a single 250-kg bomb. As these missiles could only be aimed by using the cross-hairs of the fighter's normal Revi gun-sight, it meant diving on the target. Nobody was overly keen to fly on these sorties. But as a senior ensign hoping to become an officer, the Staffelkapitän kindly allowed me to take part in every fighter-bomber mission flown. I suppose I ought to have felt privileged.

Walter was my regular number 1 on these sorties. Apart from the boss, he was the most experienced combat pilot in the Staffel. He had been awarded the German Cross in Gold back in February. Because of its size and shape, this medal, worn on the right breast of the service tunic, was commonly referred to as the 'fried egg'. Had it been earlier in the war, Walter's present score would have more than qualified him for the Knight's Cross. The first of these prestigious decorations had been presented in 1940 for a total of 20 aerial victories. But by 1943 the requirement had quadrupled to 80. And by the end of 1944 totals of 100 or more had to be achieved before the award was conferred. The Knight's Cross alone could therefore not be regarded as a true measure of any particular recipient's performance in combat when compared to another's. The goalposts were moved too often to allow any such comparisons to have any meaning.

On one Jabo sortie our task was to destroy the railway line east of Lyuban which the Soviets were using to bring supplies up to the front. It was an unpopulated area, covered in peat bogs and vast tracts of forest. Taking care to cross the front line with sufficient height to keep well clear of ground fire and light flak, we set course eastwards. At the estimated time the target hove into view. We dropped down to 500 metres before lining ourselves up with the tracks and commencing a shallow dive. We released our bombs and watched their fall. They hit the cinder bed of the track, but then bounced back up into the air before exploding harmlessly in the peat bog alongside. Disappointed, we turned away and headed towards home.

Walter climbed steadily throughout the return flight. By the time we were over Siverskaya – or the 'Gartenzaun' (garden fence), to use the standard Luftwaffe codeword for a unit's home base – we were at an altitude of 7,000 metres. But still Walter continued to climb. We were in a gentle left-hand turn, flying in tight formation, with me tucked in on the inside close beside Walter. I was aware of him watching me.

It was at that moment that my wing leading-edge slots popped open, an indication that I was in danger of stalling. If I stayed in the inside position, and if Walter continued to fly this close to stalling speed, I would not be able to hold the Gustav very much longer. I had no other option but to try to change sides; to take up station on Walter's right – on the outside of the turning circle. The throttle was already fully forward, I could not get another ounce of power out of it. So I eased off slightly, sacrificed a little height, and began to slide under and behind his aircraft.

Suddenly I found myself caught in his propeller wash. My machine rocked violently and then – with its wings remaining almost perfectly level – began to rotate about its vertical axis. There was no response from either stick or rudder pedals, the controls were completely slack. As the Me 109 started sinking towards the ground, whirling round and round like the blades of a helicopter rotor, the 360° of the horizon passed in front of my eyes; revolving slowly at first, but then with ever-increasing speed. I applied full rudder with all my might, I pushed the stick forward as far as it would go – nothing!!!

I was in a flat spin. We had not been taught how to deal with this, the most dangerous and feared situation any pilot could find himself in. Nobody in his right mind subjected himself voluntarily to this manoeuvre. But I *had* heard all about the horror stories. If I couldn't get the Gustav into a normal spin – in other words push the nose down below the horizon – so that I could initiate standard recovery measures, there was only one way out: by parachute.

I had one last chance, the large tailplane trim wheel down to the left beside my seat. If I could alter the trim to make the machine sufficiently nose heavy, maybe that would enable me to get it pointing earthwards. I began to crank the wheel with all my might. Walter's voice crackled peremptorily in my headphones. Ignoring normal R/T procedure, he yelled in clear language: "Norbert, get out! You're in a flat spin!!!" A fact which hadn't escaped me. But thanks to the earlier climb I still had plenty of height in reserve, and thus a little more time before it became absolutely necessary to bale out.

The altimeter still showed 6,000 metres as I continued cranking the handwheel furiously. Although I was securely strapped into my harness, my head was being flung from side to side against the canopy. At last I could begin to feel the nose going down. The machine revolved even faster for a few seconds and then suddenly I was out of it – out of the flat spin and in a normal steep spin, nose pointing almost straight downwards.

This was something I had been shown how to handle during training. I applied full opposite rudder and held the stick pressed forwards with both hands. The spinning motion slowed down and stopped. But I was still diving vertically towards the ground. The altimeter had unwound to just 1,000 metres and the airspeed indicator was showing 650 km/h as I gently eased the stick back. The Gustav's snout came up and with 500 metres to spare I was flying straight and level.

I'd done it. Wasting little more time, I turned back towards the field and touched down. I taxied to my dispersal point, switched off my engine and reported to Walter, who had already landed and was waiting for me. "That was a close thing, old son," he said. "But well done."

There was still the little matter of the Soviet supply line, however. We were later sent off to have another go at it. This time we did not attack lengthwise along the track. Instead, we carried out our approach from the side. And we did not aim at the rails themselves, but at the earth embankment they had been laid upon. The bombs, fitted with percussion rod fuses to maximise their blast effect, exploded on impact, sending fountains of earth into the air, together with some sizeable chunks of rail. That was one supply line well and truly severed – at least for now.

Walter had another little habit. After touching down in a normal three-pointer he would give a dab on the brakes – just enough to raise the tail back up in the air – add a touch of throttle, and drive his aircraft back across the field to dispersal like a car. Those of us landing in his wake, who taxied in the normal manner, weaving slightly to be able to see ahead, would then be chided tongue-in-cheek for our tardiness. This was to have unforeseen consequences for me not long afterwards.

Another Jabo mission I took part in was targeted at the goods stations and marshalling yards in Leningrad where the supply trains were unloaded. Reconnaissance had shown that these trains were often packed close together on adjoining tracks. But Leningrad, as we all knew, had the strongest flak defences of the entire northern sector.

On this occasion my number 1 was to be Unteroffizier Pomberger. We took off from Siverskaya in the pre-dawn darkness, using the blue-white tongues of flame from our exhaust stubs to keep station and to get into formation once airborne. Setting off on a long climb north-eastwards, we crossed the front line over the peat fields to the east of Mga and continued on a little further before reversing course to approach Leningrad with the rising sun behind us. Night had given way to the first flush of dawn. The stars faded in the cloudless sky as the sun rose. Light seeped across the Russian landscape like the tide coming in over a flat sandy beach. From 5,000 metres it was a beautiful sight as the amorphous grey carpet beneath our wings gradually assumed form, shape and colour.

But we had little time to romanticize over the wonders of nature. By the time we reached Leningrad we had to be at 7,000 metres; a tough haul when toting a 250-kg bomb. As the city came into view we opened up into a wider formation than usual, knowing full well what lay in store for us. The goods yards where the supply trains entering the city from the east ended their journey were clearly visible, as were the trains themselves, some of the engines enveloped in steam.

As we crossed in over the city the muzzle flashes of the anti-aircraft guns winked up at us. We began the 'Flak Waltz' – up a little, down a little, left a little, right a little. The gunners had their eye in. Flak bursts blossomed exactly level with – but fortunately in between – our two widely spaced Gustavs. It was time to start the dive; gently at first, but then ever more steeply, trying all the while to keep the target centred in the sights.

At 3,000 metres we pulled back the three marks on the stick that would put us at exactly the right angle to launch, pressed the bomb-release switch, and banked away to watch the bombs disappear beneath us. It took several seconds before explosions erupted on the ground. One of the bombs must have hit a munitions train, to judge from the fireworks display that resulted. The other struck a building in the yards, causing it to collapse in on itself. There was still a lot of heavy flak, but it was behind and above us. The gunners had been unable to follow our steep descent.

The main railway line supplying Leningrad from the Russian heartland to the east had to cross two rivers, the Volkhov and the Neva, before reaching the city. The bridges spanning these two rivers – that over the Volkhov at the town of the same name, the one over the Neva at Schlüsselburg – were thus of considerable strategic interest to the German High Command. If one or other of these multi-piered structures could be destroyed, it would deal a major blow to the Soviets' supply network.

As the Volkhov bridge lay beyond the range of even the heaviest of our artillery, the job of knocking it out had been given to the bombers and Stukas of Luftflotte 1, the air fleet that controlled all Luftwaffe units, including JG 54, on the northern sector of the Russian front. But as the Neva bridge at Schlüsselburg could be targeted by heavy railway guns, its destruction was the responsibility of the army.

Among the biggest of these railway guns was that known as the Adolf K (E). This monster from the Krupp factory had a calibre of 406 mm, a barrel length of 20.3 metres, weighed 323,000 kg (317 tons), and required a crew of sixty to man it. At a range of 30 kilometres the fall of shot could be anywhere within a circle 250 metres in diameter. It was not a very accurate weapon. To hit the bridge or one of its support piers would therefore be a matter of pure luck.

In the first half of May engineers had begun to lay curved spurs along the stretch of track from which the gun was being fired. Aligned with the general target area, the main track was sufficient for coarse pointing of the weapon. Fine laying was done by carefully moving the gun to exactly the right spot along one of the curved sections. Fire control was carried out from the air by an artillery spotter in the back seat of a twin-engined Me 110 reconnaissance machine. A Rotte of our Fw 190s had to provide fighter escort for the Me 110 during every shoot. For as soon as the spotter appeared overhead whole squadrons of Soviet fighters would be scrambled from the airfield outside Schlüsselburg with orders to shoot it down and thus bring a halt to the fire control process. These escort missions alternated with our continuing fighter-bomber sorties.

On 20 May 1943 I again flew as katschmarek – the Luftwaffe term for a wingman – to Walter on another Jabo strike. Our target on this occasion was a road junction in a village quite a way behind the Russian lines along the Volkhov front. Walter used a map to work out our route and estimate our flight time to the objective. The rest was routine: take-off, approach flight, attack and back home to Siverskaya. We encountered no opposition in the air. The bombs had hit their target, but the damage wouldn't hold up the Soviets for long. Their working parties would soon have it repaired.

We circled the base before landing. I touched down just behind Walter, who pulled his usual trick of lifting his tail off the ground and driving his Gustav back to dispersal. I didn't want to waste time, and so followed his example. All went splendidly. I also drove across the field on two wheels and then let the tail sink back down onto the ground as I approached the dispersal area, where the mechanic was waving both arms above his head – the signal for keep coming.

Normally when taxiing, the procedure was to weave slightly from side to side in order to allow the pilot to see ahead. If he kept in a straight line, his direct forward vision was obscured by the bulk of the engine cowling filling the windscreen. But, reassured by the mechanic's waving, I did just that. I rolled straight on in to dispersal.

What I hadn't realized was that the figure in the black overalls was not my chief mechanic, but a newcomer to the ground crew. He wasn't familiar with our ground movement signals. So when he saw me heading directly towards another parked Me 109, he began waving his arms wildly in the air to warn me. The correct signal would have been to hold his arms crossed above his head. This would have brought me to an immediate halt. Under normal circumstances this would be followed by one arm, either right or left, being held straight up to indicate which brake to keep on, while the other arm beckoned slowly forwards, meaning pivot the aircraft about the locked wheel and then switch off engine.

Whether or not the new mechanic knew this second part of the procedure quickly became immaterial. The propeller and engine cowling of the other Me 109 suddenly loomed up in front of me. There was an almighty crash. My own propeller came to an abrupt stop – buried in the other fighter's wing.

This was a classic example of a ground collision, or 'taxiing damage'. In such incidents any damage caused was automatically assumed to be the fault of the pilot of the machine in motion. And I had just severely bent two valuable combat aircraft. A cut-and-dried case for court martial and the end of my flying career. It would be pointless to lay the blame on the mechanic. But I had been in the same situation once before: when I wrote off the Bücker back in LKS 3 at Beelitz. On that occasion I had got away with a strong reprimand. Could I pull the same stroke again – admit responsibility and request due punishment? First of all, I would have to report to Walter. But he just shook his head and asked: "Did you *have* to do that?" before adding, "I've already spoken to the boss. You're to go and see him in his quarters."

I set off gloomily on foot around the perimeter track. Before I had got far I saw a car pull away from the barracks area and head towards me in a large cloud of dust: the boss! When he spotted me, he stopped the car. I went across to him to make my report, thinking as I did so, here we go again: "Oberfähnrich Hannig, two Me 109s damaged by ground collision on returning from a mission. I request my punishment."

The Staffelkapitän was of small, compact stature. When he got excited the veins in his forehead swelled visibly. But now his blue eyes regarded me quite calmly. And when he spoke, his voice, to my surprise, was equally calm – almost soft: "If the court martial people think they can simply take my best people away from me, they've got another thing coming! Not this time. Get in."

I climbed in beside him. He turned the car round, put the accelerator to the floor and raced back to the barracks block. He told me to wait in my quarters until I was sent for. Then he drove off to Gruppe HQ to discuss the matter with the Gruppenkommandeur. An hour later the summons came. I was to report to his office in full equipment and wearing my steel helmet. When I entered he was seated at his desk: "Stand to attention, Hannig. I am placing you under three days' close arrest, effective as of now, for negligence in that, on 20 May 1943, you damaged two combat aircraft. Place of confinement will be set up here. The Duty NCO will arrange all further details. Any questions?"

I had no questions. After saluting with my hand to my helmet, I about-turned and left the room. The Duty NCO was waiting outside – it was my chief mechanic. The room he shared with three others was to be my detention cell. It was quickly re-arranged and I moved in an hour later. As the regulations stated that no soldier could be punished twice for the same offence, my being arrested lifted the threat of a court martial.

Instead of having to exist on dry bread and water, my mechanic brought me in the best of everything. The door to my 'cell' wasn't locked and I had a bed with clean white sheets. At this rate, I thought, I should just about be able to hold out for three days.

On the first evening the boss came in to see me, accompanied by the Staffel's Senior NCO. I was asked to describe the incident again. His nods and smiles as I recounted exactly what had happened spoke volumes without his having to say a single word. As the boss looked around the room, the Senior NCO turned to me: "What do you what for reading material, the Bible or *Mein Kampf*?" he enquired.

Apparently this was also part of the regulations. Anyone under close arrest was permitted one of these two books. The boss was obviously taken by surprise, for he asked, "Have we got anything of that sort around here?" Flight had to admit that we hadn't – but was sure we could get hold of both books from somewhere. I refused the offer with thanks. The Duty NCO had already supplied me with plenty of reading matter.

On 21 May I could really relax and enjoy being under close arrest. I could sleep for as long as I wanted to, had more than enough to eat, plenty to read, and could chat to my guards, all of whom were members of the ground crew. They really spoiled me in return for my not having implicated their new boy in any way.

But on 22 May I heard that there had been a dogfight west of Schlüsselburg between the two Fw 190s escorting the artillery spotter and a number of Russian fighters. Walter had been leading the Rotte, but another katschmarek was flying as his number 2. After being hit in the engine, Walter had been forced to put down on the emergency landing strip at Mga, just behind the front lines.

This strip was nothing more than a pocket handkerchief-sized clearing in the woods, surrounded by tall firs, and with a good half of its area still wet and boggy. Walter had attempted a wheels-down landing, but the undercarriage immediately sank into the mushy surface and the Focke-Wulf had somersaulted. The two cables anchoring the pilot's bullet-proof head armour snapped. The slab of heavy armoured-steel plate, which was intended to protect the pilot when under attack from the rear, had slammed down on Walter's neck crushing one of his vertebrae.

When he was rescued from the wreckage Walter had still been alive, but paralysed from the neck down. He was taken to the field hospital at Mga, where he had implored the staff to put him out of his misery: "Shoot me, for pity's sake shoot me! It's hopeless – I'll never be able to move again."

His mind was perfectly clear and he fully realized the situation he was in. The boss visited him in hospital and was obviously still deeply affected by the tragedy when he told us about it later. After three days Walter Heck died and was laid to rest in the field cemetery. I was tortured by thoughts of not having been there to help. If I had been flying on Walter's wing, could I have somehow prevented his being hit? It was too late now.

On the day after Walter's emergency landing Luftflotte 1 began its campaign to destroy the Volkhov bridge. The first attack was to be carried out by a Staffel of Ju 87 dive-bombers, escorted by two Schwärme of Fw 190s from 5/JG 54. This called for a near-maximum effort from the Staffel and my services were required. At 09.00 hours I was released from close arrest. Sixty minutes later I was flying number 2 to Xaver, the quiet taciturn Swabian. But Xaver, who uttered barely three words during the course of the day on the ground, was a sharp as a knife in the air.

We had been ordered to provide close escort for the Stukas. This meant staying with them throughout, even during the dive, and protecting them from attack on the return flight. Once back over friendly territory our leader would waggle his wings – we had no radio contact with the dive-bombers – the Stuka leader would waggle his in response, and our task would be over.

The outward flight took us out over the familiar landscape of the Volkhov forests. We passed over the front line running through the peat bogs, undisturbed by flak. The Stukas flew in a very neat and close formation, almost wingtip to wingtip; they made an imposing sight. We criss-crossed close above them, first flying some 100 metres out to one flank and then returning back over the formation before heading the same distance out over the other.

The River Volkhov was crossed some distance upstream from the bridge. After a few minutes the Stukas began a wide turn to port which would take them, and us, up to the line of the railway. Another left-hand turn and the formation was now heading westwards, back along the glinting steel tracks and straight towards the bridge. There was not an enemy fighter to be seen in the sky.

The Stukas split into Schwärme and began to dive on the bridge. We eased back on our throttles and went down alongside them. At 300 metres they released their bombs and started to pull out. The Russian flak emplacements surrounding the bridge were firing for all they were worth. Angry orange and red fingers of tracer reached out at us but failed to score a single hit. We raced away at ground level and, once safely out of range of enemy fire, climbed up to re-form and set course for home.

The bridge was hidden in the fountains of water thrown up by the exploding bombs. But when a high-altitude reconnaissance aircraft overflew the target an hour later the supply trains were still crossing the bridge. The attack had been a failure.

Three days passed before the next attempt was made. This time the attacking force was made up of two Gruppen of Stukas – but the result was the same. The bombs exploded all round the bridge, but again no damage was inflicted. The supplies continued to roll into Leningrad.

By this time even the northern sector of the Russian front was beginning to feel the heat of summer. Our special issue winter clothing, the two-piece sheepskin flying suits, were returned to stores and exchanged for summer kit consisting of lightweight grey trousers with large patch pockets on the thigh, and a zippered flight blouse. For some reason the blouse I was given was white, presumably once part of some dandy's special order.

In the early mornings, when it was still cool, we would collect dry kindling in the woods bordering our dispersal area, light a camp fire, and sit around it in our deckchairs swapping stories and experiences while waiting for the day's orders to arrive.

On one particular morning, 27 May, Xaver and I were scheduled to fly the next mission. It turned out to be another escort job protecting the spotter aircraft for the big guns still trying to knock out the Neva bridge at Schlüsselburg. The artillery spotter, in an Me 110 as usual, was to arrive over Siverskaya at 10.30 hours and fire a green flare, signalling us to start, before he set course for the front. The radio call-sign for our Rotte was a perennial favourite: Edelweiß 1 and 2. We taxied over to the take-off point five minutes before start time and saw the Me 110 approaching from the south. Once overhead, the green flare was fired as arranged, and we began to roll.

We quickly caught up with the twin-engined machine and everything seemed to be going to plan. But shortly before we reached the front line our interceptor station, which listened in to the radio traffic from all the local Soviet airfields, came on the air: "To all cyclists in area Schum, to all cyclists in area Schum. The fighters at Schum have been given the order to scramble, Frage Viktor?" Cyclists was the codeword used in radio transmissions to refer to friendly fighters. That meant us.

Xaver acknowledged: "Edelweiß to Anton 1, Viktor, Viktor." Anton 1 was the call-sign of the station on the ground. Schum was the Russian airfield south of Schlüsselburg. The Soviet fighters were being sent up against us. We could already see the field quite clearly, and could even make out the plumes of dust being raised by the LaGG-3s – the fighters we knew from experience to be stationed there – as they took off.

The LaGGs began to spiral slowly upwards in a loose ball. They were in no discernible formation. In fact, the enemy pilots seemed to be displaying no flight discipline at all. Nevertheless, we managed to count the number of individual machines making up the swirling mass. There were sixteen of them. If it came to a fight we would be facing odds of 8:1. We positioned ourselves between the Me 110 and the Ivans still gaining altitude above their field to the south. Our weapons were switched on. We were ready.

Meanwhile the Me 110 continued to go about its business, spotting for the huge railway gun. Every time the order to fire was given, other batteries in the area would also open fire in order to prevent the Soviet sound locators from pin-pointing the weapon's exact location. From the air we could see muzzle flashes along a whole section of the front flicker in unison.

A few seconds later an enormous spout of water or column of earth would climb skywards from the immediate vicinity of the bridge. Apparently satisfied that he had done all he could, the Me 110 broke off and waggled his wings as he headed back towards the front line. It was the signal that we were no longer required.

Released from our escort duties, Xaver immediately focused his attention on the enemy fighters. He climbed above them, flying a wide turn to starboard with me following tucked in behind on his right. One of the Russians detached himself from the untidy gaggle and started to loop. When near the top he loosed of a burst of fire almost straight up in the air – no danger there.

Another of the Ivans then attempted a clumsy sort of Immelmann that brought him up almost level with us. Quickly realising his error he tried a desperate break to port, only to present his pale blue belly in front of Xaver as if on a plate. From a range of 80 metres Xaver couldn't miss. The brief salvo from his 20-mm cannon tore the wooden LaGG apart.

"Abschuß!" Xaver announced matter-of-factly, claiming the destruction of the enemy machine.

"Viktor, Viktor," I confirmed, "Congratulations!"

The explosion marking the end of their comrade had sent most of the Ivans diving away to safety. Xaver's voice on the R/T: "Now it's your turn. I'll cover you."

One of the bolder Russians climbed up to make an attack on us. His shots were wide. As he half-rolled away to seek the protection of the depleted pack below, the five-pointed red stars on his wingtips stood out clearly against the pale blue undersurface. I slammed my throttle forward, captured him in my sights and, at a range of 150 metres, opened fire. My guns hammered. I could smell the cordite even through my oxygen mask. Pieces flew off the LaGG as it shuddered under the impact. Trailing a long banner of black smoke it spun earthwards. "Abschuß!" I yelled.

But a kill could only be confirmed if an enemy machine exploded in mid-air, was seen to crash into the ground, or if the pilot baled out. And my LaGG, although obviously damaged and emitting copious amounts of smoke, was still airborne.

"He's still flying. Have another go at him," Xaver advised me calmly. And so I tried again. After quickly checking my tail – Xaver on the right, all clear to the left – I pushed the throttle forward and winged over towards the tell-tale trail of smoke. The LaGG grew rapidly larger in my Revi gunsight as I mentally checked off the range... 100 metres, 80 metres, 50 metres... fire!

This time it was Xaver who shouted "Abschuß!" for me. The Russian fighter had been blown apart. But there had been an explosion in my own machine as well. I felt myself spinning. My canopy was covered in oil. I couldn't see a thing but acted instinctively. I managed to pull out of the spin and get back on an even keel. But to keep flying straight and level I had to deploy almost full left aileron. What had happened?

Luckily the windshield cleaner, a tiny tube which sprayed fuel on to the armoured glass windscreen, was still working and I was able to use this to clear enough oil off the canopy to be able to assess the damage.

About one square metre of my right wing had been ripped open from the leading edge back to the main spar. The right undercarriage leg was dangling free in the slipstream. And the barrel of the cannon projecting from the right wingroot was no longer there – the weapon had been split open back to the breech. A shell had exploded prematurely! The annular oil tank in the nose of the machine had obviously been punctured too, for oil was flowing back along the right-hand side of the fuselage. The engine would not keep running indefinitely under these conditions. But we were still behind enemy lines, and to bale out now would mean certain capture and maybe death. Xaver had taken in the situation at once. "Norbert, jump," he shouted. "You're on fire!"

But there were no signs of flame or smoke in the cockpit. During those few interminable seconds fighting to regain control of the machine immediately after the explosion I had, however, completely lost my bearings. I wanted desperately to get back over friendly territory and, if possible, put the Focke-Wulf down on the emergency strip at Mga – despite Walter's fate being still fresh in my mind. "Xaver, get me back over the front line to Mga!"

"Turn right," he instructed. Neither of us were bothering with correct R/T procedure by this time. I carefully eased the machine into a gentle turn. "Now keep straight ahead on this bearing – you're pouring black smoke."

I couldn't have cared less about the smoke. My oil pressure was sinking fast and the temperature climbing rapidly towards the red. There wasn't much time left. The engine could seize at any moment. But the LaGGs had spotted the trail of smoke too and were coming back in to finish me off. There were four of them: one pair approaching from the right and level with me, the other pair curving down high from the left. Xaver, who had been sticking like glue to my tail, turned towards the two on the right and opened fire. The Ivans sheared off and disappeared. "Norbert, look out! Indians coming in left high!" he warned.

I looked up and saw the two LaGGs above me to port winging down in a copybook bounce. I couldn't just sit there and wait for them. Temporarily abandoning my run for the front line, I turned into them and fired my remaining guns, praying I wouldn't suffer another premature. Committed to their dives, the Russians flashed past close beneath me. Their canopies were half-open and for a split-second I glimpsed their light blue overalls, tan flying helmets and the large black square-framed goggles, through which they both seemed to be staring straight at me. Xaver was now firing at them too and they must have decided to give up on me, for they didn't return.

I eased my machine back on course. I was now down to 1,500 metres. The oil pressure gauge was showing zero and the needle of the temperature gauge next to it had almost disappeared off the clock. Automatically checking to my rear I was horrified to see yet another machine coming up behind me some 150 metres on the right. Almost without thinking, I wrenched the willing Focke-Wulf round yet again and blindly opened fire at my latest tormentor.

"Don't shoot, it's me," Xaver's voice remained remarkably calm as he evaded my wild fusillade, thank God.

Once more I turned back towards the front line, which I finally crossed at a height of 500 metres. Soon afterwards I spotted the village of Mga with its church and there ahead of me – almost hidden among the tall fir trees – was the ridiculously tiny clearing which was the emergency landing strip. I tried to ease back on the throttle, but the engine didn't respond. The control linkage had been damaged and the engine continued to run at three-quarters power. The only way to reduce speed would be to switch off the ignition and come in dead-stick.

The last of the tree tops whipped past just below me at an alarming rate – I was doing twice the speed I should be – ignition off, and try to float the Focke-Wulf in quickly, mindful of the damaged wing and dangling right mainwheel leg. I avoided the marshy patch that had claimed Walter, but couldn't get her down. The trunks of the firs at the end of the strip were rushing towards me. I would have to go round again.

I hit the ignition. The engine spluttered but didn't catch. I grabbed for the primer pump and tried again. With a howl of complaint the engine burst back into life and lifted me clear of the trees. I continued to turn gingerly to the left. But before I could line her up for a second approach a loud metallic bang told me that the engine had finally given up the ghost. Propeller windmilling, the only chance of getting down now was to try a side-slip. And if I could hold her for a moment just before touching down left wing low, maybe the sideways motion would shear off the dangling right undercarriage leg and allow me then to make a normal belly landing.

It worked – after a fashion. The dangling leg broke off all right, but so did both wings and the rear fuselage. Instead of the hoped-for customary belly landing I found myself careering across the surface of the field behind the engine . . . and nothing else! After much banging and rattling about I finally slid to a stop in the marshy area I had tried so hard to avoid. But at least I was down.

After all the noise, the uncanny silence that followed was almost deafening. But then I became aware of a hissing noise – the fuel tanks are going to go up, I thought. I quickly unfastened my harness and tried to crank open the canopy, only to find that the crank handle to the right of the instrument panel had also been damaged by flying splinters and was immovable. It was only now that I noticed a large hole, the size of a dinner plate, on the right-hand side of the cockpit. My guardian angel had certainly been working overtime.

But I still had to get free. Twisting halfway round in my seat, I used both hands to lift my right knee up high enough to be able to jam the sole of my flying boot against the canopy jettison lever. I trod down hard and the cartridge exploded, sending the canopy flying off. This caused my only injury of the day: a nasty graze on my back. I stood up and saw steam rising from the overheated engine as it lay in the water – that explained the hissing noise. Climbing out on to the forward cowling, I waved up at Xaver who had been circling overhead all the while. He waggled his wings in response before setting off back to Siverskaya.

In the meantime the Mga fire crew had arrived on the scene. They laid their ladders across the swampy surface and I scrambled across them to terra firma. Handshakes all round, and then they gave me a lift back to flight control which was housed in an earthen bunker. I sank down on a wooden bench outside the entrance, took out a cigarette and tried to light it. But reaction had set in. My hands were shaking so badly I couldn't strike the match. Somebody gave me a light and I dragged the smoke down into my lungs. It did me a power of good. The shaking stopped and I felt the tension lift.

I was still sitting there when a half-track motorcycle combination pulled up. Two army sergeant majors clambered off. They were infantrymen, and obviously old sweats to judge from the decorations they wore: Iron Crosses, First Class, and close combat clasps on their breasts; tank destruction patches on their sleeves. They came over to me, saluted and one enquired amiably:

"Can you perhaps tell us whether the pilot who just tried to land here managed to pull it off – or did he buy it?" "Why do you want to know?" was my natural response.

The second one answered in a broad Bavarian dialect: "We were watching the dogfights from the front line. Two of ours against a whole bunch of Ivans. When the smoking Focke-Wulf flew back over our positions we let fly with everything we had at the Ivans chasing him. We reckon we got a couple of them. But our guy was obviously in serious trouble. We've had a small bet on the outcome. I say the pilot made it and survived." He then indicated his companion, "He's convinced he couldn't have. There's a bottle of cognac riding on it."

"I'm delighted to say you've won," I told the Bavarian, "the pilot's still alive. It was me." They were a bit taken aback at first, but then hastened to offer me their congratulations on my lucky escape. They even suggested that I should return to the front line with them and help dispose of the winnings. Sadly, I had to decline this generous invitation. Xaver would no doubt be turning up soon in the Staffel's Klemm runabout to take me back to Siverskaya. The two sergeant majors wished me all the very best and took their leave. And, sure enough, the little Kl 35 arrived not long afterwards. It bounced across the uneven grass to flight control and Xaver climbed out. I rose and prepared to make my report as protocol demanded. But I didn't get the chance. Xaver gave me a friendly hug, clapped me on the shoulder and said: "Come on, get in. The boss and all the others are waiting for us."

As indeed they were. Back at Siverskaya I was able to make a full report to the Staffelkapitän, including details of my first victory, the damage caused by the shell bursting in the barrel of the cannon, and my subsequent attempt at an emergency landing. The boss listened attentively, his eyes shining.

"Congratulations. Very well done. But I knew, I knew it. I knew you wouldn't disappoint me." He slapped his thigh in obvious delight. I could only imagine that he was referring to what he had said to me after the ground collision, and that he now felt that his faith in not letting me be court martialled for damaging the two Gustavs had been justified.

The next day saw another attack on the Volkhov bridge. And this time it was not to be entrusted solely to the Stukas. A full Geschwader of He 111 bombers was also to take part. I was again assigned to fly as number 2, or katschmarek, to Xaver. We were to provide close escort for the leading Gruppe of Heinkels. The situation on the ground had changed somewhat. The Russians had assembled a large concentration of flak guns to defend the bridge. They had also increased the area's fighter defences and were keeping them on full alert. Almost the entire strength of JG 54's two Gruppen – with the exception of our own airfield defence flights – was to be involved in the operation.

The unit's Experten, those highly decorated members of the

Geschwader who already had large numbers of enemy aircraft to their credit, were given a freie Jagd role and not tied to the bombers. Allowed to range far and wide, they had the best chances of scoring. Next came those flying indirect escort, who could engage any enemy fighter getting closer than 500 metres to the bombers or dive-bombers they were protecting. Finally there were the pilots, and this included Xaver and myself, who were assigned to direct escort duties. We were to stick close to the bombers – no further than 100 metres away at any time – and provide the last line of fighter defence before the bombers' own gunners opened up.

The planning of the raid called for the high-level bombers to arrive over the target just as the dive-bombers were completing their attack. Accompanying the lead Gruppe of Heinkels, we were thus able to witness the curtain of flak thrown up as the Stukas ahead of us tipped over into their dives. It seemed almost a miracle that none was hit. Then it was our turn. As the Heinkels began their bomb run the sky ahead of us was suddenly transformed into a seemingly solid black wall of explosions.

Ordered to stay close to our charges, we had no option but to grit our teeth and accompany the Heinkels as they ploughed straight ahead into this inferno. It was my first experience of being inside a box barrage of anti-aircraft fire – a twilight world of swirling smoke intermittently illuminated by the flash of bursting shells. The minutes seemed like hours, but finally we were through. It was an even greater miracle that not one of our fighters had suffered the slightest damage. The Heinkels had not been so lucky. Two put down at Gatschina during the return flight so that crew members wounded by flak splinters could be rushed to hospital.

As had been expected, most of the freie Jagd pilots returned with further victories under their belts. Some of the indirect escort had also managed to score. We of the close escort, who had been able to fend off the few Soviet fighters that succeeded in penetrating the outer defence screen, measured our success by the fact that not a single bomber was shot down. The raid itself had been yet another failure, however. Reconnaissance later established that the supply trains were still getting through to Leningrad unhindered.

By now it was June. The dark greens of the fir forests were becoming mottled by the lighter hues of the fresh foliage on the deciduous trees and the temperature was still rising. The day-to-day routine of sorties flown in either Rotte or Schwarm strength continued without pause. The state of readiness for each of the three Staffeln dispersed around the field was rotated on a twenty-four hour basis: we would be held at fifteen minutes' readiness on the first day, at an hour's on the second, and then be stood down on the third. The mornings of our days off were occupied in sports activities and domestic chores. Our laundry was done by local Russian women, but we were responsible for looking after everything else; darning socks, keeping our uniforms and equipment generally neat and in good order, and so on. The afternoons were spent relaxing, usually reading or writing letters home.

Looking forward to one such day off, we were therefore more than a little surprised to read the following daily orders posted up on the Staffel's bulletin board: "10.00 – 12.00 hours: Drill parade, to include pilots, in full marching order: field uniforms, helmets and boots. Rifles to be carried and ammunition pouches worn. Pilots to borrow rifles from ground technicians."

The order bore the signature of Leutnant D. He was the unpopular character I have already mentioned; the one I recognized from my time at Werder. If anything, he had become even more supercilious and demanding. He flew as wingman to the Staffelkapitän. We wondered if this was not an act of personal sacrifice on the boss's part. Nobody else liked him or wanted to fly with him.

To give just one example of his behaviour. One afternoon not long before Walter's death he had come into our room. He was carrying a pair of dirty shoes and said to me: "Hannig, clean these shoes for me. I need them immediately." He threw the shoes down at my feet. A sudden silence descended on the room. Everybody was looking at the young Leutnant. What was I to do? I couldn't disobey the order of a superior officer. I was just about to pick up the shoes when Walter got to his feet, saying quietly: "Leave the shoes where they are, Norbert." Turning to our unwelcome visitor he added, "Herr Leutnant, please pick up those shoes yourself or I will report this matter to the boss." Outwardly completely calm, Walter reached for his belt and cap. The Leutnant hesitated, now unsure of himself. Then he grabbed the shoes and left the room without another word.

Was this now a delayed response – his way of getting back at the NCO pilots who made little attempt to hide their dislike of him? Having borrowed all the necessary warlike accoutrements from members of the ground staff, we fell in outside the barracks together with those of the ground crews not actually working on the aircraft. The flight sergeant called the parade to attention and reported to the Leutnant. With the boss and the other Staffel officers watching the entire performance, we were marched off towards the sports field. "A song!" the Leutnant ordered in a loud voice.

Someone in the front ranks immediately suggested a popular if somewhat derogatory ditty about army life and started us off with the first line: "Oh, how lovely it is to be a soldier... three... four!" Realizing he was being made to look a fool, the Leutnant interrupted us before we had got very far. "Not that song!" he yelled, "Another one!" This time we struck up with "The blue dragoons", whose lyrics not even he could object to. Then somebody made a loud remark. This resulted in a peremptory "Quiet in the ranks," which only heightened the tension still further. And so we arrived at the sports field.

There the drill turned into an absolute shambles. When a left turn was ordered, some promptly turned right. Confusion reigned as we marched up and down bumping into each other. By this time some were muttering and swearing under their breath, others were laughing out loud. The young Leutnant was helpless.

The flight sergeant stepped into the breach with conviction. He marched us around the cinder track bordering the sports field. "Down on the ground!" he yelled suddenly. We threw ourselves flat on the sharp lumps of coke. "On your feet! At the double!" We jumped up and began running. It was like being back in basic training camp. "Air attack!" We buried our noses in the coke again.

My neighbour was swearing softly to himself, "If he doesn't pack this in soon, I'll..." I didn't get to hear the rest. But of one thing I was certain. This morning's little episode had opened up a huge gulf between these two and the rest of the Staffel – a gulf that would not be all that easy to bridge.

The proceedings were eventually brought to a close by the approach of a car bearing the Gruppenkommandeur's pennant. The boss came over and called us to attention before reporting to the Kommandeur. The pair had a brief exchange of words about some matter or other, and then the drill was declared over. The Leutnant took charge again and marched us back to barracks. Upon his command to sing, we decided to try once more: "Oh, how lovely it is to be a soldier," we trilled. And this time he let us continue until we got back to our quarters and were ordered to fall out. It was my last parade with helmet, rifle and ammo pouches for the rest of the war.

Since Walter's loss, his place in our room had been taken by Feldwebel Zander, or the 'Count of Demyansk' as he was known. His speciality was knocking down Pe-2s. He already had ten of these twin-engined Petlyakovs to his name. They had mostly been the reconnaissance machines which regularly appeared over the front, flying singly and at great height, in the early mornings. The first freie Jagd mission of the day, which allowed one to stalk these intruders, was a much sought-after assignment. I was therefore delighted when Zander opted to take me along on one.

Our call-sign was 'Rotkäppchen' (Red Riding Hood), I recall, and the weather was ideal for our mission. A solid layer of high cloud covered the base, but off to the north, in the direction of the front, this gave way to clear blue sky. We took off and headed northwards in a steady climb. Almost as if on cue ground control, Anton 1, came on air: "To cyclists in area Schum, single furniture van nearing the front, heading north, Frage Viktor?" (Just as 'Indian' was the codeword for an enemy fighter, so a 'furniture van' was any hostile bomber.)

We were still flying just below the cloud base and could not yet see any sign of the intruder. But at the edge of the cloud we broke out into brilliant blue sky and suddenly there he was: a small dark shape about 2 kilometres away dragging a long condensation trail behind him – the furniture van!

"Rotkäppchen 2 from 1, attack," Zander ordered as he increased speed to close in on the enemy machine and get into firing position. A few columns of smoke on the ground far below indicated that we were crossing the front line. I took up station on Zander's right to watch him at work. He opened fire at 400 metres but his rounds exploded harmlessly behind the Ivan, which was now clearly identifiable as a Pe-2. Closing the range to 300 metres he loosed off another burst, bracketing the enemy aircraft. Alerted to our presence, the Russian recce pilot poured on the gas and dived away in the direction of Leningrad.

But we were faster and quickly overhauled him. A third salvo at 200 metres had no visible effect on the fleeing Petlyakov. By the time we had approached to within 100 metres of the enemy the 'Count of Demyansk', and Pe-2 specialist, was out of ammunition. His magazines were empty.

"Guns jammed," Zander reported over the R/T, "Rotkäppchen 2 take over the attack." Needing no second bidding, I slid behind and below the Pe-2 so that the dorsal gunner could not get a clear shot at me. At a range of just 80 metres I pressed the gun button. My rounds chewed their way across his fuselage and right wing. His starboard engine burst into flames. I pulled off to one side and saw the pilot and gunner beginning to climb out of their seats. They managed to escape just before the machine turned over onto its back and began a near vertical dive to the ground where it exploded in a ball of fire.

There was the usual exchange over the R/T, with me reporting the kill and Zander confirming and offering his congratulations, before we set course for home. It was now my turn to swoop low over the base waggling my wings to signify a victory. In contrast to the aftermath of my first kill, when I had ended up in the swamp at Mga, it was a moment to savour.

The highlight of our by-now familiar daily routine – whether it be the sense of expectancy felt when at readiness, the excitement of ops, or the relaxation of our off-duty hours – was undoubtedly the arrival of field post. My parents wrote regularly from home. I heard from all three of my brothers. And one day there was a letter from Gisela, the girl I had met in Heiligenbeil. I replied to them all as soon as I could. Correspondence was the one tangible link to the Homeland we were all fighting for.

And in our case much of that fighting seemed to be taking place over one particular spot: the Volkhov bridge. It was not long before another attack was ordered by HQ Luftflotte 1. This time it was to be an all-out effort, we were told, and *had* to succeed. As well as the two usual Stukagruppen, the force was to include a full Kampfgeschwader each of He 111s and Ju 88s. I and II/JG 54 were again to provide the fighter cover. This assemblage of aerial hardware, well over 200 aircraft in all, led one wag to liken the forthcoming operation to the annual Reich Party Day flypast at Nuremberg. "Only not quite so much fun," another added. And he was right. The crowds below would not be cheering and waving at us; they'd be doing their damnedest to shoot us out of the sky.

As before, I was to fly wingman to Xaver and we were again charged with direct escort of the leading Gruppe of the He 111 formation. We crossed the front at a height of 4,000 metres and climbing. It was a perfect day, not a cloud in the bright blue sky. As we weaved back and forth we could clearly see the crews of the bombers bathed in sunlight behind the glass of their canopies. Several batteries of heavy flak opened fire on us shortly after we entered enemy airspace. But the Heinkels maintained their tight formation and held rigidly to their course.

The dive-bombers were again scheduled to open the attack. We could see them, and their fighter escort, well ahead and some way below us as they approached the line of the railway to the east of the bridge. Then, to our astonishment, thick white clouds of smoke began to billow from both banks of the River Volkhov. As the Stukas turned to make their run in to the target the bridge began to be swallowed up in the smoke screen. Soon it had disappeared entirely and could no longer be made out from the air at all. This did not deter the Stukas. They continued to follow the tracks westwards until just short of the location of the now invisible bridge. Then they commenced their dives.

This was the moment, obviously at a given signal, that the bridge's immediate anti-aircraft defences all opened up simultaneously. Tracers of light flak spun fiery webs. Large-calibre shells stained the sky in the Stuka's path with the dirty smudges of their explosions. We watched as the dive-bombers plunged unhesitatingly through this maelstrom and down into the smoke.

We had been following the same approach route as the Stukas. Now we were heading west along the railway lines towards the river and the site of the bridge crossing. The Stukas had already re-emerged from the smoke screen and were making their escape at ground level. As we came into range the flak barrage suddenly rose to meet us. It was almost as if a ghostly hand had lifted it bodily and placed it directly in front of us. In reality, of course, there was a very able Russian fire-control officer somewhere down below us orchestrating the bridge defences.

As the Heinkels droned steadily onwards towards the objective the sky – a brilliant azure blue just the moment before – became black. The bright orb of the sun turned blood-red, as if seen through smoked glass. Again there was the feeling of entering a world of dark, all-enveloping smoke lit by the flash of explosions. Xaver's machine was just a silhouette; the bombers mere shadows. The force of the exploding shells was throwing our machines about violently. I suddenly had the impression of a Heinkel flying close above me. That couldn't be right. I had been turned completely upside down! A quick half-roll brought me upright and put the bomber back where it belonged: beneath me. The shape of Xaver's Focke-Wulf loomed close and I latched on to it. I had lost all sense of time, but suddenly we were through, back into the welcome glare of the sun shining in a cloudless blue sky. We'd made it.

But two of the bombers had been hit and had dropped out of formation. They turned back towards friendly territory, escorted by some of the freie Jagd fighters who had not accompanied us into the box barrage. Both made it back to airfields on our side of the lines, although one had to come in on its belly.

While we had been running the gauntlet of flak with the bombers, dogfights had been raging all around us. We could hear the excited voices of the pilots in our headphones. Triumphant cries of "Abschuß!" were interspersed with urgent warnings – "Look out, he's on your tail!" "Break!" "Pull up!" "I've been hit," somebody shouted, "returning to garden fence."

Slowly the hubbub subsided as the Ivans began to disengage and make off back to their own bases. But suddenly the unmistakable Austrian tones of Nowotny, the Kommandeur of I Gruppe and one of our leading Experten, came over the R/T: "There's another one! Pauke, Pauke!" – attack attack!

There were still about a dozen of our fighters in the area, including Xaver and myself. We had been released from our close-escort duties as soon as the Heinkels were headed safely back for home. Everybody was eager to have a crack at the lone Ivan. The racket started up again. "Wo ist horrido?" – "Where's the tally-ho?" – one pilot asked. "You're in it," another answered. "Let me at him," a third voice interrupted. Even Xaver wanted to get in on the act.

We caught sight of a Yak with unusual red, white and blue markings on its rudder. We had heard about a group of French volunteers who were fighting for the Soviets. Was this one of them? As we all continued to get in each other's way the enemy pilot, whatever his nationality, skilfully avoided every one of our passes. He twisted and turned, split-essed, barrel-rolled and zoom-climbed with such agility that not one of us could keep him in our sights long enough to get in a telling shot – not even Nowotny.

After about five minutes of these hair-raising aerobatics Nowy, as the CO of I Gruppe was commonly known, decided enough was enough: "To all pilots, let him go home, he's earned it." The Kommandeur's machine broke away and we all followed. The Yak promptly disappeared in the direction of Schlüsselburg.

Reconnaissance confirmed that this latest attack had finally achieved the required result. The bridge had been hit and one span had collapsed into the river. Mystifyingly, however, supply trains continued to roll into Leningrad. Several days were to pass before it was discovered that the Russians, presumably as an insurance against losing the bridge, had been busy laying a camouflaged branch line which crossed the river by an underwater bridge built some 7 kilometres downstream from the original structure. The tracks, just below the surface of the water, could only be made out if the weather conditions were exactly right. They would be a difficult target to hit. But our bombers were not given the opportunity. They were urgently needed elsewhere.

When I arrived in the east at the end of March 1943 the epic battle of Stalingrad had just been fought and lost. Many historians regard this as the turning point of the war on the eastern front. But although it was the first major defeat of the German Army – and undoubtedly represented a disaster of unparalleled proportions – the military situation was not irretrievable. It was the failure of the 1943 summer offensive on the central sector which was to set in motion the unstoppable Soviet advance that took them all the way to Berlin.

This offensive, codenamed Zitadelle and designed to eliminate a huge bulge in the front to the west of Kursk, was to result in the biggest tank battle of the entire war. To support the mass of German armour being assembled on the ground, Luftwaffe units from all other sectors of the front were transferred in to the Kursk area. This is where Luftflotte 1's bombers had been sent. And much of JG 54 was to follow. All of I Gruppe was ordered down to the central sector to participate in Zitadelle. But of II Gruppe only our 5 Staffel was involved. 6 and 7 Staffeln were to remain behind as sole guardians of the northern sector.

On 1 July every serviceable Fw 190A-5 of 5/JG 54 took off from Siverskaya for the flight southwards, via a refuelling stop at Vitebsk, to a forward landing ground near Orel-South (which was, in fact, on the northern shoulder of the 'bulge'). The ground crews and all necessary equipment were airlifted down in three Ju 52 transports.

The German attack was launched at 03.30 hours on 5 July. But I missed the opening of it. I had been detailed to wait behind until a major overhaul being carried out on one of our fighters had been completed and then fly this machine down later.

It was not until 8 July that I was able to stuff the flight sack containing my personal gear into the luggage space of the Fw 190 and take off from Siverskaya. Following the lines of the major supply highways running southwards – left-hand wheel, right-hand track – the flight went smoothly. We had been issued with detailed maps of the Orel area, showing the exact locations of the many landing fields scattered about the region. It was mainly flat open country, veined by the tributaries of the River Oka that ran through it.

The forward landing ground itself, which rejoiced in the nickname of 'Diamond Valley', turned out to be just a wide expanse of grassland without a building or tree to be seen. The aircraft stood out in the open, dispersed a little further apart than usual against the possibility of air attack. The pilots lived under canvas, occupying two-man tents made out of groundsheets buttoned together and erected over holes dug in the ground. Except for this latter feature, also intended to provide a measure of protection in the event of an air raid, it all reminded me rather of the summer camps I had attended as a boy.

The ground crews also lived in tents. Everybody had to improvise, but operations carried on as usual. Bowsers were on hand to refuel the aircraft. The signals section had laid lines to I Gruppe HQ, from whom we received our operational orders and to whom we submitted our claims and loss returns, plus various other reports. This no doubt kept them happy and contented, shuffling papers and waging their own little paper war. Our meals were delivered from the field kitchen in ration containers.

On arrival I reported to the Staffelkapitän, who then sent me over to Ede's tent where there was still a space free. Everybody seemed pleased to see me, but the strain of the past days was clearly etched on their faces. Successes had been achieved, but a price had been paid. The following day I was back in the air flying on Xaver's wing for the first of a long succession of sorties providing cover for Stukas, artillery spotters and bombers operating along the northern flanks of the Kursk battlefield.

On 14 July we were scheduled to fly escort for a Staffel of Ju 87s. By this date, having failed to penetrate the strong Russian defences, the German attacks against the Kursk salient were already being called off. Many units had been given orders to retire back to their original jumping-off positions. In doing so, one group of infantry had lost contact with its rearguard, which had been cut off and surrounded by Russian troops and was now holed up in a station along the railway line leading north-eastwards out of Orel towards Tula.

The infantrymen were about to mount a local counter-attack to rescue their trapped comrades and the Stukas were being despatched in support. We rendezvoused with the dive-bombers above our landing field. As they were flying at an altitude of only 800 metres, the events on the ground were clearly visible to the naked eye. The rescue party sent up red flares to indicate their position. The Stukas formed into a large circle, a battle formation which allowed every machine to select its own objective and dive on it separately. For this mission they were carrying only their 50-kg underwing bombs. These could be launched singly, which meant that each aircraft was also able to carry out several attacks on specific targets such as machine-gun emplacements, trenches, mortar positions – even individual Russian soldiers.

Circling above the Stukas to give fighter cover, we saw our infantry leap from their armoured half-tracks and storm the station building. Moments later they reappeared, shepherding the rearguard survivors, several of whom were carefully carrying a makeshift stretcher fashioned out of tent halves; presumably a wounded comrade. As there were no enemy fighters about Xaver and I joined in the ground action, strafing the surrounding Russian positions to keep their heads down while our own troops climbed back aboard their carriers. Green flares signalled mission completed as they set off for the front lines only a few kilometres away.

The Stukas continued to watch over them until they reached the safety of German-held territory. There the leading dive-bomber waggled its wings to thank us for our services, and we turned away for our temporary home near Orel.

This little incident formed just one small part of the general withdrawal from the Kursk area. As it spread and gathered momentum we too were forced to vacate Diamond Valley. But even in retreat the troops retained their down-to-earth sense of humour. A new expression was coined mocking the official communiqués which spoke reassuringly of straightening the lines and advancing to prepared defensive positions: "Forward, comrades! We've got to pull back!"

Our first port of call after departing the forward landing ground had been Orel-Main. This was the scene of a prank which could have had serious consequences. The hangars at Orel-Main had already been prepared for demolition before we arrived there. We discovered another of the airfield's lesser amenities situated not far from our assigned dispersal area. This was a typical rural German water-closet, or Klo, which in those days could be found in many a garden back home. It was a small wooden structure, not unlike a sentry-box, but with a door on the front which, as was customary, had a small opening near the top cut in the shape of a heart. It was a little piece of Germany in the middle of Russia, and much more civilized than our usual outdoor 'thunder-boxes'.

But when a pilot of I Gruppe came across a petrol drum nearby still full of fuel he announced, "The Klo has got to be prepared for demolition as well." Whereupon he opened the door of the little hut, rolled the drum inside and started attacking it with a pick-axe until the petrol began to gush out. He then came out, closed the door carefully behind him and lit a small rolled-up piece of paper. He stuffed this home-made torch through the heart-shaped hole, but nothing happened. He tried a second time – still nothing.

We shouted at him to stop playing the fool, the petrol could go up at any moment. But he wouldn't listen. For his third attempt he picked up a complete newspaper, set light to it, went up to the door and pushed his hand holding the blazing paper through the opening. There was one almighty bang and the whole lot exploded. But our hero was lucky. The door shielded him from much of the blast, although he received severe facial burns and had to be rushed off to hospital. There he was luckier still. It was decided that his injuries were not the result of self-inflicted wounds – which would have meant an automatic court-martial – but of plain stupidity.

From Orel-Main we had to make two further withdrawals, to Karachev and Bryansk, before finally returning to Siverskaya on 20 July. We quickly settled back in alongside the other two Staffeln, and soon everything was the same as it had been before our departure for Zitadelle less than three weeks earlier.

On the northern sector during that time the Russians had been trying to push the front line southwards away from Leningrad, but without much success. Our pilots, flying with their usual Rotte or Schwarm strength, had been involved in a number of fierce dogfights. But there had been no major actions such as we had experienced around Orel. Then on 30 July our Gruppenkommandeur, Hauptmann Jung, was shot down and killed in a clash with Soviet fighters over Mga.

His replacement was Hauptmann Erich Rudorffer, who was posted in from JG 2. Rudorffer was a highly experienced pilot who already had 74 victories to his credit, all scored against the western allies over NW Europe and North Africa. Yet despite these successes in the air, he was a somewhat reserved, even shy, type on the ground. He always kept his Knight's Cross in his pocket; only putting it on display round his neck when we had important visitors.

I myself was presented with the Iron Cross, Second Class, by our Staffelkapitän on 9 August and could not suppress a thrill of pride. I had already flown more than fifty missions and was slowly becoming one of the 'old hares', as experienced pilots were known. But I too was beginning to feel the effects of constant ops – my eyes had taken on a slight yellowish tinge.

On the afternoon of 14 August Walter Nowotny paid us a call. He wore the Knight's Cross like our boss. The two of them got on well together. On that particular day our Schwarm – Xaver, Tangermann, Zander and myself – had been held at readiness from 15.00 to 16.00 hours. When we returned from dispersal and entered the mess the others were sitting around enjoying a cup of coffee.

As we had not met before, I had to introduce myself to Nowotny. He scrutinized me closely before turning to the boss and saying: "If you want to keep him, you'd better send him on leave fast."

"Why's that?" our Staffelkapitän asked. Nowotny replied: "Look at his eyes. They're already yellow. He needs a rest."

This brought an immediate and unexpected reaction from the boss. "Chiefy," he yelled loudly, "Chiefy!"

The Staffel warrant officer came running to see what the trouble was. The boss pointed to me. "Make him out a leave pass at once, and make sure he gets a place on tomorrow's courier flight." "And you," he turned to me, "go and pack your things immediately."

I wasn't going to argue. Thanking the boss, I saluted and dashed to my room to start packing. The Ju 52 courier machine carried out a daily return flight from Berlin to Siverskaya and back. I was given a leave pass running from 15 August to 7 September. It would be my first time home on leave from the front and it was a marvellous stroke of luck. My three brothers and I had already arranged by letter that we would try to get simultaneous leave and meet at home around the end of August. It was a bit of a long shot, of course. Although Jochen was not too far away on the Volkhov front, Günter was still up in Norway and Kurt, the eldest of us, was somewhere down on the central sector. But at least I would now be certain of keeping our appointment.

On 15 August I climbed aboard the good old 'Auntie Ju' and settled down to enjoy the trip back to Berlin Tegel. It would make a pleasant change to be flown as a passenger and not to be at the controls myself, continually quartering the sky for hostile aircraft. I was looking forward enormously to my unexpected leave; to drop in on Göttchen while in Berlin – but above all to get home and see my parents, my sisters and our old dachshund, Hexe. I was full of plans to visit friends and relatives. The war was a million miles away, on another planet.

As an Oberfähnrich I was already entitled to wear certain items of officer's uniform. But these were not obtainable at the front. I had therefore been authorized while in Berlin to pick up an indent form from the local Luftwaffe HQ which would allow me to purchase my officer's equipment off the peg at the clothing stores. Funds were no problem. My pay was being transferred each month into my post office savings account. At the front we existed solely on our extra flying pay. But as there was nothing to buy out there, most of this money was also saved whether we wanted to or not.

I planned to stay for two nights in the Soldatenheim in Berlin before setting off on the journey home to Hermannsdorf. Next morning I kitted myself out in my new finery, including officer's cap, belt and dagger. Also armed with some less lethal items – a bunch of flowers and several tins of Schoka-Cola chocolate – I made my way round to the Alte Jakobsstraße. My little surprise worked. Margot and her room-mate had been on duty the night before and had the afternoon off.

We greeted each other warmly. I was in the best of spirits, laughing and joking about the times we had spent together while I had been training at Werder and Werneuchen. It all seemed so long ago now. But I couldn't help noticing that the girls were much more subdued than normal. Göttchen told me several times to calm down and be serious. I asked why? I hadn't had the chance to relax like this for a long time and I intended to make the most of it.

She looked at me silently for several seconds. "I've got some bad news for you," she said softly, her eyes brimming with tears. "Kurt has been killed. We heard from your father."

My cheerful mood vanished in an instant as I struggled to take in what she was saying. Kurt, my eldest brother – the one I had looked up to all my life – gone? My next thoughts were for my parents and the family. I had to get home as quickly as possible. I took my leave of the tearful girls, thanking them for breaking the news to me – it must have been very hard for them – collected my things from the Soldatenheim, and caught the night train.

Arriving at Siegersdorf the following morning, I walked the four kilometres to Hermannsdorf; my daily route to and from school as a boy. I reached home shortly after nine o'clock. Crossing the schoolyard I went in by the back door which we always used. Mother was busy in the kitchen. Father was teaching in the classroom.

As soon as mother saw me standing there the tears started to run down her cheeks. I took her in my arms. In a tiny voice she said, "How lovely that you're here. You were the one we were always most worried about. And now it's Kurt that's been taken." She stifled a sob and I stroked her hair gently.

Father had heard us and came hurrying into the room. "My boy. Thank God that you're safe and sound." He gave me a hug and clapped me on the shoulder. I had to struggle to get a grip on myself. I was on the point of bursting into tears as well. "It was his fate, father. It was meant to be. What else can I say?" Indeed, what else could I say to my parents. My words of comfort seemed so inadequate.

Two of my sisters now attended school in Bunzlau and didn't get home until the afternoon. The younger one threw herself into my arms and we held each other tightly.

Father showed me a copy of the obituary he had placed in the Bunzlau daily paper. It said all there was to say. But two phrases in particular caught my attention. The first of these read: 'Gave his young life... for Volk and Fatherland...' The accepted wording of these sad notices, which were now beginning to fill columns in every paper in the land, nearly always stated, 'for Volk, Führer and Fatherland'. By deliberately omitting the almost obligatory middle word of the three, father was indicating quite clearly that in his view his eldest son had fallen in action fighting for his people and his country – not for the current political regime.

It was a brave thing to have done. But as the announcement had been made in the name of the whole family, and included the details of his surviving sons – all three of us in uniform and fighting at the front – there was not a lot the local party big-wigs could do about it.

The second phrase was even more startling: 'He fell on 14.7.1943 near Orel as the leader of his troop.' 14 July was one of the days I had been flying in the Orel area. I asked father whether he had any further details, but sadly he hadn't.

The whole extraordinary story was to come to light a few days later, however. Kurt's deputy, a young Leutnant serving in the same troop of mechanized infantry that my brother had commanded, had gathered together a number of his personal effects before the burial and had been looking after them ever since. Now home on leave himself, he had contacted my parents requesting permission to return Kurt's possessions to the family in person.

They were few enough to show for a life, but precious beyond compare: Kurt's wallet – containing a photo of him receiving Holy Communion in the field in front of his men – his purse, some letters that he always carried with him, his Iron Cross, Second Class, and his officer's cap.

Our visitor then explained in detail what had happened:

> "On 12 July our troop was ordered to act as rearguard for the regiment as it fell back along the railway line leading from Tula down into Orel. The Russians were pushing hard, and on 13 July they got behind us and cut us off. We barricaded ourselves in one of the stations along the line and radioed for help. This was promised for the following day.
>
> "We held our position throughout the night. In the morning the Russians attacked us with mortars. The CO was hit in the chest by a shell splinter. It must have penetrated his heart for he died instantly. There was nothing we could do for him.
>
> "Then our troops counter-attacked, supported by Stukas and fighters. While they kept the enemy busy we managed to escape. We brought the CO with us – we didn't want to leave him to the Russians – and were later able to bury him in the military cemetery in Orel."

The young Leutnant fell silent. Sitting on the sofa beside mother, my father squeezed her hand tightly without saying a word. Their tears were flowing freely. I asked the name of the station where all this had taken place, and the exact time the counter-attack had gone in. Incredibly, it was the very attack that Xaver and I had supported when escorting that

Staffel of Stukas. I had witnessed the soldiers carrying the stretcher out of the station – not knowing that it bore the body of my own dead brother.

The tragedy cast a pall of grief over what was to have been a happy homecoming. We each coped with Kurt's loss in our own way. Father sat at the keyboard for hours on end playing the harmonium. Mother busied herself quietly in the kitchen and the garden. Even the three girls, usually so boisterous, were quiet and at times almost withdrawn. Günter arrived home the following week, and Jochen shortly afterwards. We were to have been four. Now we were just three. But when we went to visit friends and relations Kurt was always with us – in our thoughts and in our conversations.

Despite the pervading air of sadness the leave was over all too soon. On 7 September the others accompanied me to Siegersdorf station. A quiet handshake, a final wave from the train window, and I was on my way back to the war.

The first part of the journey was on the local line via Liegnitz to Breslau. There I would change on to the leave train departing for East Prussia with troops returning to the northern sector of the Russian front. But my travel warrant instructed me to detrain at Königsberg, the East Prussian capital, and make my way to the Geschwader's rear-area base at Heiligenbeil, where I would receive further orders.

When I got off the local train at Breslau the leave special for Vienna was about to depart from the platform opposite. Suddenly I heard my name being shouted loudly above the general hubbub, "Norbert, Norbert, over here!" It was Unteroffizier Rommer, my chief mechanic. I ran across to him and he quickly filled me in with all the latest Staffel news before his train began to pull away.

"Eckert's been killed in a crash – Paul Bienecke shot down, baled out and in hospital – the boss shot down behind enemy lines, parachuted and missing – Xaver Müller brought down by light flak, exploded and killed." He named several others who had been posted, before adding hurriedly, "Leutnant Lang has taken over the Staffel. They're waiting for you. You're going to be needed out there. Hals- und Beinbruch – all the best."

The Vienna train started to move. A quick wave of thanks to Rommer and I had to dash to catch my own connection for East Prussia. In the train I did a quick mental calculation. When I had joined them back at the end of March I had been number twenty-six on 5 Staffel's pilot roster. Now at the beginning of September, twelve had been killed or reported missing, seven posted, and only seven of that original twenty-six were left.

At Heiligenbeil the sense of urgency was palpable. On arrival I was immediately ordered to take the following morning's courier flight out to Schatalovka, SE of Smolensk on the central sector, where 5 Staffel was now based, and report back on duty. There was no time to arrange a meeting with Gisela. I had to be content with leaving her a short handwritten note.

I made the trip as dorsal gunner aboard the Ju 52 transport, sitting in the open position atop the fuselage behind the fully-armed, ring-mounted MG 34 machine gun, ready for any eventuality. I had learned to operate the MG 34 at the air college, but my skills were not put to the test. The flight passed uneventfully.

From my vantage point I had a panoramic view of the countryside unrolling beneath me. Once again I was struck by the differences in the culture and conditions between west and east as the model-like farms and villages gave way to straggling communities of thatched mud cottages surrounded by uncultivated fields. At Schatalovka I was to experience at first hand just how primitive living conditions really were for much of the rural population of the Soviet Union.

Our forward landing ground took its name from the nearby hamlet. This was typical of many, a collection of straw-thatched wattle-and-daub cottages strung along an unmade road which, during the autumn rains and spring thaws, became a bottomless river of mud. Inside each cottage was a large wood-fired oven that was used to bake bread and which, in winter, the family would sleep around for warmth. On either side of the stove was a partitioned room; the one serving as a bedroom in the summer, the other a communal living room. The walls were whitewashed, and the clay floors stamped hard and covered with fresh straw.

The members of the Staffel were quartered in the hamlet. When a comrade and I arrived at the cottage to which we had been assigned, we were met at the gate by an elderly couple bearing the customary gift of bread and salt. We had been taught the correct response to this ceremonial greeting. We each took a piece of the proffered bread, sprinkled it with a little salt, thanked our hosts, and ate it before entering the cottage.

Inside we were ushered into our bedroom. A thick feather quilt covered each of the two beds. On the wall hung two pictures of Russian soldiers, both showing a group of about company strength formally posed in front of a barracks building. The old man went across to these photos and pointed to a figure in each: "He – my son. He also. Both in war. God protect them and you also."

These few simple words in broken German were deeply touching. The old man's obvious sincerity moved us both. Every morning the elderly couple would come out to the garden gate to see us off. Every evening they would be waiting to welcome us home – just as they would their own sons. We brought them some of our cold rations and some coffee, and had great difficulty in dissuading them from kissing our hands in gratitude. At nights the feather quilts proved too heavy for comfort, however. We preferred our familiar olive-green Russian sleeping bags.

We were not to stay at Schatalovka for long. A few days later the Staffel was moved further south still, to one of the complex of airfields surrounding Kiev, the capital of the Ukraine.

Kiev-West had large, solidly-constructed hangars and workshops, paved taxiways and a firm grass surface. Pilots and ground crews were accommodated in a barracks block in the city itself and were taken to and from the airfield each day by bus. Here there was no longer any contact with the Russian civil population other than those officially employed by the local military administration to carry out kitchen and cleaning duties.

In the Kiev region German forces were falling back on the River Dniepr. Our job, in addition to flying escort missions for reconnaissance aircraft and bomber formations, was primarily to help cover the troops' withdrawal and protect them from Soviet air attack. The heavily-armoured Il-2 ground-attack aircraft, or Sturmovik, was a particular menace.

Despite its recent losses, the Staffel's morale was high. The new Staffelkapitän, Leutnant Emil Lang, was liked and respected by all, both in the air and on the ground. The feeling of everybody pulling and working together couldn't have been better.

Since my return from leave I had become the regular katschmarek of Feldwebel Reinhold Hoffmann. Like me, 'Lerge' was a Silesian. He had joined 5 Staffel a few months before me, had already flown 200 missions and had nearly 40 victories to his credit. As my number 1 he reminded me very much of Xaver. We flew well as a team, operating together as if with one mind. Very soon we had established ourselves as the Lerge Rotte. We even used Lerge's nickname as our radio call sign. It was a Silesian expression, used to describe someone who was a bit of an artful or crafty type.

I flew mission after mission on Lerge's wing; sticking to him like glue. We never became separated in a dogfight. I watched his tail, and he in turn coached and encouraged me. Under his expert tutelage I added another five enemy aircraft to my score. When we landed after the last – which had taken my total to seven – and reported back to the Staffelkapitän, the latter congratulated me warmly, then laughed and said: "Guess what, Hannig, before I can put you in for the Iron Cross, First Class, you're going to have to make it 10."

Up until this time the number of victories required to win the Iron Cross, First Class, had been seven. But I wasn't unduly concerned by the fact that another three had now been added to that figure. When I had first volunteered to join the Luftwaffe and become a fighter pilot it had been out of a sense of duty. I wanted to help defend my country. The winning of medals had not entered my head. And now that I was at the front I found that, to most people, decorations were almost an irrelevance. There were the glory-seekers of course. But the vast majority placed far greater value on winning the trust and respect of their comrades rather than awards.

Nobody fostered that sense of camaraderie better than our new CO, 'Bully' Lang. He addressed us with the familiar "du". And although many of his subordinates, including myself, continued to use the more formal "Sie" in reply, it was in deference to the man, not the superior officer. Discipline did not suffer in the slightest. When things became serious every order given was obeyed instantly.

Above Kiev the Dniepr was a very wide sluggish river flowing down from the north. Its western bank along that stretch consisted of undefended swamplands. The city itself stood on the same western side, but on a high plateau. A steep embankment led down to the river, which narrowed at this point. It was here that the road and rail bridges spanned the stream, giving access to the flat country to the east across which our ground forces were retreating. Below the city the river widened out again as it continued on its journey down towards the Black Sea. South of the city the western bank also levelled out into open country.

As the army fell back on the Dniepr it was ordered to carry out the same 'scorched earth' policy the Soviets had used to try to stop our invading troops in 1941. After the civilian population had been evacuated everything that might prove of use to the advancing enemy was either destroyed, burned or blown up. As we patrolled east of the river the sights that greeted us – burning villages, abandoned livestock roaming the deserted landscape – brought home to us the true and ugly face of war.

These tactics apparently succeeded in slowing the Russian troops to such an extent that, in some areas, our retreating army units lost contact with the enemy altogether. It was then the special task of our fighters to fly reconnaissance missions to establish exactly where the Soviets were and in which directions they were heading. The closer our forces got to the Dniepr, the more they were being funnelled into the approaches to the Kiev bridges, the only available crossing points. This meant that huge stretches of the river's banks to either side of the city were being left wide open. Advancing on a broad front, the Russians could appear on the Dniepr anywhere along these sectors – and at any time.

But the enemy was proving extraordinarily difficult to locate. As Lerge and I set out on yet another of our special reconnaissance flights, we orientated ourselves on those villages where ground engagements had last been reported. From there we flew northwards. And then we flew southwards. We scanned the empty Ukrainian landscape for enemy columns, signs of tank tracks, figures in olive-brown uniform – nothing.

Our fuel was beginning to run low. We would soon have to head

home. The 'red lamp', the warning light that indicated we were now on
reserve tanks, began to flicker. We had just ten minutes flying time left.

"Lerge 2 from 1. Back to the garden fence. Time to 'Luzie Anton',"
came from Lerge over the R/T, informing me that we were to return to
base and land. The phonetic initials Luzie Anton – LA – were the code
for landing.

But just before we reached the river I caught a fleeting glimpse,
ahead of us and off to the left, of a panje wagon, three saddled horses,
and a group of about five Russian soldiers bent over a map. They
suddenly looked up at the sound of our engines, I saw the blur of their
faces ... but then we hurtled past low above them and they were gone.

"Lerge 1 from 2 – did you see that? A group of them standing on the
bank next to a panje wagon."

"Viktor, Viktor! We've got to get back. Luzie Anton!" Lerge shouted.

We climbed to clear the embankment on the west side of the river,
lowered our undercarriages as we passed over the city, and quickly came
in to land. We were certain of what we had just seen: the Russians had
reached the east bank of the River Dniepr before all our troops were
safely back across the bridges. We reported the fact immediately, which
caused no little surprise and dismay.

On 8 October I received a surprise myself – but was not in the least
dismayed – when the Gruppenkommandeur, Hauptmann Rudorffer,
drove across to our dispersal area. Lang stood to attention to make his
report, but Rudorffer gestured for him to relax. It wasn't an official visit.
Instead, he called across to me: "Hannig, come over here. I've got
something for you."

He reached into his trouser pocket, presumably not the one his
Knight's Cross was in, and pulled out a pair of officer's shoulder straps.

"You were commissioned Leutnant effective as of 1 June this year,
but we've only just received notification from the personnel department.
The shoulder straps are mine. I've taken the Hauptmann's stars off them.
My heartiest congratulations." As he took my shoulder straps off and
replaced them with his own everybody crowded round to offer their
congratulations. That evening quite a party developed and substantial
inroads were made into the bar's stock of liquid refreshments.

A week later came another change. By now I had over one hundred
ops of all kinds behind me as a katschmarek, or wingman. The
Staffelkapitän decided the time was ripe for me to be elevated to the
number 1 slot and lead a Rotte of my own. This meant I would be
responsible not just for my own survival in the air, but for that of my
number 2 as well. I recalled the words of our old Geschwaderkommodore Hannes Trautloft when we first arrived at Gatschina: "It is
far more important to me that you bring your wingman back safely than
that you return alone with a victory claim."

In other words, be constantly aware of the man on your wing and never fly in such a way that would expose him to unnecessary danger. Put bluntly: forego the chance of a kill if it imperils your katschmarek. Between Walter Heck, Xaver Müller, Lerge Hoffmann and myself there had developed a mutual and instinctive understanding that hadn't needed to be put into words. If, for example, I found I had an enemy fighter on my tail, I would make a diving turn away at full throttle while my number 1 immediately began to climb.

If the Russian pilot stuck to me, my leader would come down behind him and, more often than not, shoot him down, If the enemy chose to climb after my number 1, he would then dive away and I would be in a position to get on the Russian's tail. We christened this manoeuvre the 'yo-yo' after the up and down motion of the children's game. It was not something that had been taught in the schools. It had evolved out of experience at the front.

I was assigned one of the new replacement pilots as my wingman. Before our first mission together I carefully explained to him all the situations we might encounter, the things that were important, and how he was to react to each.

The call-sign of our Rotte was 'Taube' (Dove). My newcomer settled in well and followed instructions to the letter. Then one day, while escorting some Stukas, we were bounced by a pair of La-5s. By this time the Russians were also flying in twos and fours; adopting not only our combat formations of Rotten and Schwärmen, but also many of our tactics. They had become much more dangerous as opponents.

I turned into the leading La-5 as he dived on me. He curved away to the left but remained at the same height. Meanwhile his wingman, who was a long way behind, went into a loop that would bring him down behind my katschmarek. So I shouted a warning over the R/T: "Taube 2, watch out, he's coming down on your tail!!"

But instead of pulling a tight turn and diving away, my number 2 remained steadfastly in position behind me. He hadn't grasped the situation. I yo-yoed after my La-5 setting him up for an attack, but kept a close eye on what was going on behind me. "Taube 2 – break immediately! Break, break!!"

But still he remained in position, a sitting duck for the second Russian. There was only one thing to do. Abandoning my attack, I dived away in a steep turn myself. My number 2 followed obediently in my wake, but not before he had taken a couple of hits in his engine and oil cooler. The enemy pilot broke off as I held my turn in towards him. My wingman's machine was by now trailing a long banner of black smoke.

Fortunately we were behind our own lines. Below us was a large field of stubble where the golden Ukrainian wheat had already been harvested and gathered in; the ideal spot for a belly-landing. After returning to base I borrowed the Staffel's Fieseler Storch to go and fetch my number 2. He admitted that he had not seen the Russian fighter coming out of its loop onto his tail until it was too late. He first became aware of its presence when the bright red pearls of tracer began flashing past his cockpit. Then he heard and felt the strikes on his engine, saw the black smoke pouring out, and decided it was time to put down as quickly as possible.

This event taught me a valuable lesson. For the rest of my time in Russia not one of my wingmen took a single hit from an enemy fighter.

The month of October was dominated by our ground troops' withdrawal across the Dniepr. To the south of Kiev the Red Army was close on their heels. But where was the enemy to the north of the city?

The eastern bank of the river was still covered in thick green vegetation. The west bank above Kiev was, as I have already mentioned, a region of marshes and swamps. It was considered impassable, and therefore no defensive positions had been established in that area. In the skies all was quiet. The Russian air force was only evident when called upon to support a local ground offensive.

When it did put in an appearance, however, their machines now outnumbered ours 10:1 or more. Then, to paraphrase a popular song of the period, the heavens did not just 'hang full of violins', but full of enemy aircraft as well. Our only advantage was that the enemy's supply of properly trained pilots was not keeping pace with the number of machines being produced. There were very few Russian fighter pilots on a par with our own highly successful Experten. The vast majority lacked combat experience. This helped to compensate for the numerical imbalance – and also goes some way towards explaining the significantly higher scores our pilots achieved in the east compared to the other fronts.

Towards the end of October I was ordered to fly yet another reconnaissance sortie upstream from Kiev to try to establish the whereabouts of the Red Army. It was a sunny late autumn day of unlimited visibility. There was no action of any significance to be seen either on the ground or in the air.

I led my wingman north along the river at an altitude of about 300 metres. But we could make out no signs of the enemy's presence. After twenty minutes we reversed course and flew back down along the river towards Kiev. Still nothing, either close to the river or on the flat plain stretching off to the eastern horizon; no columns of troops or vehicles – not even a cloud of dust.

Then, just before we reached the city, something in the undergrowth along the river's eastern bank attracted my attention. Among the greenery there seemed to be several small patches of withered foliage. Unable to account for this – why should these particular bushes be turning brown when those all around were still obviously flourishing? – I ordered a full 360° and went back for a second look.

I soon had my answer. Dispersed in the thick shrubbery below were a number of tanks and other vehicles camouflaged with branches. It was this camouflage, no longer fresh and already turning brown, which had caught my eye. Wanting to make absolutely certain, I made another complete circle and came in from the north to carry out a strafing run.

"Kleeblatt (Cloverleaf) 2 from 1, open out a little and keep a close watch. Am attacking the camouflaged vehicles below us."

"Kleeblatt 1 from 2, Viktor, Viktor," was the response as my wingman took up position off to my right.

I dived down on the suspect area, lining the cluster of brown patches up in my sights before letting fly with all barrels. My rounds exploded among the bushes from which, no doubt on a given signal, there suddenly erupted a storm of return fire. The troops below had obviously been watching my manoeuvres, but had not opened up on me sooner for fear of revealing their positions. Luckily their aim was off – too short. I jinked away at ground level until out of danger and then we headed back to Kiev to report that Soviet troops had reached the banks of the Dniepr to the north of the city as well.

In fact, the tactical reconnaissance boys discovered corduroy roads of felled logs laid through the swamps on the western bank. The enemy was already across the river in some strength and the capital of the Ukraine was in danger of being encircled.

On 26 October I had been awarded the combat clasp in gold for flying 120 operational missions. Exactly one week later, on 2 November, II/JG 54 received instructions to vacate Kiev immediately and retire to Fastov. The transfer order had a sting in the tail, however, courtesy of the Luftflotte Commander, General der Flieger Seidemann: six aircraft and a skeleton ground crew were to remain behind at Kiev-West "to support the city's defenders".

5 Staffel drew the short straw. The six pilots selected were Leutnant Lang as Staffelkapitän, Leutnants Hünerfeld and Hannig, Feldwebel Hoffmann, and Unteroffiziere Groß and Paschke. Together with a dozen mechanics, we were the ones who would be staying put.

The rest of the Gruppe took off, the ground personnel following by vehicle along those roads still open to the south-west. It was in this direction that the landing ground at Fastov lay, some 45 kilometres away.

The huge expanse of Kiev-West was suddenly deserted; its hangars empty. As evening approached we towed three aircraft into each of the two hangars and closed the doors. Leaving four of the ground crew armed with machine pistols to stand guard, the rest of us set off on foot for the barracks in the city. There were road blocks everywhere and to have driven in would have been difficult, if not impossible.

The Russian barracks complex was surrounded by a 3-metre high brick wall. A paved road ran past in front of it. A large gate gave access.

Inside, three-storey barrack blocks were arranged in open U shapes along either side of an almost straight inner road. Everything stood abandoned and empty. An eerie silence enveloped the whole place.

We went into the U-block nearest the gate and decided to occupy three rooms on the top floor of the wing parallel to the road. There was no electricity, but we dared not show a light anyway. We would take it in turns – in pairs, one pilot and one mechanic – to keep watch. From the end windows there was a commanding view of the main gate, the road outside, and the nearby buildings. The first night passed quietly.

In the early hours of 3 November the Russians opened their offensive against Kiev. Launched simultaneously from both the north and south, the enemy's plan was clearly to surround the city and take it by storm. We had made our way back out to the airfield before first light. The infantry soldiers guarding the road blacks let us pass without any trouble.

With the rising of the sun the Red Air Force arrived to add its weight to the assault. We had no telephone link to our Geschwader, or to any other higher Luftwaffe command. How we chose to "support the city's defenders" was entirely up to us. We opted to fly in our usual Rotte formations; taking off straight from the hangars whenever the sky above the airfield was free of enemy machines. Hardly were our undercarriages retracted before we found ourselves in the midst of hordes of Russians. But they probably didn't even notice our presence as we 'roof-hopped' across the burning city before attempting to gain height. As the day progressed the enemy's numbers grew and we each managed to score. Below us all hell had broken loose. Everywhere you looked there was total chaos and confusion.

After sunset we serviced our machines in the hangars and then returned to our barracks on the western outskirts of Kiev. By now the road blocks had been strengthened by artillery. As we clambered over them the gun crews stared at us as if we were men from the moon. They obviously hadn't expected to see a bunch of pilots in flying overalls apparently taking part in the street fighting.

The enemy's pincer tactics were working. The city was almost completely surrounded and the chances of getting out of it in one piece were fading rapidly. The noise of cannon fire had been growing louder throughout the day, but it lessened considerably during the hours of darkness. And so we spent the second night in our deserted barracks. Leutnant Lang had gone across to a nearby infantry command post to find out what the situation was – hopeless, he was told.

At dawn on 4 November the noise of battle flared up again; the rumble of artillery, bursts of machine-gun fire, even individual rifle shots could be heard. We kept the hangar doors closed, waiting for the first Russians to appear overhead. Instead, two war reporters turned up, requesting permission to cover our activities. One carried a camera and wanted to film us for the weekly newsreels, the other was a correspondent. Both were in uniform and wore the insignia of Oberfeldwebeln.

Lang outlined the plans for the day. He would fly the first mission with Unteroffizier Paschke as his wingman. If the Russians were still about, he would also take the second with Unteroffizier Groß as his number 2. Lang was not far short of his hundredth victory and he was understandably eager to add to his score. The third Rotte would consist of Lerge Hoffmann, whose total was standing at 48, and myself. If necessary, a fourth Rotte would go up later.

But things didn't quite work out that way. Suddenly the sky was filled with the noise of aircraft engines and a veritable armada of enemy machines roared past low overhead; formations of US-supplied Boston bombers and heavily-armoured Il-2 ground-attack aircraft in groups of a dozen or more. Above and behind them came their fighter escort: La-5s, Yak-7s and more 'Americans' – Bell Airacobras. Some of the fighters were flying in twos and fours, others in larger gaggles.

The whole lot passed by just to the north of us before beginning a wide turn to attack the positions of our infantry defending the northern edges of the city. Not a single machine bothered to investigate the apparently abandoned airfield of Kiev-West off to their left.

Lang took off with Paschke close behind him as soon as the leading formations were safely past. As the two fighters disappeared westwards we hurriedly closed the hangar doors behind them. After thirty minutes the pair returned and taxied back into the hangar before switching off their engines. Lang jumped down from the cockpit swearing like a trooper. After despatching two Il-2s all four of his cannon had jammed. He immediately climbed into another Focke-Wulf that was standing ready and, the moment the sky was clear of Russian aircraft, took off again, this time with Unteroffizier Groß on his wing.

A good hour passed before the pair reappeared. They came in fast and low from the west, landed without any wing-waggling and rolled straight up to, and through, the opened hangar doors. Lang had claimed no fewer than 7 enemy aircraft destroyed. Groß had got two. Both began to describe their experiences between grabbing bites to eat from the food container; it was already lunchtime. Meanwhile the ground crews were busy on both aircraft, re-arming and refuelling them, and then turning them around so that they were pointing towards the hangar door ready for immediate take-off.

It was then that Lang turned to Lerge and me as we were getting ourselves ready to fly the next mission: "Look, how about letting me and Groß go up again? I'm still a few short," – by which he meant he still needed a few more kills to reach his century. What could we do but stand down and let Lang have the third mission as well. It was harder for Lerge than for me. He required just two more victories to make his 50.

Lang and Groß took off again at about 14.00 hours. By now the Il-2s, which were operating from a forward landing ground on the east bank of the Dniepr only some 15 kilometres away, were passing almost directly overhead, wheels down, in unbroken procession. They were lifting off from their field and – without even bothering to retract their undercarriages – heading towards us before swinging north, attacking the German positions with guns, bombs or rockets, and then returning to base to re-arm and start all over again. The whole process, excluding the attacking part, was not unlike the circuits and bumps we had flown while training.

Some sixty minutes later our Rotte came back in to land. This time we had witnessed two of Lang's kills. We had been standing in the hangar doorway watching the approach of another group of Il-2s and their fighter umbrella when we spotted our Focke-Wulfs behind them. Lang closed right in on one of the La-7 escorts, fired a short burst at a range of some 50 metres, banked quickly left, got on the tail of another and gave it the same treatment. Both La-7s broke up in the air, a wing snapped off one, and pieces of aircraft came crashing down to the ground near where we stood. Neither pilot stood a chance. One war reporter was filming it all like mad, the other scribbling furiously.

The result of this third mission: Emil Lang had added another 5 to his score and Fred Groß 1. Now Lang was just two short of his 100, and Lerge Hoffmann still 2 shy of his 50. Both wanted to make the most of this unique opportunity. I deferred yet again. And at about 16.00 hours Lang took to the air for a fourth time, with Hoffmann as his katschmarek.

Wave after wave of Russian aircraft continued to fill the sky. They seemed completely oblivious to the fact that German fighters were operating in the area and scoring successes. The city's flak defences continued to bang away as well, bringing down a number of enemy machines. But our combined efforts couldn't alter the situation. The Soviets' superiority in numbers was too overwhelming.

Meanwhile, members of the ground crew had been busy making up a congratulatory placard, bearing the number 100 surrounded by oak leaves, ready to present to the Staffelkapitän upon his return with the hoped-for century. Slowly the Russian attacks began to abate. The enemy's operations for the day were winding down and the skies grew quiet. As if to compensate, the sounds of the ground fighting became louder and seemed to be getting closer.

At last Lang and Lerge returned. They taxied to a halt in front of the hangar, switched off their engines and slid back their canopies. "Made it. Another four." Emil Lang told us with a broad smile. Laughing, he accepted the mechanics' congratulations together with their placard bearing the magic number 100. Then he climbed out of the cockpit, jumped down from the wing of his machine and went across to meet

Lerge who saluted, hand to the peak of his cap, and reported: "Unteroffizier Hoffmann returned from mission. Two kills. My congratulations on your four."

Both had achieved their goal. The correspondents captured the whole proceedings on film. Photographs were taken, the story was written up and documented. Two months later Lang's achievement of 4 November 1943 featured on the front cover of the 13 January 1944 issue of the prestigious *Berliner Illustrierte Zeitung* weekly magazine. The full page photograph showed a beaming Emil Lang being borne in triumph on the shoulders of the mechanics. The caption underneath read: 'Eighteen in one day: the victor returns.' What nobody knew at the time was that Lang's feat was, and would remain, the world record for the highest number of enemy aircraft shot down by a fighter pilot in a single day.

That same evening the two war correspondents left Kiev – there was still a narrow corridor leading westwards out of the city – and so they missed the events of the night ahead.

The aircraft and vehicles had been safely stowed away in the hangars and we had returned to our barracks building on the edge of the city. We had impressed upon our ground crews once again the importance of not showing a light or making a sound during the night. Each of them had also been given a bottle of Crimean champagne that had no doubt been taken from one of the quartermaster depots in the city before the Russians could get their hands on it.

Now we three officers were watching the events outside from our top-storey window. Some 500 metres beyond the main gate of the barracks complex stood the first German road block of Kiev's inner defence ring. The darkness was constantly rent by the flash of explosions. Bangs and crashes sounded continuously from all around us. Suddenly, above the background din, we became aware of the rattle of tank tracks on the road outside the gate. The vehicles halted, their engines grumbling. Then they started up again, coming closer. The leading tank fired a shot and we distinctly heard the metallic clatter of the empty shell case as it was thrown out and bounced onto the roadway.

We looked at each other in alarm. They were right outside! We saw the first tank nose its way cautiously through the gate. It was followed by four others, all laden with Russian infantry. The tanks came to a stop in front of our block. A searchlight clicked on. Slowly its beam fingered the face of the building on the other side of the road from us.

Orders were barked in Russian. There was a lot of shouting and yelling as the soldiers jumped down from the tanks and ran into the barracks. The searchlight swung across to our side of the road, illuminating the block to our left. The beam crept towards us. We dropped to our knees and crouched below the sill of the window as the room behind us was suddenly bathed in glaring white light. A tremendous racket was coming up from the ground floor where the

Russians were kicking down doors and smashing furniture.

We crept out on to the landing. At the head of the stairs stood a box of hand grenades 'for emergencies'. None of us took one. We were all waiting to see what would happen next. The noise below slowly subsided until all was still again inside the building. We went back to the window and looked out cautiously, showing as little of ourselves as possible. The Russians must have decided the barracks were deserted after all and not worth searching further. The infantry were climbing aboard the tanks, which turned and lumbered out of the gate before heading back off towards the west. We slowly breathed out.

As dawn broke on 5 November we woke the ground crews who, incredibly, had slept the night through and noticed nothing – perhaps the champagne had helped! Our little group set out for the airfield. The road blocks along the way were all still intact and at the field everything was as we had left it the evening before.

Lang now decided that we too should leave for Fastov. To stay in Kiev any longer would be pointless. The five serviceable Focke-Wulfs would be flown out. The ground crews, and one pilot, would follow on by road. Lang would have to lead the flight, but he wanted one of us two officers to be in command of the ground party. Preferring not to give a direct order, he suggested that the fairest way of deciding would be to draw for it. Udo Hünerfeld and I agreed. Lang took two matches and broke the head off one of them: "The one who gets the short match leads the ground column, OK?"

We both nodded. Lang hid his right hand behind his back for a moment and then held his fist out to us; the two matches projecting an equal length. The older man got to choose first. That was Udo. He picked the short match and so was placed in charge of the ground party.

We five took off as soon as possible in order not to delay the ground crews' departure any longer than was necessary. They would be facing by far the greater risks. At Fastov they had been expecting us daily. We were welcomed back and quickly put in the picture. Another transfer had already been ordered – to Byelaya Zerkov, 30 kilometres to the south. Udo turned up with the ground column before nightfall. They had managed to make their way out of Kiev by keeping to the side roads and had got through without incident. 5 Staffel was back together again.

The following morning – 6 November, the day Kiev was finally recaptured by the Red Army – we moved to our new base. Byelaya Zerkov was a pre-war Russian airfield close to the main Kiev-Odessa highway. It had fallen undamaged into German hands in 1941 and its flight control and admin buildings, hangars and workshops still stood beside the large expanse of grass-surfaced runway. A little further back there were extensive accommodation blocks and married quarters for the original permanent staff.

In contrast, the many landing grounds in the area were simply open fields chosen for their proximity to roads or railway lines. This eased the problems of supply, but the personnel manning and operating these strips would either have to live under canvas, in summer, or be quartered in the nearest Russian village when the winter set in.

We fighter pilots were also very much dependent upon weather conditions. As we had not been trained in instrument flying we could not operate in low cloud or poor visibility. When such conditions kept us on the ground 'qbi' was said to be in force; this being the radio code for bad weather.

Missions flown in marginal conditions called for added alertness. You never knew when an enemy pilot trained in the art of blind-flying might appear out of a cloud and take a pot-shot at you. That nearly happened to me. I had been ordered to fly a patrol along the front line. The cloud base was solid 500 metres above the ground. I flew the required leg, but saw nothing. There were no signs of any movement on the ground either. I turned and headed back – still nothing.

Despite the layer of cloud above me, the sense of inactivity all around caused my attention to wander. It therefore came as quite a shock to see a shape, just a shadow at first, emerge out of the cloud diagonally off to the right ahead of me. If the enemy machine – the large red star on his fuselage left no doubt as to his identity – had appeared *behind* me it might have been a very different story. As it was, I reacted instinctively: a little more throttle, close in on him – 100 metres, 80, 50 – let him have it with all six barrels. The enemy pilot hadn't seen me and couldn't have known what hit him. The machine tipped over and exploded on the ground. I returned to base and made a low pass with wings waggling: Abschuß!

Fortune favoured me again a few days later. A group of Il-2s were attacking some troops dug in on the edge of a village. Our forward air observer on the ground reported the presence of the 'furniture vans' and vectored us onto them. My wingman and I found ourselves approaching the Soviet machines from almost directly abeam. Selecting a target, I allowed for enough lead and pressed all the buttons.

The tracers reached out towards my chosen victim. My shells exploded in the middle of his fuselage and tore the entire cockpit canopy away. The machine reared up and then fell away on one wing, crashing into the ground behind one of the larger cottages in the village. I turned my attention towards another of the Il-2s now retiring at full speed. I positioned myself directly astern of this second Russian so that his rear gunner could not fire at me without being in danger of shooting his own tail off. I adjusted my speed to his and sat there patiently, well within range, awaiting my chance.

That chance came when he had to climb slightly to clear some trees. Keeping a little below him I was able to get in a burst at his oil cooler.

His engine caught fire and he pancaked into the ground. Another Ivan that wouldn't be returning to base.

My number of victories was now into double figures. And on 1 December the Staffelkapitän pinned the Iron Cross, First Class, on the breast of my tunic. These Iron Crosses had stories of their own to tell. They were conferred at the discretion of a panel at rear-area HQ. The unit commander at the front would first submit a recommendation. This would then be scrutinized, evaluated and pronounced upon by the rear-area authority. If granted, the unit commander would be informed by teleprinter. The medal itself would be despatched from the rear by courier, which could take days or even weeks.

The official date of award of the decoration, however, was the day of receipt of the teleprint. Rather than having to inform a pilot that he had won the Iron Cross – "but it hasn't turned up yet" – this led to unit commanders pinning their own Iron Cross on to the breast of the new recipient and being without a medal themselves until the other one arrived, which they would then wear. My own decoration, for example, had first been presented to Kommodore Hannes Trautloft. He then passed it on to my original Staffelkapitän, who in turn handed it over to Emil Lang, who had now presented it to me.

At Byelaya Zerkov we were accommodated in the original officers' married quarters. As a Leutnant I was given a room of my own that was heated by a pot-bellied iron stove. It was a luxury I was more than grateful for. The Russian winter had set in. Snow, ice and fog brought flying to a standstill; qbi conditions were in force for days on end.

While we were condemned to inactivity, the Red Army continued to advance westwards. Christmas was approaching. The weather remained atrocious and operations were out of the question.

On the day before Christmas Eve elements of a Waffen-SS division moved into our building. They had been pulled out of the front line ready to be sent as a 'fire brigade' unit to shore up another sector. The entire eastern front was now in a state of constant retreat. But wherever these battle-hardened veterans were deployed they stood like a bulwark against the oncoming Soviet tide. But once they were moved elsewhere it was all too soon a case of 'Forward comrades, we've got to pull back' again. This was one of the bitter truths of the situation in the east by the end of 1943. Our army divisions had suffered enormous losses. The survivors were worn out and battle-weary. They were no longer capable of offering the same level of resistance to Russian pressure as the often better-equipped and stronger Waffen-SS units.

In the morning I watched the Waffen-SS men drilling outside our quarters as if they were on the barracks square back home, oblivious to the snowstorm raging about them. By the afternoon they had marched to the station, entrained, and were gone.

The weather grew steadily worse. Heavy blizzards alternating with thick fog still kept us pinned to the ground. The many recent moves meant that we had had no post for a long time. The only thing coming our way was the Red Army, and that was getting nearer by the day. Imbibed in sufficient quantities, the vodka, brandy and liqueurs helped to lift the worst of the gloom, but it was a forced kind of gaiety. For most of us the festive season was a time of waiting and wondering what lay in store.

The waiting, at least, was soon over. On 27 December orders were received to retire to Tarnopol at once, regardless of current weather conditions.

In clear visibility this would have posed no problems whatsoever. You simply had to follow the road westward out of Byelaya Zerkov for about thirty minutes, make a 20° turn to port, pick up the main Vinnitsa-Lemberg (Lvov) highway and then stick to this until you reached Tarnopol. In foggy conditions, and with the rolling landscape covered in a thick mantle of snow, it was a different matter entirely. The horizon would be difficult, if not impossible, to keep in sight. Distinctive terrain features were few and far between. Lose track of the all-important roads and you were in real trouble.

The entire Gruppe was divided into individual Rotten. Each pair would take off at five to ten minutes intervals, visibility permitting. Lang, the ex-Lufthansa pilot and therefore trained to fly on instruments, would take two wingmen with him: Unteroffizier Koller and myself. With his experience he could quite easily have climbed through the cloud into clear air above. But this would have meant abandoning his two hapless katschmareks to their fate. And so he remained below the cloud layer, leading us out along the road that ran west from Byelaya Zerkov.

The road was full of retreating troops, some nearly invisible in their white winter camouflage smocks, the majority sticking out like sore thumbs against the snow in their green and grey uniforms. One or two of the columns shot at us as we flew by close overhead, prompting Lang to move us out well off to the side of the road.

After thirty minutes Lang made a slight left turn. Leaving the road behind us, we followed close on his tail as he struck out across open country on a bearing of 250° that would take us WSW towards the Vinnitsa highway. The terrain started to become more hilly, forcing us to climb. At the same time a thick fog began to descend. Suddenly we found ourselves flying along a blind valley which ended in a large bowl. Hills reared up all around us, their summits blanketed in fog. With the weather closing in rapidly, we had to get down in a hurry. The question was – where?

Below us in the centre of the bowl was a perfectly flat area of snow; obviously a frozen lake. From its banks the land rose gently at first, but then climbed steeply into the fog. To one side of the lake stood a factory building with a single tall chimney, alongside it the huts of a small village.

If we tried a landing on the lake would the ice bear the weight of our machines? And what lay hidden below the snow on the slopes of the lakeshore? If the ground underneath it was too uneven, a wheels-down landing could easily result in a somersault. But a belly-landing in this God-forsaken spot would automatically mean that the aircraft would be lost, and with it any chance of continuing our flight to Tarnopol.

Lang circled the factory chimney several times, with us trailing obediently behind him, while he decided on his course of action. Finally his mind was made up. The R/T crackled: "Kleeblatt (Cloverleaf) 2 and 3 from 1: I'm going in wheels-down. I'll land up the gradient from the edge of the lake. If I crack up, you two belly-land and get me out. Frage Viktor?"

Koller and I acknowledged. I tucked in close beside Lang, following his every movement – lowering my undercarriage and flaps when he did – to get a feel for the approach and to watch how he did it. He went in very low over the frozen lake, chopped his throttle as he reached its edge, touched down, bounced a few times, and rolled to a stop.

I did another circuit and then landed beside him. Koller followed me down. Our three Fw 190A-6s had come to rest in the snow twenty metres apart from each other, in a neat row almost as if lined up for inspection, somewhere between Vinnitsa and Tarnopol. We switched off our engines, clambered out of our machines, and went into a huddle to discuss our situation. The results were far from encouraging:

- not one of us knew where we were;
- the machines were standing in a ploughed field covered in snow;
- our weapons consisted of one machine pistol that Koller had brought along with him, and the two 7.65-mm pistols that Lang and I had at our belts; and
- we had no provisions or personal effects of any kind with us; they, together with our sleeping bags, were with the ground party now hopefully making their way westwards.

We decided the first priority was to find out where we were and then, if at all possible, persuade the villagers to help us construct some sort of strip so that we could take off again when the weather cleared. Leaving Koller to guard the machines, Lang and I began to crunch through the snow towards the factory. We crept around the side of the building and peered out along the village street. A uniformed figure carrying a rifle was coming towards us. Pistol in hand, Lang whispered: "Hang on, we'll ask this character."

As the armed man came around the corner we sprang out in front of him. He nearly jumped a foot in the air, shouting: "Not shoot! I work Kommandant. You come."

He was a Hiwi – a Hilfswilliger, or foreign volunteer – engaged by the local military commandant and probably employed as the village policeman. He took us to the hut that served as the office of the commandant, who turned out to be an army Oberfeldwebel. The sergeant major saluted. We explained our predicament to him and what we hoped to do about it. He said he would get his people to mount guard on the aircraft overnight, offered us quarters in a hut at the end of the village, and was helpful in the extreme.

We fetched Koller, were given food and drink, and spent a quiet night. When we went back out to our aircraft the following morning there were no guards to be seen. They, together with the sergeant major, had quietly decamped during the hours of darkness. What now?

Despite its isolated location, we discovered that a small road wound along the valley floor. Small groups of retreating German troops were beginning to trickle along it, all heading westwards. Some were still carrying their weapons, others were unarmed. But the faces of all of them were deeply etched with battle fatigue and exhaustion. We could expect no help from that quarter.

Then, in the afternoon, we saw a small convoy of trucks carrying quadruple 20-mm flak guns approaching. This was more like it. We flagged them down and immediately recognized the Leutnant in charge. The group had been part of Kiev-West's anti-aircraft defences. An agreement was quickly reached. The Leutnant and his flak troop would willingly guard our three Fw 190s parked out in the field in exchange for the diesel fuel we had found in a small dump in the village. His vehicles had been running low. Now each was topped up to the brim and the troop's onward journey was assured.

In the meantime we had inspected the field a little more closely. We had been very lucky. Our approach and landings had been made in line with the ploughed furrows. Had we landed *across* the iron-hard ridges we would almost certainly have come to grief. But any thoughts of constructing a strip to allow us to take off again could be forgotten. Our only hope – and it was a very slim one – was that the Soviet advance along this part of the front would be brought to a halt before it engulfed us. Then, perhaps, our aircraft could be dismantled and recovered. Otherwise, the only option would be to blow them up. But we didn't even have the means to do this. The flak Leutnant did, however, and so agreed to stay with us a little longer.

The news we got from the troops still straggling through the village was not good. They told us that the enemy was not far behind them. The Leutnant set a deadline. He would have to pull out by 30 December at the latest, or the road to the west might be cut and his little convoy of vehicles trapped.

On the morning of 30 December a single tank came down the road carrying a load of wounded infantrymen. Lang waved down the vehicle and had a few words with the commander. Another deal was struck. The tank commander was prepared to stay the coming night in the village with us if the flak Leutnant would take charge of the wounded. This was agreed and the wounded were transferred to the trucks before they made their departure. The tank was also desperately short of fuel and was quickly filled from the drums of diesel we had found in one of the village cellars.

Another night passed uneventfully. But towards noon on 31 December we spotted several files of tiny brown figures emerging from the tree line and beginning to snake down the hillside towards us. "There they come," the tank commander stated quite matter-of-factly. "Time to get going. All aboard."

Koller and I climbed onto the rear decking of the tank. The heat of the engine and our fur-lined flying overalls would protect us from the cold. Lang was in the turret with the commander. It had been decided that our aircraft would each be destroyed by a single round of cannon fire from the tank. Lang had asked to be allowed to fire the shot intended for his own machine. His first attempt at 80 metres was too high. Obligingly the tank commander ordered his driver to advance fifty metres. From just 30 metres away not even a 100-victory air ace could miss. Three shots in rapid succession and all three Focke-Wulfs began to burn. Their undercarriages collapsed and the aircraft exploded one after the other.

The tank trundled out of the village. After a short distance we left the road and began to bulldoze our way across country in the rough direction of Vinnitsa. Koller and I clung on as the vehicle lurched and swayed beneath us. The fog had long gone and as darkness fell the night sky became a jewelled canopy of coldly glittering stars. We reached another road that was completely deserted, followed it for hours through woods and fields, and finally arrived in Vinnitsa. The tank commander insisted on delivering us right to the airfield, where we thanked him and his crew profusely and said our goodbyes.

At Vinnitsa we found a number of our comrades who had managed to make it through this far by air. It was New Year's Eve. An impromptu party got underway and on the stroke of midnight – strictly against all regulations – a spectacular firework display erupted as every weapon in the place was loosed off. The year 1943 had come to a close.

And the result of our withdrawal from Byelaya Zerkov? Of the 24 machines of II/JG 54 that had taken off, just one reached Tarnopol, twelve had put down here at Vinnitsa, and the remaining eleven – including our three – were scattered over the surrounding countryside. It was the single greatest Russian success against our Gruppe on any one day of the entire campaign. But not one of our fighters had been hit by either air or ground fire. It was all down to the fog.

In our old sector to the north, the Red Army had finally succeeded in driving the German forces back from the gates of Leningrad. Our ground troops were retreating to the Narva-Pleskau line along the Estonian border. But for us pilots of JG 54 there was little time to dwell on thoughts of old stamping grounds now lost. After three days all but one of our missing pilots had been found and brought back to Vinnitsa with hardly a scratch between them to show for their forced landings. A Ju 52 took us 'orphans' to Cracow in Poland to collect replacement aircraft. From there we were ordered to fly directly to the Gruppe's new base: Stara Konstantinov, a forward landing ground situated between Tarnopol and Zhitomir.

Our lost pilot was to rejoin us six weeks later. As an ex-instructor at a training school he was rated for instrument flying. On taking off from Byelaya Zerkov he had immediately climbed through the cloud layer and set course south-westwards. When his fuel ran out he got back down through a hole in the clouds and belly-landed. By then he was well inside friendly territory, but had been ordered to remain with his machine until a recovery team could be sent out to retrieve it.

The Russian winter still had us in its grip. The fresh falls of snow on our new landing ground were rolled hard so that we could continue to take off and land. Ops remained very much the same as before. We were engaged primarily in protecting our front-line troops from low-level air attack. It had all become routine. We even accepted our nomadic life style as normal. When we transferred from one base to another each pilot took with him just what he would carry on an operational mission: his front ID card and his pistol. Everything else would follow by baggage train. Despite increasing difficulties the system worked well. Throughout my whole time on the Russian front none of my possessions were ever lost or stolen.

Our day-to-day existence at the front had its lighter moments too. On one occasion a little black panje pony turned up on our airfield. Nobody seemed to know where he had come from, but he was completely tame and very friendly. He took bread from our hands. Youthful memories stirred within me. Perhaps he would let me ride him? I stroked his neck and gently rubbed his muzzle. He returned my display of affection, nudging my arm with his shaggy little head. Holding his mane, I swung myself up onto his back and trotted off. He responded to my leg and arm movements just like our old farm horse back home. In the evening we took him back with us to the cottage where we were billeted and presented him to the owner. The old man was overjoyed at the unexpected gift and loudly called down God's blessing upon us.

We were to spend only a few days at Stara Konstantinov. The front had been stabilized for the moment and we were recalled to Vinnitsa, where we were once again housed in the airfield's accommodation blocks.

By now I had been elevated to the position of Schwarmführer and was leading formations of four or six machines. Not long after returning to Vinnitsa I was ordered to take a small Kommando of half-a-dozen fighters down to Uman to help provide air cover for troops fighting on the southern sector. Uman was another peacetime Soviet base that we had captured intact and which had so far remained undamaged. The Luftwaffe airfield servicing companies responsible for the upkeep and maintenance of the larger bases we occupied employed various measures to ensure they remained operational during the winter months. Grass airfields would have the snow on half their surface rolled flat for aircraft to use. At paved bases such as Uman the runway would be shovelled clear, the snow banked up high on either side, and sand or grit laid to prevent the exposed area of runway from freezing over again.

Unfortunately the gritters at Uman had been concentrating their efforts along the end of the runway where machines normally touched down. But a pilot cannot use his brakes immediately upon landing. He has to wait until his aircraft has settled fully on the runway before attempting to slow it down – and at Uman that area remained untreated and was completely smooth and slippery.

I went in first, touched down safely enough, but then realized that my brakes were gripping unevenly. The nose of my machine began to swing to the left but the aircraft continued to slide in a straight line down the centre of the runway. I took my feet off the brakes and awaited the inevitable. The nose swung further to the left and I executed a neat pirouette – I was by now travelling too slowly to call it a ground-loop – and backed gently into the wall of snow alongside the runway where I came to a stop.

My five comrades were still circling above. Once I had taxied clear, I radioed for them to land in the opposite direction to me and not to apply their brakes until they hit the gritted stretch. All five got down safely.

In the far south the spring arrived earlier than we had been used to in the north on the Leningrad front. By the end of February the thaw was already beginning to set in, and with it came the mud. As the snow melted, grass airfields had to be allowed to dry out properly and the surface harden before ops could be resumed. Many units based on grass were therefore transferred to paved fields for the duration of the thaw period. At Uman, for example, we heard that we were to be joined by a Staffel from JG 52.

Our six Focke-Wulfs had been assigned to airfield defence duties. This entailed keeping a Rotte at constant readiness. Two aircraft were positioned in line with the end of the runway at all times. If an emergency flare was fired from the HQ building they could then be scrambled immediately. The runway at Uman was laid out on a NE-SW axis. Aircraft taking off and landing had to be particularly careful when a west wind was blowing. If a cross-wind caught them and a wheel left the runway it would almost certainly sink into the still soggy ground. At high speeds this could easily result in the aircraft somersaulting. And even if the machine was moving only slowly it could well end up on its nose. JG 52 were still flying the Me 109G. This type's notoriously weak undercarriage meant that landing on a paved runway in a cross-wind was not at all easy.

Sure enough, when my turn came to take over the readiness Rotte one of JG 52's Messerschmitts was already standing on its nose alongside the runway, tail high in the air. We called a machine in this undignified pose a 'flyer's monument'. I was still admiring the pilot's handiwork when a green flare suddenly shot up from ops HQ with a loud whistle: emergency scramble!

I stabbed the inertia starter, closed the canopy, pushed the throttle forward and started to roll. I was still accelerating down the runway when I was overtaken by a Pe-2 flashing past low overhead. As I looked up I saw quite a fair-sized bomb drop from its oil-streaked fuselage. The missile hit the concrete in front of me, bounced, and buried itself in the grass next to the runway before exploding. By that time I was well past. As I started to lift off a second Petlyakov overtook me. It followed the first into a wide turn to starboard, making for the front line and safety.

Wheels now up and at full throttle I was rapidly gaining speed. I turned sharply inside the two bombers and quickly caught up with them. A burst of cannon fire sent the nearest one down not far from the airfield perimeter. It took me several more kilometres to close into position and despatch the leader. All the while my number 2 was following me with his wheels down. He had flown through the dirt and debris thrown up by the explosion of the bomb that had just missed me and was unable to retract his undercarriage. Despite his reduced speed he was near enough to witness and confirm my two bombers, both of which crashed inside our lines.

At the beginning of March the Red Army launched a major offensive against our forces in the southern sector. On 10 March they recaptured Uman. Ten days later they were to take Vinnitsa.

Before these attacks began, however, we had been ordered to return to the northern front with a three-day stopover at Warsaw en route to allow the machines to undergo a complete overhaul. That meant three whole days of special leave in the city's Soldatenheim; the luxury of a hotel room with bath, hot running water, a real bed and carpets on the floor, together with the prospects of excellent meals and evenings spent in a box at the theatre or opera. The contrast between life in the Polish capital and life at the front could not have been greater, even if the two were now only an hour's flying time apart.

After our break in Warsaw we continued northwards via Insterburg and Riga to Petseri in Estonia. This was an airfield 40 kilometres west of Pleskau in Russia – the old Estonian-Russian border ran almost midway between the two – and south of Lake Peipus. Our missions were very much as they had been in the southern sector: protecting the retreating ground troops from low-level air attack by Il-2s and engaging the Ilyushins' fighter escorts.

At Petseri we were, for the first time, no longer operating from Russian soil. But somehow or other one became used to the constant withdrawals, the losing of territory previously fought for and won, and the inexorable approach of the Red Army towards the borders of the Reich. One also became inured to the losses. You accepted them as the hand of fate and attempted to close your mind to them – but always there was that nagging thought that tomorrow it might be you.

In the north it was appreciably colder. Although most of the landscape was now free of snow, the surface of Lake Peipus was still frozen over and covered in a blanket of white. I was flying a freie Jagd with my wingman not far from the lake when I spotted a pair of Russian fighters below us approaching from the direction of Pleskau. It was already afternoon and the sun was in the western sky at our backs. Perfect conditions for a bounce. Over the R/T I alerted my katschmarek of my intentions before winging over into a steep dive.

My speed built up rapidly. I was soon on top of the rearmost Russian who was trailing a considerable way behind his leader. A brief stab of the gun button and the enemy machine, now identifiable as a Yak-9, belched a thick column of black smoke. His nose tipped forward and he went down almost vertically into the lake, leaving a large round black hole in its otherwise pristine white surface. The other Ivan, alerted by my streaks of tracer, had immediately executed a sharp about turn and was now fast disappearing eastwards at low level. It had been my twenty-first victory on the Russian front.

Towards the end of March we moved some 180 kilometres southwards to Idriza, just back across the Russian border. Here we were witness to another form of Soviet aerial warfare: night harassment. Idriza was surrounded to the north and east by a low line of hills. Several quadruple 20-mm gun positions had been set up on the crests of these hills as part of the airfield's flak defences.

One night as we were just about to retire to our quarters we heard the sound of a ratchety aircraft engine from somewhere overhead. This was the distinctive noise made by a Russian U-2. These antiquated biplanes – nicknamed 'sewing machines' for obvious reasons – were armed with small 2-kg bombs and employed by the Soviets to attack our lines and rear areas during the hours of darkness. Although indiscriminate and causing little material damage, these nuisance raids were part of the enemy's nocturnal war of nerves. And this particular one seemed to be heading our way.

Suddenly three searchlight beams sliced the blackness. They quickly coned the intruder. Pinned like a moth, the bumbling Polikarpov didn't stand a chance as 20-mm anti-aircraft fire was poured into it. It fell to the ground trailing smoke and shedding bits behind it. The searchlights clicked off. All was dark and quiet again. A few minutes later there was another brief chatter of fire from one of the gun positions up in the hills – they had just been credited with the kill.

On the evening of 29 March as I was passing the ops room on my way back to my billet the Kommandeur, Hauptmann Rudorffer, called me over. "Hannig, you've just been posted to the Ergänzungsgruppe at Liegnitz as a fighter instructor. You'll leave on tomorrow's courier flight for the depot at Heiligenbeil. There you'll get your papers and receive further orders. I'm sure you'll do a good job. We need well-trained replacements. I wish you Hals- und Beinbruch!"

My Staffelkapitän, Leutnant Emil Lang, had already been informed. He too wished me all the best. That evening I said my farewells to my comrades over a few rounds of drinks. The following morning I returned my special flying clothing and equipment to the stores, formally reported my departure, and made my way out to the flight line to climb aboard the Ju 52 transport. Once again I experienced the pleasure of sitting back – *inside* the good old Auntie Ju this time – and being flown by somebody else.

With every minute that passed I could feel the war, the front, and the misery and suffering of the Russian civilian population receding behind me. Little did I know what awaited me in Germany.

CHAPTER 4

Fighter Instructor in the Homeland

After landing back at Heiligenbeil I reported to the Geschwader's rear-area detachment based on the field. The officer in command, a Hauptmann, greeted me warmly, promising me every assistance and asking me all about conditions at the front. I learned for my part that before taking up my duties as a fighter instructor at Liegnitz I was to be given three weeks leave.

Liegnitz was the provincial capital of Lower Silesia, and not all that far from my home. I would be flying over the very area where I had grown up as a boy. But before catching the train to Silesia I wanted to see the girl I had met in Heiligenbeil who had written me so many Feldpost letters while I was in Russia. I had replied to every one of them and a bond had developed between us. I therefore rang the personnel department on the base and asked if she was free after work. Gisela was very pleased to hear from me and we arranged to meet. We had lots to talk about. We went for a long stroll together, chatting and enjoying each other's company so much that I decided to delay my departure for an extra day.

Gisela accompanied me to the station to see me off. I hadn't been able to tell my family that I was coming. Their surprise and obvious delight at my appearance was therefore all the greater. My parents and sisters had begun to come to terms with the loss of Kurt, and the house had regained some of the joy and laughter of old. I couldn't wait to get out of my uniform and into my Lederhosen and comfortable outdoor clothes. I took Hexe for walks through the nearby pine woods. The peace and tranquillity in the stillness of the forest were a tonic. At home I listened to father play his harmonium and let mother spoil me atrociously.

After an idyllic week of doing nothing but relaxing, I set out to visit other members of the family who meant so much to me: my grandmother and aunts at Grottkau in Upper Silesia, and my uncle and aunts in Leipe, where we had always stayed during the holidays as children. I also went to Zobten on the Bober to see old friends and acquaintances.

114

I had spent ten years growing up in Zobten and the church, the houses, the fields – almost every stone – brought childhood memories flooding back. The cherry trees in the gardens and along the roadside had just begun to blossom, the weather was lovely, and the air mild with spring. Silesia was still a backwater and a haven of peace. The war could have been a million miles away. Unfortunately, however, it wasn't. And I still had my part to play in it. On 21 April 1944 therefore, back in uniform, I reported to the office of Jagdgruppe Ost at Liegnitz.

Unlike their RAF Operational Training Unit equivalents, the Luftwaffe's Ergänzungs units remained in a near constant state of change and development throughout the war. In 1940 each Jagdgeschwader had begun establishing its own Ergänzungsstaffel. This was a rear area squadron designed to give newly qualified fighter pilots a final polish before they joined their parent Geschwader at the front. As the need for replacement pilots grew, most of these Staffeln were expanded into Gruppen. Later, these Gruppen were in turn detached from the control of their individual parent Geschwader and formed into autonomous units. Initially known as Ergänzungsjagdgruppen, they were subsequently redesignated simply Jagdruppen. There were four of them, named after the points of the compass: Nord, Süd, Ost and West. Finally, during the winter of 1944-45, these four Jagdgruppen would be amalgamated to form Ergänzungsjagdgeschwader 1.

A link between the operational training process and 'parent' front-line units was retained throughout, however. Each training Staffel within the overall organization, whatever the latter's current make-up, was responsible for readying new pilots for its own specific Geschwader. Its instructors consisted of experienced pilots from that Geschwader withdrawn from ops for the purpose. One of the two Liegnitz-based Staffeln of Jagdgruppe Ost, for example, prepared pilots for service solely with JG 54. The Staffel's instructors were all drawn from the Geschwader's front-line Gruppen. I was now to be one of them.

The Staffelkapitän of 1/JGr Ost was Oberleutnant Udo Hünefeld, he of the short match drawn when it had been time to vacate Kiev-West. Our shared experiences there and at Byelaya Zerkov had formed a link that now grew into a close friendship. There were ten other instructors in addition to Udo and myself: Leutnant Heino Cordes, Oberfeldwebels Karl 'Ede' Brill, Siegfried Müller and Paul Brandt; Feldwebels Michael Kossatz, Richard Raupach and Hans-Joachim Kroschinski; and Unteroffiziere Fritz Luer, Hans Michelka and Artur Lueneburg.

Several, including Udo and Ede of course, I knew from II Gruppe in Russia. The others came from other Gruppen within the Geschwader. All were 'alte Hasen'; veterans wearing the Iron Cross, First Class, and combat clasps in gold. They accepted me wholeheartedly into their tight-knit little community. There was an air of easy informality about the unit. Everybody used the familiar "du" irrespective of rank. But this did not lessen the sense of purpose and dedication. What counted here was experience and the ability to pass on that experience to those we were sending to the front to join our comrades. The instructors may have formed a club of their own – but it was a club which recognized the importance of the job it was doing.

There was no formal training involved in becoming an instructor. It was just something you got on with and did – but only after first wading through the usual paperwork. Once I had completed the necessary formalities I was assigned quarters in the officers' barracks block. I shared accommodation with Leutnant Gotthard Neubauer, the Staffel's TO, or technical officer. With an entrance hall, living room, bedroom and bath – all fully furnished – my new home was a vast improvement on some of the billets I had occupied in recent months.

Liegnitz was a well-established base with all the usual admin and services buildings. Other blocks housed the trainees and ground crews. But most of the major maintenance work on the aircraft was carried out in a large tented hangar. Although the Allied round-the-clock bombing offensive against Germany was gaining strength daily, Silesia had yet to feel its full weight. Not a single bomb had so far fallen on the town of Liegnitz and no civilians had been killed.

It was against this relatively peaceful background that I began my career as a fighter instructor. Each of the Staffel's instructors was in charge of three trainees. As a group of four, this allowed the standard combat formations of Rotte and Schwarm to be demonstrated and practised. The pupils fell into two categories. They were either green youngsters straight from training schools, or experienced operational pilots from other types of units – mostly disbanded bomber Gruppen – now converting onto fighters.

My first trio of pupils were all officers. They had previously been training-school instructors themselves and possessed a vast wealth of flying experience. But they were complete novices when it came to operational flying and combat tactics. It was my task to impart to them the knowledge I had gained at the front. If I succeeded they would hopefully not only survive, but become a welcome and useful addition to the Geschwader's front-line strength.

But even at this late, indeed final, stage of a fighter pilot's training there was still one glaring deficiency. I was unable to provide them with any sort of gunnery practice, against either air or ground targets. The complicated art of aerial marksmanship was taught by pure theory alone. There were no ranges and no aerial drogues to allow the trainees to put this theory into practice. There was not even an official manual to explain the complexities of deflection shooting, the amount of lead required to hit a target, and other such essentials. Instructors had to devise their own teaching aids and get the fundamental principles across as best they could. Pupils would receive their first practical demonstration at the front where, if they were lucky, they would find themselves flying as wingman to a number 1 who could show them how it was done.

At Liegnitz we began in the time-honoured fashion with type familiarization. The cockpit layout and controls would be explained, the engine was started, the pupil was allowed to get the feel of the machine while taxiing on the ground, and then would come the take-off. As there were no two-seater trainer conversions of the Fw 190 yet available, a pupil's first flight was also automatically his first solo. After a few circuits and bumps my initial group of trainees were conversant with the basics of the Focke-Wulf. There had been no problems and everything had gone smoothly.

Next on the agenda came formation take-offs and flights. An instructor would take his three pupils up in turn to practise close-formation flying, demonstrate how to execute turns together, and show his wingman the various positions to adopt in combat. With each of these flights lasting from 60 to 75 minutes, it meant the instructor was in the air for anything between three to nearly four hours every morning or afternoon. As replacement pilots were urgently needed on all the fighting fronts, we flew every day; Sundays and holidays included. This constant pressure put a great strain on the instructing staff and short periods of compulsory rest and relaxation were introduced at intervals throughout the course.

Within a short time my three trainees had fully mastered the Fw 190A-4 and A-5. Now I could begin to show them the 'tricks of the trade' of a front-line pilot: the stall turn and dive, slip turns, flick half rolls and, of course, the yo-yo. I pushed them and myself hard. But a drop of sweat now might save a lot of blood later.

Less strenuous were the straightforward formation flights. There were no restrictions imposed on our training programme. I led my pupils on cross-countries at low level and at altitude, preparing them for both ground-strafing sorties and high-level escort or interception missions. We avoided flying low over Liegnitz and other built-up areas. But the rest of the Lower Silesian countryside surrounding the base became our playground. So I got to see the landscapes I had known as a boy from an entirely new perspective as we flew over familiar villages, rivers, woods and streams.

But the most impressive sight of all was without doubt the nearby chain of mountains separating Silesia from the Protectorate of Bohemia and Moravia – today's Czech Republic – to the south. The largest of the chain were the Riesengebirge (Giant Mountains) and the tallest peak of all the 1,605-metre-high Schneekoppe – literally Snow Summit. On its peak were a hotel, weather station and transmitter mast. The summit commanded breathtaking views across the rolling Silesian hills. But the only way up was by two narrow paths – one steeper and even more difficult than the other.

We had it easier. With my three pupils echeloned to starboard I flew a course keeping us to the right of the lower mountain crests as I headed towards the bulk of the Schneekoppe. Approaching level with the ridge line 200 metres below its summit, I ordered the Schwarm to begin a left-hand spiralling climb around the mountain's conical rocky flanks. Hikers higher up on the two paths waved down to us as we circled up towards them. Reaching the summit I called my three trainees into close formation and we roared over the hotel and weather station. Another order and they slipped seamlessly into line astern as I went into a steep dive into the valley below. Leading them back out across the foothills it was then just a short ten-minute flight back to base.

Our trip to the Schneekoppe had been an exhilarating experience. But there was a serious purpose behind it too. My three pupils had kept station impeccably. They had obeyed my every order and had changed formations smoothly and without fuss. It had provided them with invaluable experience. And for some of our trainees that experience was going to be put to the test much sooner than they expected – certainly before they were despatched to the front.

The American daylight bombing raids on Germany were growing heavier. In the early days of their offensive, when the US bombers lacked fighter cover, our homeland defence units had been able to inflict severe damage on them. Since the advent of the P-51 long-range escort fighter, however, our own fighters were coming under ever more pressure. There were simply not enough of them to combat the increasing menace of the Americans' attacks.

Then somebody realized that there was an untapped pool of highly experienced fighter pilots scattered throughout Germany: the instructors serving with the Ergänzungsgruppen. Orders immediately went out that the individual training Staffeln of these units, each of which consisted of no fewer than 12 instructors and 36 pupils, were to set up a so-called Einsatzstaffel – operational squadron – from among their existing members.

Every Einsatzstaffel was to be made up of three Schwärme; each Schwarm to comprise two instructors and two pupils. The instructors would be the Schwarm and Rotte leaders. Their two wingmen were to be chosen from among those trainees nearing the end of their course and considered best suited to the task. Whenever warning was given of the approach of enemy bombers all training would immediately be suspended and the Einsatzstaffel, six instructors and the six selected pupils, would be put on readiness.

At Liegnitz I was one of the instructors forming part of 1/JGr Ost's Einsatzstaffel. While carrying on with the training programme as usual, our little group-within-a-group awaited the coming of the Americans. And late in June 1944 they came.

Our radar and monitoring services had been tracking the enemy formation's route since its assembly over England. It set course out over the North Sea, crossed the Schleswig-Holstein peninsula and continued into the Baltic. Level with the Oder estuary the bombers would turn 90° to starboard and begin the final leg down to their objective: the Meseritz hydrogenation plant midway between Frankfurt an der Oder and Posen (Poznan).

By this time all training had been shut down at Liegnitz and the twelve Fw 190A-6s of the Einsatzstaffel prepared for take-off. When I climbed into the cockpit of my machine and checked the controls I discovered that a screw was inhibiting the full travel of the throttle. This had the effect of reducing engine output by ten per cent, which was a justifiable measure on a training aircraft. It helped to protect the engine and increased its number of flying hours. But in combat it could mean the difference between life or death if maximum engine power was not available.

When I asked the mechanic why this locking screw had not been removed his answer was, "Orders from above. They say enemy fighters aren't normally to be reckoned with in this part of the world – only those escorting bomber formations."

The order to scramble was given. We took off in Schwärme, the Staffelkapitän leading the first with me heading the Rotte alongside him. Next came Heino Cordes and Michelka with their wingmen, followed by the two remaining Schwärme. I knew none of the trainees flying the wing positions. They were all pupils of other instructors.

It was about 11.00 hours on a beautiful summer's day; a blue sky with patches of cumulus sailing along between 1,000 and 4,000 metres, drawing little herds of shadows across the face of the peaceful sunlit landscape below. We climbed steadily northwards, the direction from which the enemy would appear. As we climbed we checked our R/T and switched on our weapons. The 'armed' indicator lights came on and the clicking of the cannon breeches could be clearly heard through our lightweight summer helmets – all part of the routine for the old hares among us, but a new experience for the six trainees.

"To all cyclists, to all cyclists! Furniture vans now Hanni 7000, course east over the Baltic north of Rügen..."

Hanni was the codeword for Höhe, or height. In other words, the enemy bombers were now north of the Baltic island of Rügen still heading eastwards at an altitude of 7,000 metres. The Staffelkapitän acknowledged receipt of the report with a "Viktor, Viktor" as we continued to gain height northwards. The intention was to climb to the same altitude as the bombers and attack them head-on. Each Schwarm was flying echelon right. I was in the number 3 slot to the leader. On either side of me the two trainees were holding station well.

Again the controller's voice sounded in my ears: "To all cyclists, to all cyclists! Furniture vans turning south direction Wollin, Hanni 7000... I repeat..." At a combined closing speed of something like 800 km/h the distance between our two formations was now diminishing rapidly. With about 200 kilometres, or fifteen minutes to go before estimated time of contact I was keeping a sharp lookout ahead for the first sign of the enemy bombers. We would have very little time to position ourselves properly for a frontal attack, and the firing pass itself would be over in a split second. We would probably be able to score a few hits, but actually to bring down a bomber would be a matter of pure luck.

We were now at exactly 7,000 metres ourselves, heading due north with the ribbon of the Oder on the left far below us. Suddenly I spotted them – tiny shapes reflecting flashes of sunlight like a glittering shoal of small silver fish. But this was no shoal of fish. It was a seemingly unending stream of heavy bombers.

I immediately reported my sighting: "Kleeblatt 1 from 3, furniture vans far ahead, same altitude." As I spoke I glanced across at the Schwarm leader. His engine was emitting tiny puffs of smoke. His speed fell off and he began to lose height. Obediently we three followed him down. Reporting an engine malfunction he waved us away: "Kleeblatt 3, take over the Schwarm – 2 close up on 3." The leader's machine turned away and disappeared beneath us. As his number 2 moved into position on my left wing Heino Cordes' Schwarm flew past overhead towards the now clearly visible enemy bombers.

We climbed after them trying to regain our lost height. We saw Heino and his Schwarm wade straight into the leading squadron of bombers with all guns blazing. Suddenly there was a huge fireball in the sky. One of the enemy had exploded. Then it was our turn. We had not been able to get back up to the bombers' altitude in time. With my wingmen tucked in close on either side of me we attacked the formation from below, pouring our fire into their silver bellies.

As we broke through above them we became aware of condensation trails lancing down towards us. In bunches of four, these could only be the bombers' top cover fighter escorts. Within seconds I had four, then eight, and finally twelve Mustangs sitting on my tail. But while I was flying close above the stream they were unable to open fire on me for fear of hitting their own bombers. This dubious sanctuary did not last long. The high combined closing speed which had protected us during our frontal assault on the bombers now worked against me and I soon found myself hurtling past the last squadron in the formation and out into clear sky beyond.

I immediately began to yo-yo; turning steeply, diving and climbing, climbing and diving. My pursuers didn't seem to know what to make of my Russian front aerobatics. They clung on grimly behind me, but couldn't hold me in their sights long enough to get in an effective burst. I spied a welcome bank of cumulus ahead of me and slightly below. After three more complete circles I was directly above one of the larger clouds. I yanked the stick to the left back into my belly and trod hard on full right rudder. My machine spun down into the cloud.

In my temporary haven I let go of the controls. The trusty Forke at once righted itself and I shot out from the bottom of the cloud into sunlight again. Where were the Mustangs? I looked up and saw them circling the cloud-top above me. I put my nose down and got out of there fast.

While I had been dealing with my own problems my earphones had been filled with the sounds of the dogfights raging all around me. "He's on your tail – break, break!"... "My engine's on fire, baling out."... "I can't control her"... "Belly-landing."

Then I heard a familiar voice, "I've got one right behind me! Heading south at ground level..." It was Heino. I looked down and spotted a lone Focke-Wulf fleeing southwards. A P-51 was sitting right on his tail and three others were following close behind in line astern. Heino was hedge-hopping at zero altitude fishtailing wildly –that is, he was keeping the machine's nose straight but was tramping hard on left and right rudder in turn. The pilot of the P-51 was trying to follow his yawing movements and get into a good firing position. But every time Heino saw the Mustang starting to slide behind him he would slam on opposite rudder and the Ami's shots were going wide – mostly.

"Hang on, Heino," I shouted, "I'm coming down." I dived towards the ground as fast as my doctored throttle would allow. At a range of 300 metres I loosed off a few bursts at the three P-51s bringing up the rear of the chase. When they spotted my cannon shells exploding on the ground around them they broke into a 360° turn which put them out of the running for a while.

Now I could concentrate on the Mustang sitting behind Heino. He showed no sign of abandoning the pursuit. But if I wanted to knock him off Heino's tail it would have to be a team effort. Heino would have to move out of the way the instant I said so. Otherwise the fire I directed at the P-51 might hit Heino's machine directly ahead of it as well.

I edged in closer, "Heino, get ready – left rudder *now!*" Heino had just put on right rudder. By reversing almost immediately he took the American pilot by surprise. The Mustang was still fishtailing full right rudder and suddenly there was empty sky in front of him. I had the clear field of fire I needed. At this range I couldn't miss. And at this altitude the result was inevitable. The Mustang's nose went down a fraction and it cartwheeled into the ground. The other three P-51s which had been closing in behind me broke off and climbed away to rejoin the formation high above.

I closed up alongside Heino. "Any idea where we are?" I asked in plain language. "My red light's starting to flicker." "Haven't a clue," he answered, "but the Oder should be coming up soon."

The river came into sight. We gained a little altitude so that we could scan the countryside for signs of an airfield. As soon as we saw one we lowered our undercarriages and went straight in. We taxied across to the airfield buildings, switched off our engines and climbed out. After slapping each other on the shoulder we examined our machines. Heino's had 21 bullet holes in its fuselage and wings; mine only 17. But nothing vital had been hit. Engines, undercarriages and controls were all in good working order. All we had to do was re-fuel and set off back to Liegnitz.

There we reported to the Gruppenkommandeur, Major Viktor Bauer, in the officer's mess. The post-mortem on our mission was sobering and said all that needed to be said about the futility of pitting penny-packets of Luftwaffe fighters against the might of the American bomber streams. Our twelve Fw 190A-6s had been sent up against a force of some 250 American B-17 bombers escorted by dozens of P-51 Mustang fighters. And the result? One fighter landed undamaged with engine trouble, two returned damaged – Heino's and mine – five made emergency or crash landings, their pilots wounded or dying, and four pilots baled out; two being shot and killed in their parachutes by enemy fighters. The effect this catalogue of disasters had on the other pilots can be imagined.

One of the two pilots who took to his parachute and lived to tell the tale later described what had happened to him:

"My machine was hit and caught fire as I flew through the bomber formation. I baled out but didn't open my 'chute until I had fallen well clear of everything that was going on. I finally landed in a potato field. I quickly got out of my 'chute and cleared off as fast as I could. Then I saw a Schwarm of Mustangs coming down in a line. I dived between two furrows of potatoes and made myself as small as possible. The Mustangs strafed my parachute one after the other and shot it to shreds. Fortunately they didn't spot me."

The air war had certainly changed, and not for the better. But we had little time to dwell on such things. The following day training resumed as usual. The combat units desperately needed replacements – especially those engaged in the defence of the Reich itself, as we now realized ourselves from bitter experience.

The firepower of an individual Schwarm was far too weak to have any effect on a bomber stream. To increase our fighters' effectiveness a new attack formation was introduced. A Staffel of twelve machines would fly in two arrowheads. The leading Vee was to consist of seven fighters in tight formation. The second Vee of five would fly behind and slightly below the first. The Staffel would attack from ahead, holding this formation and opening fire together upon the leader's command. In this way a fusillade of forty-eight 20-mm cannon and twenty-four

12.7-mm machine-gun fire would be brought to bear on the enemy.

What was really needed, of course, was air-to-air rockets which could be discharged from outside the range of the bombers' defensive fire – or larger calibre cannon and faster aircraft. These things were all under development or in the pipeline. Some had even reached the production or delivery stage, but we saw precious little evidence of them.

Instead, we readjusted our flying-training programme to concentrate on practising and perfecting the new Staffel arrowhead formation to be used in frontal attacks on the American bomber streams. Demonstration and teaching of the traditional Rotte tactics employed in fighter combat and designed to increase the chances of survival in a dogfight came a very poor second. And to instil both into our fledgling fighter pilots we had a grand total of just twenty-five flying hours.

To add to these difficulties there were the usual day-to-day problems that beset every unit. The Staffelkapitän went down with appendicitis and had to go into hospital for an operation. I stood in as acting Staffelkapitän and took over responsibility for the training. Everything carried on the same. The instructors got together to discuss and work out the day's programme before the start of flying and we simply went from there.

Taking off seven aircraft at a time demanded more concentration from all concerned. But once in the air it was purely a matter of formation flying with either three or two machines holding their positions each side of the leader. At the end of a flight the aircraft opened out into extended formation and they kept to this distance when landing.

I also assumed temporary command of the reconstituted Einsatzstaffel. Little more than a week after our first disastrous mission enemy bombers were again reported to be heading our way. This time they were coming up from the south, from US bases in Italy, and were heading for the synthetic-fuel plants in Upper Silesia. We were alerted and placed on readiness, as was a Staffel of Me 109s of JGr West operating out of Breslau-Gandau.

The mission plan called for us to rendezvous with the Messerschmitts over Breslau. They were to provide high cover for us while we attacked the bombers, taking position 500 metres above and behind us to keep the enemy fighters off our backs.

We scrambled from Liegnitz and headed towards Breslau. By that time the enemy bomber formation was reported to be at 6,000 metres above the Neusiedler lake SE of Vienna. The Me 109s were waiting for us over Breslau. They were a little higher than us and I noticed that they still flew in Schwärme of fours. I waggled my wings in recognition as arranged, fully expecting the Messerschmitt leader to do the same. Instead he came barrelling down behind us, giving every indication that he was getting ready to attack. What did this character think he was doing? I swore out loud over the R/T: "You b- idiot! We're cyclists! Get off our tails!!"

I rammed the throttle forward – I'd made sure that all the Einsatzstaffel machines had had those damned inhibitor screws removed – pulled up into a steep climb and easily eluded my would-be assailant. But our carefully rehearsed arrowhead formation was in tatters as individual Me 109s and Fw 190s began to mix it in a wild melee high above the historic rooftops of Breslau. The scene was enough to make anyone's hair stand on end. Finally we managed to persuade the Me 109 pilots that we were fully paid-up members of the German Luftwaffe too. And after a few last rolls and loops they at last desisted.

All the while the bombers had been heading northwards from the Neusiedler lake and were now about to cross into Upper Silesia. My wingman, one of the trainees, had stuck close by me during the confusion over Breslau. Major Knappe was an ex-bomber pilot with a dry sense of humour. Now he addressed me over the R/T in simple speech: "Tell you what, Hannig," he suggested, "why don't we surround them and take them prisoner – you go round to the left, I'll go round to the right, and we'll meet up on the other side."

It was a tempting suggestion, but reality intervened when the bombers hove into view. We were off to the left of the approaching formation and would have to curve in to the right. I couldn't see any escorting fighters.

"Achtung – am attacking!" I came in about 300 metres above the right-hand bomber of the high squadron. Matching my speed to his, I side-slipped down towards his tail, got in close behind him and aimed at his two starboard engines. Pieces flew off his wing as my shells struck home. Bright flames streamed from his engines . . . I continued to fire . . . an inferno erupted as his wing tanks went up. As I dived away I saw the bombs tumbling from his belly.

My fighter suddenly shuddered and I heard a loud rattling noise. I had been hit by return fire. I steepened my dive to get out of danger. All seemed in order, but as I began to pull out of my descent both undercarriage legs flopped down and locked. Try as I might I couldn't retract them again. The little 'wheels down and locked' indicator rods sticking up out of each wing refused to budge. Although there was still no sign of any enemy fighters, it was unhealthy to remain flying around for too long with my undercarriage on display for all to see. And to attempt a three-pointer on the uneven ground below would be tantamount to suicide; the risk of flipping over on to my back was too great. I had to find the nearest airfield, and quickly.

I spotted one on the edge of a fair-sized town not far away and made straight for it. It turned out to be Grottkau where my grandmother and two aunts lived. But there was no time for a visit. Leaving my Focke-

Wulf to have its damage assessed, I grabbed my parachute and quickly organized a lift to the station to make my way back to Liegnitz by train.

This time we had suffered no casualties. After the skirmish over Breslau, the others had all returned to base without making contact with the enemy. My katschmarek, Major Knappe, was the only other pilot to have attacked the bombers, but without apparent result. He too got back safely. I heard later that the Messerschmitt Staffel had not escaped so lightly.

These were the only two American incursions into the area during my time instructing in Silesia. We were permitted to carry on with our training programme undisturbed after this.

Later in July I was pleasantly surprised to see a copy of an official manual explaining the rules and techniques of aerial gunnery. Such a handbook had long been lacking. It was published and distributed by the Luftwaffe High Command and the author was an officer on the Staff of the General of Fighters – none other than my original Kommodore when I first joined the Green Hearts of JG 54: Oberst Hannes Trautloft.

Although officially listed as Publication D.(Luft) 5001 and marked with the stern warning 'Not to be taken on operations!', the handbook's title *Tally-Ho, the fighter pilot's shooting primer* and the cartoon drawing on the cover set the tone. Here for the first time were laid out, clearly and concisely, such things as the rules governing deflection shooting, easy ways to judge an enemy's distance, common mistakes and how to avoid them, and much more. Unlike so many official publications, the whole pamphlet was presented in an entertaining and light-hearted manner and was illustrated throughout by the talented pen of Hannes Trautloft himself (see illustration section). Many pilots even maintained that their clay pigeon shooting skills improved dramatically after they had studied it.

The training of new pilots was no longer able to keep up with the high rates of attrition being suffered by the front-line units. A recent attempt to mount a renewed bomber and intruder offensive against England had proved a costly failure. It was first scaled down and then abandoned altogether. A number of the units involved were disbanded. Experienced and fully-trained bomber pilots could volunteer for conversion to fighters as a way of avoiding conscription into one of the Luftwaffe's infantry field divisions.

We received three such officers. One of them, a Major, wore Oak Leaves. The other two, both Hauptleute (captains), sported Knight's Crosses. Together they constituted the trainee element of a Schwarm and they became my responsibility. This posed something of a problem. I was a mere Leutnant with just an Iron Cross, First Class, on my tunic. How was I to go about training, and therefore inevitably telling, three highly decorated superior officers what to do? The easy-going Major

Knappe had been an exception. I had never faced this kind of pupil before.

I realized it all boiled down to just one basic question: could this trio of experienced bomber pilots survive in combat as fighter pilots, or would they simply be sitting ducks – shot down the moment they encountered the enemy? There was only one way to find out.

Type familiarization on the Fw 190 – take-offs and landings – posed no problem for them at all. It was at the next stage, formation take-offs, that their difficulties began. As was customary I took each of them up in turn as my wingman to demonstrate the basic Rotte. We got off the ground together. But their years as bomber pilots had ingrained in them the habit of lifting off gently and maintaining a straight course until a sufficiently safe height had been gained to allow them to commence a slow turn to either port or starboard. By contrast a fighter pilot would retract his undercarriage and flaps almost before his wheels had left the ground, pour on the coal and be ready for any eventuality the moment he was in the air.

To them it was second nature to carry out all control movements carefully and in a coordinated manner. We, on the other hand, worked quickly and instinctively, often jerking the throttle and stick about, twisting and turning, zooming and diving as the situation demanded. If they couldn't develop such reflex actions in the short time available to them they would be dead men on their first op. And that was a fate I wanted to spare them if it was at all in my power.

But after three training flights nothing had changed. They were still painstakingly coordinating their ailerons and rudder movements. Their formation flying and station keeping were impeccable – their practice dogfights a catastrophe. Two or three turns and I would be on their tails every time. Back on the ground I expressed my concerns and made the following proposal to them:

> "One of you please choose the machine you think is the best of all those we've got here on base. I'll take one of those you've just been flying. We'll climb to 3,000 metres and I'll begin to dogfight. If I'm not sitting on your tail in position to fire within three minutes, you *may* just stand a chance of survival in combat."

They were a bit taken aback at first. But then they went into a brief huddle and agreed to my suggestion. It was decided that the Major with the Oak Leaves would be the one to accept the challenge. He selected a brand new Fw 190A-6 while I took the machine he had just been using. We took off and climbed to 3,000 metres. "Kleeblatt 2 from 1 – ready?" I asked. "Viktor, Viktor," he replied.

I immediately slammed home the throttle, went into a steep diving

turn to the right, pulled out sharply, and yo-yoed upwards. Looking back
I could see my katschmarek way behind me just beginning to recover
from his initial dive. By the time he was climbing I was already on my
way back down again, nose-diving past him as he clawed for height. In
less than two minutes I was directly behind him, the A-6 filling my
sights. His attempts to shake me off his tail were fruitless.

We went through the whole rigmarole twice more with exactly the
same result. After that he conceded defeat. We flew back to base in
perfect, tight formation before opening out for the landing. All three
thanked me for the convincing demonstration, took themselves off the
course and offered their services elsewhere.

It was a different story with those young trainees fresh from the
flying schools. Here was raw, untutored talent. They were eager to learn
and quick to master the bravura style of flying necessary to become a
fighter pilot. We hoped that the lessons and experiences we were able to
pass on to them from our own time in combat would enable them to play
a useful role when they reached their front-line units. Nearly all went on
to fly with JG 54. And as the Geschwader remained split between west
and east – III Gruppe was now part of the Reich's defence organization,
the other Gruppen still on the Russian front – most were given the
opportunity to choose the theatre of operations in which they wished to
serve.

If truth be told, German fighters were facing increased odds on all
fronts. My own II Gruppe had undergone a number of changes as a
result of casualties and transfers. On 2 April Albin Wolf had taken a
direct flak hit while engaged against Yak-9s near Pleskau. Feldwebel
Mieszala had been forced to bale out after suffering engine failure. Both
had been killed. My long-time number 1, Lerge Hoffmann, had been
promoted to Leutnant at the beginning of May. Posted to III Gruppe in
defence of the Reich, he had quickly added six heavy bombers to his
score, only to lose his life when his damaged machine somersaulted as
he attempted an emergency landing after combat on 24 May. Emil Lang,
promoted to Hauptmann and awarded the Oak Leaves, had taken over as
the Gruppenkommandeur of II/JG 26 in France. 7 Staffel's Leutnant
Helmut Grollmus had died in a dogfight over Viipuri in Finland on 19
June.

Whenever one received news of a comrade's death something
remarkable happened. All normal feelings seemed somehow to switch
themselves off. The mind imposed iron control on the body. There were
no tears, no wailing, no outward signs of grief or mourning. Had there
been, one would have run the risk of becoming obsessed by thoughts of
one's own death. The only possible way to express how one felt was to
honour the fallen friend's passing.

So it was with Lerge. He and I had flown over forty missions together. We had fought against superior odds and each had been able to rely totally upon the other. But nobody can escape his fate. And now that he was gone I wanted to pay my last respects to a true comrade and a good friend.

Lerge came from the tiny village of Petersdorf in the Riesengebirge mountains. He had been taken home and was to be buried in the local cemetery there. The Geschwader had sent representatives to attend the funeral and lay a wreath. At Liegnitz I had made enquiries as to the date and exact time of the ceremony. Consequently I took off with my three pupils and set course for Petersdorf. We circled high above the little church in order not to disturb the service, waiting for the funeral procession to appear. The sun was shining; the mountains seemed near enough to touch.

When the church door opened and the mourners emerged, led by the priest and the altar boys, followed by the pall-bearers carrying the coffin, I ordered the trainees into close formation on my right wing. Throttling back, I led the Schwarm down in a wide sweeping turn to port. Coming in just over the church tower we flew low and slow along the churchyard path leading to the cemetery, above the heads of the procession, before climbing away into the cloudless blue sky. I fired a short salvo, my final farewell to Lerge, and then led my little group on over the Riesengebirge to complete the scheduled training mission.

Despite the pressure we were under, the training programme still allowed for occasional periods of relaxation. Each instructor continued to put in his three flights a day, either with a single pupil or leading his complete Schwarm. When not scheduled to fly, be it morning or afternoon, his time was his own to do with as he pleased. One favourite spot where we spent many of our free hours was the town's open-air swimming pool. Here it was just like peacetime. Surrounded by well-kept lawns and flower beds, the pool was a popular place of recreation for the local citizens, young and old alike.

Most of the young trainees were keen on sport. And over the months many of my groups would accompany me when I announced my intention to go swimming. Sometimes though they were more interested in just having fun than doing lengths up and down the pool. And whenever a few young pilots – little more than overgrown schoolboys really – got together with time on their hands one of the regular pastimes was that perennial old favourite, the game of 'Dare'.

On one occasion my group and I had made ourselves comfortable on the grass alongside the pool. Next to us a young lady was sitting on a blanket, a bathing robe and book beside her. She was just unwrapping a towel, which she had been wearing like a turban around her head, when one of the trainees came up with the inevitable, "Bet you wouldn't dare!"

It was directed at me, of course, the old man of the party. "What wouldn't I dare?" I enquired suspiciously. "Ask that young lady if you could borrow her bathing robe and towel."

"And what would I want to do that for?" I queried.

"So you could put them on and run round the pool in them!"

"And if I did – what's in it for me?"

"A crate of beer," was the prompt reply.

For a crate of beer it was worth a try. With my most disarming smile I went over to my victim, introduced myself, politely asked if I might borrow her robe and towel for a little while, and whether she would be kind enough to show me how to wind a turban? She joined in the joke and agreed with a laugh.

Suitably attired I set off on my lap of the pool. It didn't take long for the children to spot this strange apparition in their midst. With whoops of delight they joined in the chase. Soon there were so many youngsters shouting and yelling in a long train behind me that I began to feel like the Pied Piper. As a finale, I climbed up onto the 3-metre diving board, waved to the crowd, and jumped into space, the skirt of the robe flapping around my legs.

The robe and towel, both somewhat damp, were returned to their rightful owner, who graciously accepted our invitation to join us for coffee. The end of a perfect afternoon.

At the beginning of August Emil Lang, temporarily back in Germany with his new Gruppe, paid us a visit at Liegnitz. In the evenings it was the custom for us all to dine together in the officers' mess, eating at separate tables for four. In the middle of the room stood the Kommandeur's table at which he entertained guests or else shared with officers of his immediate staff. It was the rule that a latecomer, upon entering the room, would salute those present and then find himself a free place at one of the tables.

I had been on flying duty on this particular afternoon and knew nothing of Lang's visit. When I came into the mess a little later than the others I saluted at the door as was customary and looked around for a chair that was free. As soon as he saw me standing in the doorway, Lang got up from the Kommandeur's table and made his way across the room towards me, exclaiming at the top of his voice in his usual bluff, and thoroughly unmilitary manner: "Ye Gods, Hannig, are you still alive? Come here and let me have a look at you."

With that he gave me a bear-like hug, clapped me on the shoulders with his huge paws and then grasped my hand in his, beaming from ear to ear. His obvious delight at seeing me was returned in full measure. He had to go back to the Kommandeur's table but we arranged to meet later in the bar. There we swapped news and caught up on each others' recent doings. When the time came to part, he asked me: "Why don't you come and join me? I could use you. The posting wouldn't be a problem."

I thanked him sincerely for his offer, but explained that I wanted to return to our old unit on the eastern front. Pilots were needed there too. He understood. We shook hands again, wished each other "Hals- und Beinbruch", and he left. Emil Lang led his Gruppe back to the western front. Within three weeks he was dead; killed in action against American Thunderbolts over Belgium.

As my six-month tour as an instructor in the Homeland was coming to an end and I wanted to rejoin my old circle of comrades in the east, I wrote to my Gruppenkommandeur, Major Erich Rudorffer, requesting that he ask for my return to II/JG 54. In the meantime I was ordered to transfer the training Staffel to Sagan. Liegnitz's grass surface had been taking quite a pounding from the constant take-offs and landings, and was now suffering badly in the heat of high summer. Every aircraft taking off threw up a huge cloud of dust and what little grass was left was disappearing rapidly.

The move was made without difficulty. Sagan was only 80 kilometres, or 12 minutes flying time away. It was a well-equipped field and we were accommodated in similar quarters as before. But I retained the rooms that I shared with the TO at Liegnitz and took only a few essentials with me. The training programme continued without a break. The motor pool at Sagan even provided me with a BMW 250 motorcycle for my official duties, which was a great help.

During my final weeks' instructing, the Staffelkapitän was discharged from hospital. He had been passed fit for light duties only and was not yet permitted to fly. He was able to take over the daily running of the Staffel, however, and as I had just completed the training of another group of three pilots, I put in for short leave. I wanted to go up to Heiligenbeil to spend a few days with Gisela to whom I had grown very attached. Permission was granted and on 18 August I set off for Saint Axe by train.

The massive Allied bombing raids – both day and night – which were now beginning to devastate Germany's cities and kill civilians in their thousands, had not yet reached East Prussia. In this still peaceful oasis I got to know Gisela's mother, a loveable and kind-hearted lady, her grandparents and many of her other relations. All welcomed me warmly, made me feel at home and did everything they could to ensure that my leave would be one to remember.

We drove to the Haff, the long lagoon-like stretch of water separated from the open Baltic by a narrow tongue of land. Here we bathed and visited Uncle Max and Aunt Hannchen. They owned a large farm where everything was still in abundance. They offered us things to eat that I had almost forgotten existed. We borrowed a canoe from them and paddled out onto the Haff. We travelled to the provincial capital, Königsberg, where we visited the famous castle, rowed on the park lake, enjoyed coffee and cakes in the lakeside café, and browsed through the shops. On 25 August it was time to say goodbye again. But those few precious hours had been enough to make us both realize that we wanted to spend the rest of our days together – war or no war. Life suddenly had a new meaning.

Four nights later, on 29/30 August 1944, bombers of the Royal Air Force attacked Königsberg. According to the enemy's own estimate, 41 per cent of all housing was destroyed. Hardly a building was left standing in the ancient heart of the city.

Back in Sagan training went on as usual. Then, at the beginning of September, I was notified of my posting back to JG 54, the Green Hearts, on the eastern front effective as of 20 September. This meant I was entitled to another period of leave – from 7 to 18 September – prior to returning to operations. Gisela and I had already arranged to become engaged on my birthday, 12 September, in Heiligenbeil. From there I would fly directly back to my unit.

First I went home for a brief visit to my parents. They were overjoyed to see me. But I could sense their unspoken concern about my imminent return to the front. Would another of their sons be taken from them in combat? Nobody dreamed at the time that Silesia itself was soon to become a battleground; or that father would be called upon to help defend it as a member of the Volkssturm, the local Home Guard. As far as I was concerned my home province, or rather the skies above it, was already a battlefield, as my brushes with the American bombers had shown. But this was a subject that was not touched upon at home.

On 10 September father saw me off at Siegersdorf station. Arriving at Heiligenbeil I made my way out to the airfield where I was expected and provided with quarters. The next day, armed with a large bunch of tea-roses purchased from the nearby florists, I called on Gisela's mother and formally asked for her daughter's hand in marriage. There were tears in her eyes as she gave her consent, requesting only that I make her daughter happy. I assured her that was to be my sole aim in life.

The engagement party was a family affair. Despite wartime restrictions Gisela had managed to have announcements printed and everybody came. On the day Gisela wore a wine-red dress with an overlay of black lace. She looked absolutely enchanting and I was the proudest man in the world. As an engagement present Gisela gave me a little long-haired dachshund, named Füchsle or Little Foxy. With her silky reddish-brown coat and appealing, intelligent eyes she captured my heart immediately. I was to take her to the front with me and from then on we became inseparable companions through thick and thin.

Another recent arrival at Heiligenbeil was Oberfeldwebel Hajo Kroschinski. A native of East Prussia and newly married, he and I were already good friends. 'Kroschi', as he was known to one-and-all, was a highly experienced fighter pilot who had just completed his tour as an instructor at Sagan. He had brought with him two pupils who had likewise just finished the training course. We four were to form a Schwarm and return to the front together. We were ordered to collect our new machines from Luftflotte 1's depot at Bromberg (Bydgoszcz) and fly direct from there. And so, on 18 September, I said goodbye for the first time to my fiancée of just six days as my new Schwarm – four pilots and Füchsle – boarded a Ju 52 for the trip down to Bromberg.

But the situation on the northern sector of the Russian front had suddenly worsened dramatically. On 14 September 1944 the Red Army had launched a major offensive against the Baltic states. Our ground forces had been thrown back from the Narva line north of Lake Peipus and were retreating through Estonia. The Luftwaffe units supporting them were also being forced to withdraw. While the front remained volatile there was no way of knowing where our units were from one day to the next. We would have to wait at Bromberg, we were told.

There was nothing worse than this uncertainty, sitting inactive while all hell was breaking loose at the front. However, using the official telephone lines I was able to get through to Gisela at Heiligenbeil. We arranged that she should contact Kroschi's wife, Marga, and that the pair of them should come down by train to Bromberg for the weekend. We met them at the station on the Saturday and snatched a few more carefree hours together.

On 1 October we were finally given clearance to continue our journey. But we were instructed to proceed only as far as Insterburg and await further orders there. The flight took us northwards along the Vistula and then past Marienburg and Elbing to the shores of the Haff, which we followed north-eastwards, over the ruins of Königsberg, to the airfield at Insterburg.

Here, although we were only some 60 kilometres from the Lithuanian border, there was little sign of the war. The atmosphere was very relaxed, with everybody going about their normal routine under almost peacetime conditions. It was difficult to realize that the war was being fought such a short distance away. But when, after landing, I got through to Luftflotte HQ I was again ordered to wait at Insterburg until the situation stabilized. The front was still 'fluid' and the exact location of our units unclear.

With that I had to be content. Front-line troops were never given an overall appreciation of the situation. Their knowledge of events and conditions was purely local and on a strict need-to-know basis. As fighter pilots our horizons were bounded by our mission briefings and the limits of our operational area at the time – nothing more.

I was, however, ordered to telephone HQ twice daily so that I could get my little group up to the front as soon as conditions permitted and a destination could be given. In the meantime, the only jarring note to disturb Insterburg's otherwise deceptively peaceful existence was the presence of a Staffel of Ju 87s. They were being employed, without fighter cover, to attack the advancing Soviet ground forces. One evening I met the Stukas' Staffelkapitän in the mess. In the course of conversation he asked whether my Schwarm would perhaps be willing to fly fighter escort for his unit on the following day, 11 October. They had already been briefed to attack a group of enemy tanks reported to be approaching the border, and he wasn't sure whether this armoured column would have fighter cover or not. As all four of our machines were serviceable and fully-armed, I told him we'd be glad to, but that I would have to get permission from staff HQ first. This was immediately given over the 'phone; written confirmation following later by teleprinter.

At 10.00 hours the next morning the Stukas took off. I led my four Fw 190A-6s into the air shortly afterwards and quickly caught up with the dive-bombers. I waggled my wings and the Ju 87 leader responded. Contact established, I took up position with my katschmarek to the right of the formation, Kroschi and his wingman to the left.

The Stukas droned eastwards, over Kroschi's hometown of Gumbinnen towards the Lithuanian border. Above us at 1,200 metres the cloud base was solid, but visibility was good. The road the Ju 87s were following was lined on either side by an avenue of old trees, their gnarled bare branches clearly visible. The open fields bordering the road were covered in a blanket of snow. On the road itself long lines of horse-drawn farm wagons, piled high with people and their possessions, plodded along. Interspersed among them were other figures on foot, some pulling handcarts or sledges. These were refugees from the border areas fleeing westwards to escape the Red Army.

Suddenly the road ahead was empty. The Stukas slid into attack formation, line ahead. Still following the road, the leader appeared to be searching. In the distance another caterpillar-like line of refugees appeared. But they were being rapidly overhauled by a column of Russian tanks charging across the snow-covered fields to the left of the road. The Stuka leader wheeled his machines into a circle above the enemy armour and prepared to attack.

But he had been spotted. Before he could start his dive the Soviet tanks had turned sharply left, their churning tracks sending up flurries of snow as they charged straight into the refugee column packed tightly along the thin ribbon of road. Panic broke out. Horses bolted, wagons overturned, people ran into the open fields. The Stukas circled helplessly. The enemy tanks were using the refugees as a living shield. The snow was stained red where they ploughed unheedingly over man and beast. The Stuka leader called off the attack. He could not add to the carnage by bombing the tanks and spreading more death and destruction among the civilians below.

The Ju 87s returned to Insterburg and landed with their bombs still aboard. It was the one and only occasion throughout my entire time on the eastern front that a Stuka formation I was escorting had been unable to carry out its mission as ordered.

The following evening I received instructions to fly with my Schwarm to rejoin JG 54 now headquartered in the Courland to the west of the Latvian capital, Riga. Although the Red Army had reached the shores of the Baltic at Polangen three days earlier and the whole of the Courland peninsula was now separated from the main body of the German forces fighting in the east, some semblance of order had at last been restored to the front.

Our flight to Tukkum on 13 October passed without incident. We did not take the direct route over enemy-held territory, however. We first headed NW from Insterburg to the Baltic coast which we then followed almost due north, looping out over the sea to bypass Polangen. Level with the Latvian port of Libau (Liepaja) we turned back inland again and headed across the Courland peninsula to Tukkum.

Füchsle enjoyed every moment of the trip. My little dachshund had developed a real love of flying. Whenever I climbed into my machine she would be there, standing on her hind legs waiting for my mechanic to lift her up and put her in the cockpit behind me. Her place was on top of my parachute back-pack where she could look out and watch everything that was going on around us. As I flew I could sense her behind my head, her muzzle to the right of me and her long silky tail to the left.

Although I obviously didn't take her up on dangerous operational sorties, I prided myself on flying the only two-seater combat Fw 190 on the eastern front – perhaps in the whole Luftwaffe?

Top left: Winch launch of a Grunau Baby II glider, Glogau airfield, summer 1941.

Top right: The circuit completed, the glider comes in to land back at the take-off area.

Middle left: As an eighteen-year-old Luftwaffe volunteer recruit, 4/FlAusbRgt 33, Detmold, December 1941.

Middle right: March 1942. Norbert's first home leave, proudly displaying his Gefreiter's chevron.

Bottom: One of the perks of being an orderly: enjoying a few quiet moments in the corporal's room, Detmold, Christmas 1941. Note C-Class glider proficiency badge above Norbert's left breast.

Top: A Bücker Bü 181
Bestmann trainer of the type
Norbert wrote off among the
tree stumps at Beelitz.

Middle centre: Norbert
pictured with his brothers Kurt (centre) and Günter
(right) at the Döhnhoffsplatz in Berlin one Sunday in
July 1942.

Middle right: As a Fahnenjunker-Unteroffizier, LKS 3
Werder/Havel, October 1942.

Bottom left: In summer flying gear at Biarritz.

Bottom right: Preparing for the next training flight;
2/JGr West, Biarritz, March 1943.

Top left: It was still winter when Norbert arrived in Russia! Olt Kath, the Adjutant of JG 54 (left) and Norbert's future Staffelkapitän Ofw Max Stotz.

Top centre: Oberfähnrich Hannig of 5/JG 54, Siverskaya, April 1943.

Top right: "This is the cylinder that's leaking." Uffz Rommer identifies a problem, April 1943.

Left: Obstlt Hannes Trautloft, Kommodore of JG 54 at the time of Norbert's arrival on the eastern front, in the cockpit of his winter-camouflaged Fw 190 bearing the Geschwader badge.

Bottom: Off-duty pilots of 5/JG 54 relax around the campfire, June 1943.

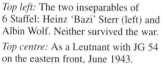

Top left: The two inseparables of
6 Staffel: Heinz 'Bazi' Sterr (left) and
Albin Wolf. Neither survived the war.

Top centre: As a Leutnant with JG 54
on the eastern front, June 1943.

Top right: Norbert with the Staffel's
master mechanic and armourer at
5/JG 54's dispersal area, Siverskaya.

Right: 5/JG 54's readiness room,
Siverskaya 1943.

Below: Stalin, Roosevelt and Churchill
in front of the flight control building at
Siverskaya, 1943.

Top left: Fw Karl Brill, known to one and all as 'Ede', is credited with scoring 5 Staffel's 600th victory.

Top right: Ofw Xaver Müller entertains everyone on the accordion as they sit around a smoky camp fire. Orel, July 1943.

Middle left: Maj Erich Rudorffer back from a mission over the Orel sector, August 1943.

Middle right: Tented accommodation and a canine friend at 'Diamond Valley' near Orel, August 1943.

Left: Kurt Tangermann (right), Rudorffer's regular wingman, with his chief mechanic.

Top left: Major Hubertus von
Bonin (left), Kommodore of
JG 54, congratulates Hptm Walter
Nowotny, Kommandeur of
I Gruppe, upon the latter's 250th
victory, 14 October 1943.

Top right: Kurt's last home leave
in Hermannsdorf; pictured with
Günter, holding the family
dachshund Hexe.

Middle left: Kurt's obituary, which
his father placed in the local
Bunzlauer Anzeiger newspaper on
3 August 1943.
The fourth line reads, 'for Volk
and Fatherland' … no mention of
the Führer!

Middle right: The Rotte of
Lt Lang/Uffz Paschke returns to
Kiev-West after the first sortie of
3 November 1943.

Above: Uffz Paschke (with scarf) describes the mission to members of
the ground crew.

Top left: After four separate sorties, and a record eighteen kills in one day, Lt Lang reaches his century. Kiev-West, 3 November 1943.

Top right: Lang's wingman, Fw 'Lerge' Hoffmann (right) claimed his fiftieth on the same mission. The pair congratulate each other.

Middle left: Norbert escorts a jubilant 'Bully' Lang back to the waiting ground crew.

Middle right: Lt Lang thanks the mechanics and armourers for all their hard work. Norbert gets in the photo too (directly behind Lang).

Left: A panje pony pays a visit and Norbert displays his bareback riding skills, December 1943.

Nummer 2   13. Januar 1944
Copr. 1944 Deutscher Verlag

53. Jahrgang   Preis 20 Pfennig

Berliner
Illustrierte Zeitung

Achtzehn an einem Tag:
Die Rückkehr des Siegers

Der Münchener Läufer Emil Lang

schoß als Leutnant der Luftwaffe an einem Tage 18 Sowjetflugzeuge ab. 18 Abschüsse, mit denen er seinen 100. Luftsieg erreichte. Nach der Landung wird Leutnant Lang von seinen Kameraden stürmisch begrüßt
PK-Aufnahme: Kriegsberichter Rudebach (Wb.)

The front page of the 13 January 1944 issue of the *Berliner Illustrierte Zeitung* featuring 'Bully' Lang's exploits at Kiev-West over two months earlier.

Top left: Fw Albin Wolf claims the 'Green Heart' Geschwader's 7,000th victory; Petseri, 23 March 1944.

Top right: Fw Reinhold 'Lerge' Hoffmann at readiness in the cockpit of his Fw 190.

Middle left: Olt Dulon of the signals section outside the ops room at Idriza, March 1944.

Middle right: View from the cockpit: Norbert's katschmarek keeping station off his port wing.

Bottom left: As an instructor with Jagdgruppe Ost at Liegnitz/Silesia, April 1944.

Bottom right: Practising the Staffel twin-arrowhead attack formation introduced to bring heavier fire power to bear on US bombers.

Top left: The rear arrowhead of five machines viewed from the port quarter.

Top right: A group of instructors relaxing in front of the workshop tent at Liegnitz, July 1944. From left to right: Lt Hannig, Ofhr Brill, Olt Hünerfeld, Ofw Müller, Ofw Raupach, Uffz Luer and three unknown.

Middle right 1: The full formation of twelve Focke-Wulf fighters seen from the rear.

Middle right 2: Four of the instructors at Liegnitz pose in front of a school Fw 190 with the JG 54 Geschwader badge, June 1944. From left to right: Fw Raupach, Ofw Kroschinski, Ofhr Brill and Uffz Luer.

Bottom: Norbert (centre) discussing the day's training programme with two fellow instructors at Liegnitz.

Top: Norbert (third from left), with his group of three trainees, enjoying the sun at Liegnitz municipal swimming pool, August 1944.

Middle left: With Lt Heino Cordes (right) after a day's instructing at Liegnitz, August 1944.

Middle right: Accepting the dare and dressing up in the young lady's bathing robe, Liegnitz pool. In his borrowed finery with Ofw Kossatz – bet won!

Left: Norbert's fiancée Gisela with Füchsle, August 1944.

Top left: A happy weekend at Bromberg with Gisela, 'Kroschi' Kroschinski and his wife Marga (on left), September 1944, before Norbert's return to the eastern front.

Top right: Ofw Hans-Joachim Kroschinski.

Above: Norbert's last wartime leave at home in Hermannsdorf, Christmas 1944. Father and Gisela (left), three sisters on right.

Right: Lt Schleinhege (front) and Lt Thyben leave II/JG 54's ops building at Libau-North on the Courland peninsula, December 1944.

Top left: With Fw Toni Meißner on the quay wall at Libau, January 1945.

Inset: Father Christmas arrives by Fw 190!

Top right: Winter sports at Libau-North: the ice slide in the garden of Norbert's quarters, January 1945.

Bottom: More winter sports: the 'Indestructible 6th' as they were known, set out on a sleigh ride. Fw Toni Meißner side-saddle on the docile panje pony; Staffelkapitän Hptm Wettstein at the reins, with Libau-North's concrete bunkers in the background.

Top left: 6 Staffel poses for a group photograph outside one of Libau-North's World War One reinforced concrete bunkers, January 1945.

Top right: The ground crews continued to work under almost impossible conditions; Libau-North, winter 1944-45.

Middle left: Lt Schulz scores the 'new' 6 Staffel's 100th victory; Libau, January 1945.

Middle right: Hptm Helmut Wettstein (right), the Staffelkapitän of 6/JG 54, with Fw Rommer on top of a bunker at Libau-North.

Below: Celebrating Schulz's achievement outside the pilot's readiness hut at Libau-North.

Top left: Norbert's Schwarm after having just returned to Libau from attacking and sinking two Soviet MTBs off Polangen. From left: Fw Meschkat, Uffz Licht, Lt Hannig and Uffz Kohler.

Top right: Commanders' conference outside a Libau-North bunker. Left to right: Oberst Hrabak, Kommodore JG 54; Hptm Wettstein, Kapitän 6 Staffel; Hptm Findeisen, Kommandeur II Gruppe, and GenOberst Kurt Pflugbeil, GOC Luftflotte 1.

Middle left: Füchsle poses beside Norbert on the wing of his Fw 190.

Middle right: Chatting to the Geschwader's MO, Stabsarzt Dr. Kurth.

Bottom: Pilots (and dogs) of 6 Staffel enjoy a respite from ops at Libau.

Top left: Uffz Kohler in the cockpit of his Fw 190, awaiting the order to scramble.

Top centre: Fw Meschkat climbs out of his machine, another mission completed.

Top right: Fw Toni Meißner's salute was a sight to behold: "Allow me to introduce myself."

Middle: The last three ex-Liegnitz trainees to reach the front. Left to right: Gefr Aufermann, Lt Tschikowski and Uffz Kohler.

Bottom left: 6 Staffel eat an alfresco lunch in front of a Libau bunker.

Bottom right: The 'hanged-man' – Ofhr Schreiber acts the fool, pretending that the beam supporting Libau-North's gas alarm is a gallows.

Top: A line-up of Me 262 jets at Lager Lechfeld in the summer of 1944. By the time Norbert and Ossi Unterlerchner arrived in April 1945 all organized jet training had effectively ceased.

Middle left: Having been ordered to fly out of the Courland peninsula with his unit, Hptm Helmut Wettstein, Kapitän of 6 Staffel, surrenders to British forces after landing at Flensburg on 8 May 1945.

Middle right: The front of the Hermannsdorf schoolhouse, Norbert's family home, in the summer of 1944.

Bottom left: The Hermannsdorf schoolhouse and utility outbuilding in the winter of 1945.

Bottom right: The Russian Kommandantur in Siegersdorf – formerly Burchard's inn.

Top left: Norbert with his wife Gisela outside their barracks home in Schleswig, 1946.

Top right: In working party battledress as a prisoner of the British, June 1946.

Middle left: The cover of *Tally-Ho, the Fighter Pilots' Shooting Primer*, a manual prepared, designed and illustrated by Oberst Hannes Trautloft.

Middle right: One of Hannes Trautloft's cartoons in the manual accompanying advice on how to bring down an enemy four-engined bomber.

Above left: The standard notification slip issued by the OKL (Luftwaffe High Command) in confirmation of a victory. This one credits Norbert with a LaGG-3 fighter at 16.10 hrs on 4 October 1943 (the 786th collective kill for 5/JG 54). But note the date at top

right: 5.12.44 … the wheels of bureaucracy grind exceedingly slow!

Above right: Page one of Norbert's Luftwaffe pilot's licence.

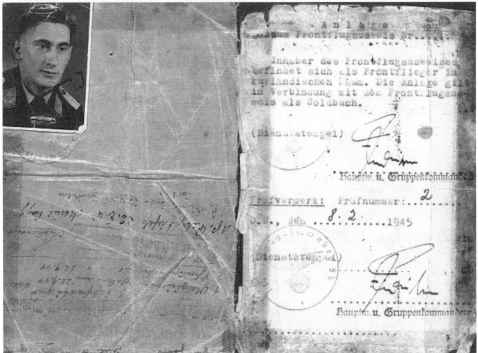

Top: Inside front cover and page one of Norbert's pay-book.

Above: Norbert's front ID card.

CONTROL FORM D.2
Kontrollblatt D.2

CERTIFICATE OF DISCHARGE
Entlassungschein

| ALL ENTRIES WILL BE MADE IN BLOCK LATIN CAPITALS AND WILL BE MADE IN INK OR TYPE-SCRIPT. | I
PERSONAL PARTICULARS
Personalbeschreibung | Dieses Blatt muss in folgender weise ausgefüllt werden:
1. In lateinischer Druckschrift und in grossen Buchstaben.
2. Mit Tinte oder mit Schreibmaschine. |

SURNAME OF HOLDER **HANNIG**
Familienname des Inhabers

DATE OF BIRTH **12.9.1923**
Geburtsdatum (DAY/MONTH/YEAR (Tag/Monat/Jahr)

CHRISTIAN NAMES **NORBERT**
Vornamen des Inhabers

PLACE OF BIRTH **POMBZEN**
Geburtsort

CIVIL OCCUPATION **SCHÜLER**
Beruf oder Beschäftigung

FAMILY STATUS SINGLE. ~~Ledig~~
Familienstand MARRIED Verheiratet
~~WIDOW(ER)~~ ~~Verwitwet~~
~~DIVORCED~~ ~~Geschieden~~

HOME ADDRESS Strasse **KAISERSTR.3**
Heimatanschrift Ort **RENDSBURG**
Kreis **RENDSBURG**
Regierungsbezirk/Land
SCHLESWIG

NUMBER OF CHILDREN WHO ARE MINORS
Zahl der minderjährigen Kinder ......

I HEREBY CERTIFY THAT TO THE BEST OF MY KNOWLEDGE AND BELIEF THE PARTICULARS GIVEN ABOVE ARE TRUE.
I ALSO CERTIFY THAT I HAVE READ AND UNDERSTOOD THE INSTRUCTIONS TO PERSONNEL ON DISCHARGE" (CONTROL FORM D.1).
SIGNATURE OF HOLDER v *Norbert Hannig*
Unterschrift des Inhabers

Ich erkläre hiermit, nach bestem Wissen und Gewissen, dass ausserdem dass ich die "Anweisung für Soldaten und Angehörige militär-ähnlicher Organisationen" u.s.w. (Kontrollblatt D.1) gelesen und verstanden habe.

II
MEDICAL CERTIFICATE
Ärztlicher Befund

DISTINGUISHING MARKS
Besondere Kennzeichen

DISABILITY, WITH DESCRIPTION
Dienstunfähigkeit, mit Beschreibung

MEDICAL CATEGORY **FIT**
Tauglichkeitsgrad

I CERTIFY THAT TO THE BEST OF MY KNOWLEDGE AND BELIEF THE ABOVE PARTICULARS RELATING TO THE HOLDER ARE TRUE AND THAT HE IS NOT VERMINOUS OR SUFFERING FROM ANY INFECTIOUS OR CONTAGIOUS DISEASE.

Ich erkläre hiermit, nach bestem Wissen und Gewissen, dass die obigen Angaben wahr sind, dass der Inhaber ungeziefertei ist und dass er keinerlei ansteckende oder übertragbare Krankheit hat.

SIGNATURE OF MEDICAL OFFICER
Unterschrift des Sanitätsoffiziers

NAME AND RANK OF MEDICAL OFFICER IN BLOCK LATIN CAPITALS **Dr. med. Ernst Vorstoffel, U-Arzt**
Zuname/Vorname/Dienstgrad des Sanitätsoffiziers
(In lateinischer Druckschrift und in grossen Buchstaben)

P.T.O.
Bitte wenden

† DELETE THAT WHICH IS INAPPLICABLE
Nichtzutreffendes durchstreichen

Top: Front side of Norbert's PoW release document.

Bottom: Fifty-four years almost to the day, after making his final wartime flight in a Fieseler Fi 156, Norbert was reunited with another Storch at Duxford in May 1999... this one even had a Green Heart painted on it!

NB: Most of the photographs in this section are from Norbert's private collection taken *in situ*, so the quality is varied.

CHAPTER 5

Final Operations over the Courland

When I arrived back at JG 54 I found that several changes of command had occurred during my six months' absence. The previous Geschwaderkommodore, Oberstleutnant Anton Mader, had been succeeded by Oberst Dietrich Hrabak. And Hauptmann Eisenach had taken over as Kommandeur of I Gruppe in place of Hauptmann Ademeit, who had been reported missing in action on 8 August.

I was to remain at Tukkum for the first couple of weeks serving in a temporary capacity as the acting Kapitän of 1 Staffel while Leutnant Heinz Wernicke, who had been awarded the Knight's Cross on 30 September for his 112 victories, was away on leave. I recognized a number of faces among the Staffel's pilots. They had been pupils of ours at Liegnitz and Sagan. The Chiefy, admin staff and ground crews, on the other hand, were all experienced old stagers. These old hares didn't need any orders from me. They knew their jobs inside out and I was happy to let them get on with things without interfering.

The Russians had continued to employ and perfect our Rotte and Schwarm tactics. But it struck me that a lot of their pilots still appeared to be lacking in front-line know-how. This was something that could not be taught; it could only be gained by experience. Another thing I noticed was that I now needed to use much less ammunition to bring down an enemy aircraft. The hours spent studying and putting into practice the rules set out in Oberst Hannes Trautloft's shooting primer had more than proven their worth.

On 1 November I finally returned to my old 5 Staffel which, to complicate matters slightly, had now been redesignated as 6/JG 54. It was based along with the rest of II Gruppe at Libau-Grobin. Situated just outside the harbour town of Libau on the Courland peninsula's Baltic, or western coast, this was a grass-surfaced airfield, well-equipped, and with brick-built accommodation blocks for pilots and ground crews in a small stand of firs close by.

Hauptmann Rudorffer was still in command of the Gruppe. I thanked him for asking for me back after my stint as an instructor. My old Staffel was led by Oberleutnant Wettstein, to whom I was assigned as

Staffeloffizier, or deputy. He had previously been a member of 1 Staffel and I had originally met him shortly after my arrival at Gatschina when I first joined the Green Hearts. He had stuck in my memory because he had chewed me out for wandering into the emergency Rotte's readiness cabin without first requesting permission. As a Fähnrich new to the front I had known no better. But that was just his manner. He was every inch the professional; open and straight as a dye. We hit it off immediately. Füchsle and I were invited to share his quarters. We found we complemented each other as a team, and were able to talk freely between ourselves when discussing the general war situation. This last required a certain amount of trust; it was not advisable to speak one's mind openly to just anybody – it could prove dangerous. But Helmut and I had that trust in each other. It was to form the basis of a life-long friendship.

There were two harbours at Libau: a commercial port and a naval base. Each was connected to the open Baltic by a canal. On the narrow tongue of land separating these two canals was a small airfield known as Libau-North. Like Libau-Grobin to the south of the city it was grass-surfaced, but could only be used in the dry season. On the seaward side of this tiny field were a number of large supply bunkers. Dating back to the First World War, their metre-thick concrete walls provided excellent protection during bombing raids.

Libau's commercial docks were the major entry point for all supplies coming in to the isolated Courland armies by sea. Air supplies were just a drop in the bucket and Libau was therefore vital for the Courland front's continuing existence and ability to fight. Naval motor torpedo boats based at Libau protected the supply ships running the gauntlet of Russian attacks. The merchantmen attempted to time their arrivals and departures from Libau so that they passed the Soviet-held stretch of coast around Polangen – where the enemy had already established an airfield – during the hours of darkness.

The Soviets had also recognized the importance of Libau, and the smaller supply port of Windau (Ventspils) further up the coast near the tip of the peninsula, to our troops. On 16 October the Red Army unleashed its first big offensive in this sector. Its aim was to cleave the Courland in two, separating the two German armies trapped on the peninsula – the 18 Armee in the western half on the Baltic, the 16 Armee in the eastern half on the Gulf of Riga – and then advance on the supply ports. But Army Group Courland put up fierce resistance and the Soviet offensive was abandoned after a week of intense fighting.

On 27 October the Russians launched a second attack, but again without success. In all, the Red Army would stage no fewer than six all-out assaults in its efforts to occupy the Courland. But although the defenders were forced to give ground from their original line across the base of the peninsula, they held on and Army Group Courland remained undefeated – but cut off from the rest of the front – until the end of the war.

During the opening weeks of the siege of the 'Courland cauldron' our missions were flown almost exclusively against the enemy's Il-2 ground-attack aircraft, either in support of the troops in the front lines or in defence of our own airfields. The Russians usually outnumbered us by at least eight-to-one. Often it was much more. Casualty figures began to rise; ours as well as theirs.

At the end of October the first snow showers fell. Mixed in with longer and heavier downpours of rain, this soon resulted in Libau-Grobin's surface almost disappearing under water, which made take-offs and landings practically impossible. By this time the Russian forces advancing along the Estonian coast to the north had occupied the cluster of islands in the mouth of the Gulf of Riga. Only the southernmost tip of the largest of these islands, Ösel, was still in German hands. Here a combat group was holding out on the narrow, finger-like Sworbe peninsula just 20 kilometres across the straits from northern Courland. This force was being supported by naval gunfire from the pocket battleship *Admiral Scheer* and heavy cruiser *Lützow*.

Now an attempt was to be made to evacuate the combat group and Luftflotte 1 was asked to provide fighter cover for the operation. Luftflotte HQ forwarded the request in the form of an order to our Geschwader HQ, who in turn passed it on to II Gruppe: "One Rotte to provide fighter cover for heavy naval units off Sworbe." The Kommandeur himself went to the telephone to talk to the staff officer at HQ, explaining that he would not be responsible for any take-offs with the airfield in its present waterlogged state. But the order stood. The mission had to be flown and a Rotte would have to take off whatever the current condition of the field.

As luck would have it, 5 and 7 Staffeln were off duty and in their quarters. It was 6 Staffel's turn to be at readiness and we pilots were gathered in the readiness hut out on the field when the Kommandeur entered. Having briefly explained the situation, he then said: "I need two men for this mission. Any volunteers?"

We all knew the score. We also knew that taking off would be a risky business. But there was no hesitation – every hand went up. I was sure of one thing. If I couldn't lift off in time and saw the edge of the field getting too close there would be only one course of action: throttle back, retract undercarriage, and slide to a stop on my belly. That might cost a machine, but not my life.

I had hoped that a couple of experienced old hares would be chosen. Instead, an ex-flying instructor, who had plenty of hours but little front-line experience, and a young newly arrived sergeant were selected to fly the mission. Despite my protests at this decision, it was final. The veterans in our little group gave the pair what advice we could before they left the hut and went out to their aircraft.

For airfield defence a number of 20-mm quadruple flak guns had been installed around the perimeter. To protect the gun sites against attack by low-flying aircraft each emplacement was surrounded by a wall of earth some 1½ metres high. These earth walls were clear to see and we were all aware of their presence. One of the gun emplacements stood close to our hut and we went outside to stand alongside it to watch the aircraft take off.

As the two Fw 190s taxied across the field to the start line their wheels were in water; their propeller wash throwing up fountains of spray. At the far side of the field they turned into the wind ready for take-off. Under normal conditions aircraft would lift off in the centre of the field, retract their undercarriages, and roar past low over our heads.

But these were not normal conditions. As the pilots opened their throttles each machine was enveloped in a solid cloud of spray which rose above cockpit level before being whipped away behind them in long streamers by the whirling propellers. Then they began to move, still half-hidden by spray. As they gathered speed their noses appeared, the forward momentum at least allowing the pilots to see ahead. But both remained firmly anchored to the ground. They reached the middle of the field still heading for us and it was clear that neither was going to be able to lift off in time.

But then the leader, by pure luck, must have hit a patch of drier grass. He yanked the machine off the ground and got clear. His number two, however, continued to plough through the slush and was now heading directly towards the gun emplacement. The pilot gave one final despairing pull on the stick. His wheels came free of the water at the last moment, only to clip the top of the earth embankment. The tail reared up, the machine somersaulted and smashed into the ground on its back.

We were running to help even before it hit. We saw that the windscreen and canopy had been squashed flat with the top of the fuselage. From inside the machine the invisible pilot was screaming for help. We tried getting underneath one upturned wing and lifting the aircraft by brute force, but it was hopeless. Steam was rising from the hot engine half-submerged in the snow and slush. The smell of petrol grew stronger as we continued our efforts. Realizing he was about to be burnt alive, the young sergeant was still screaming and begging for someone to put him out of his misery.

"Everybody back at once, everybody back... the machine's going to go up any second!" The Kommandeur had also come running to the scene. We scrambled out from under the wing and jumped clear as the Focke-Wulf exploded in a fireball. The voice from inside was stilled. I don't know if anybody had put a bullet into the unfortunate pilot. We all carried pistols and the sound of a single shot would have gone unnoticed in all the noise and confusion. It was never investigated. The remains of the aircraft and its occupant were later recovered by the airfield's fire crew. No further take-offs were ordered while the field remained under water.

At night Libau-Grobin was often subject to attack by single Pe-2 bombers. Whenever this happened we had to make a dash for the slit trenches. And we had to be quick about it. Our base was so close to the front that the interval between the siren sounding and the arrival of the bomber was only a matter of minutes. But Ivan was nothing if not consistent. Each time the attacker would drop just four 250-kg bombs in a row, one after the other. We soon got into the habit of counting the explosions. After the fourth and final one we knew we could safely climb out of the trenches and return to our beds. Scattered among the fir trees around our quarters were bomb craters left from previous raids. Personally I preferred to seek shelter in one of these. They were nearer than the slit trenches and I could take my dachshund with me. Füchsle was terrified when the Russian bombers attacked us. Her little body would tremble all over at each detonation, but she quickly calmed down when I stroked her and whispered reassuringly in her ear.

One evening when the alarm went off I grabbed Füchsle under one arm and made for the nearest crater in the woods. Crouching close to one side of the hole I waited for the four bombs to come down. A few minutes later the first hit the ground not far away. The second was closer still. The blast of the third lifted me bodily from the floor of the crater. The fourth was on the far side of me. It had been a close call. I was unscathed – but where was the dog? I could only hope that she had scampered off to find a safer place of refuge. I returned to our quarters. Nobody I asked on the way had seen her. I went to my room to fetch my torch and make a proper search. I had unrolled my Russian sleeping bag on top of the bed and there in the middle of it, quivering with fright, was my dog. As soon as she saw me she jumped up, her tail wagging excitedly. But the relief and delight at finding her unharmed were all mine.

As well as Füchsle the Staffel had another mascot. Löwe – Lion – was a rough-haired male dachshund who had been with the unit since the start of the campaign in Russia. He had long outlived his original owner and was now looked after by Feldwebel Toni Meißner. Löwe was a real character with a will of his own. He obeyed only when it suited him; he was friendly only when he wanted to be; he would go for a walk only if he felt like it; and if he took a dislike to anybody he made no attempt to hide it – in other words a true dachshund. When he was first introduced to the competition in the shape of the very feminine Füchsle all the pilots awaited the outcome with bated breath. But the two of them hit it off from the very start and quickly became a pair. They played together, wandered the base together, and ate out of the same bowl. They were adored by the whole Staffel, pilots and ground crews alike. Everybody went out of their way to be friendly and kind to the little dogs. Some even vied with each other to become the animals' particular favourites.

Whenever I flew a mission my crew chief, Franzel, would look after Füchsle for me. She would accompany me out to the machine and wait to be lifted up into her usual place in the cockpit. When this didn't happen and she realized she wasn't going to be taken along she would go and sit on the tarpaulin engine covers piled up next to dispersal. Franzel told me she would remain here watching the aircraft take off. Only when they had disappeared from sight would she leave her vantage point and roam about the dispersal area among the ground crews. Just before we returned she would take up her position again, waiting and watching for us to land. As we taxied in she would run out towards my machine to welcome me back. I can only assume that she could recognize my particular aircraft from the noise of its engine. She would always skirt the spinning propeller blades and approach from the side with her tail wagging furiously in greeting.

There were some operational sorties which we could be fairly certain would not result in contact with the enemy. And on these I occasionally took her along. Among such missions were those flying escort for minesweeping Ju 52s out over the Baltic. Having failed to capture Libau overland, the Soviets were now mining the seaward approaches and harbour entrance to the port in an attempt to stop the supplies getting through. This resulted in four special Ju 52s being stationed at Libau-Grobin. Each of these tri-motor transports was equipped with a large metal ring containing an electromagnetic coil beneath its fuselage which was used for exploding magnetic mines from the air. Three of these Junkers would fly in line-abreast along the sea lanes clearing them of the mines laid by the Soviets.

Given the trouble they must have gone to to plant the mines in the first place, the Russians made surprisingly little effort to interfere with the Junkers' promptly blowing them up again a few hours later. This is why I was able to have Füchsle in the cockpit with me. She took in everything that was going on around her. She would turn her head to follow the movements of my wingman's machine gently lifting and falling beside me. She would also watch the Junkers flying their straight and level paths and become quite excited whenever a huge spout of water from an exploding mine rose up from the surface of the sea behind them.

But I couldn't take her with me when, on 1 December 1944 – and much to my astonishment – I was suddenly ordered to attend a unit leaders' course at Landsberg an der Warthe, a town some 120 kilometres to the east of Berlin. I couldn't understand why I should have to go on such a course, and especially at a time when every pilot was desperately needed at the front. But orders were orders, and this one came direct from the personnel department of the Air Ministry. So once again I found myself climbing aboard a Ju 52 courier aircraft. This one lifted me out of the Courland pocket and deposited me at Berlin-Gatow. From here I was instructed to make my way to Landsberg by rail.

At Landsberg I was reunited with all my old comrades from the Werder Air College, none of whom I had seen since my cadet days. It seemed that our entire course – or those of us who had survived the intervening years – had been brought back together again to round off our training as unit leaders. The commander of the school at Landsberg was Major Günther Rall, a holder of the Knight's Cross with Oak Leaves and Swords. He was one of the Luftwaffe's leading fighter pilots with a total of 275 victories.

Major Rall greeted each of us individually and quickly gained our unreserved respect and admiration. Calm and intelligent, comradely and approachable, his personality impressed us all. Despite severe injuries suffered earlier in the war he was a keen sportsman. And sport, together with theoretical teaching and flying, played an important part in the Landsberg training, which was designed to instil in us all the knowledge necessary to become Staffelkapitäne and, later perhaps, Gruppen-kommandeure. The course was scheduled to last just over three weeks. It would end a few days before Christmas and we were then to return to our units.

What struck me most, however, was that the syllabus contained not one reference to the present overall war situation. Not a word was said about the Western allies' advance towards the Rhine, or the Red Army's approach to the Reich's eastern borders. The round-the-clock Anglo-American bombing offensive which was laying waste to Germany's towns and industries did not get a mention. Even our own counter-offensive in the west through the Ardennes, launched on 16 December under the codename Wacht am Rhein – Watch on the Rhine – but now better known to history as the Battle of the Bulge, was not considered to be a topic for discussion; not even amongst ourselves in the mess. In short, the general war situation was taboo. And yet we were all young Luftwaffe officers who knew perfectly well what was happening on each of our own particular fronts. The very fact that not one of us raised a single question on the subject was indicative not only of the all-pervading air of secrecy, but also of the advisability of keeping one's own counsel on such sensitive matters.

The harsh reality of Germany's plight was brought home to me a few days later. It began with an official call from Oberst Trautloft, who was still serving on the staff of the General der Jagdflieger in Berlin, to our course leader Major Rall. As Trautloft knew me personally, and was aware that I had been an instructor on Fw 190s at Liegnitz and Sagan, he had a special assignment for me and one of my fellow course members, Leutnant Lothar Kabbe, who had also spent a tour instructing on Focke-Wulfs.

We were ordered to go at once to Großenhain airfield in Saxony and there report to a Hauptmann Schloßstein. He was the Kommandeur of II/ZG 76, a twin-engined Zerstörergruppe equipped with Me 410s that had recently suffered crippling losses. Our task was to convert the unit's remaining pilots on to the Fw 190A-8.

Taking just our small packs with us, Kabbe and I arrived in Großenhain on 18 December. We presented ourselves to Hauptmann Schloßstein as instructed. He knew we were coming and had been apprised of our mission. He received us in a very sombre manner and proceeded to put us fully in the picture. Originally a long-range fighter unit, his Gruppe had been savagely mauled in action against US heavy bombers. It was then decided that they should be employed in the role of fighter-bombers. Carrying 250-kg bombs, II/ZG 76's machines were sent to destroy the bridges built by the Russians across the River Oder at Küstrin, due east of Berlin.

Before they could get to the bridges they were attacked by swarms of American Mustangs. Even as a fighter, the Me 410 was no match for the P-51. Weighed down by bombs, the twin-engined Messerschmitts didn't stand a chance. Fifteen of their number were hacked down. Only three crews, including the Kommandeur's, returned from the mission unscathed. The strain the man was under was all too apparent. We could hardly get a word out of the other surviving pilots. And these were the people we were supposed to convert to Fw 190s so that they could be returned to ops as quickly as possible, and in the company of a group of unknown replacements. Such were the lengths to which the German Luftwaffe had been reduced by the end of 1944.

Kabbe and I had been instructed to assess the situation at Großenhain and report by telephone to Oberst Trautloft in person. After listening to the Hauptmann's disturbing account of his Gruppe's recent losses I was unsure exactly what to say. But the report had to be made. I telephoned Berlin in the Kommandeur's presence and asked to be put through to Oberst Trautloft. He came on the line.

"Herr Oberst, Leutnant Hannig and Leutnant Kabbe reporting from II/ZG 76 in Großenhain as ordered. We are sitting here with the Kommandeur, who has explained the situation to us in detail." I hesitated, not quite knowing how to continue. If I painted too black a picture would it be construed as defeatism? To express any form of doubt in these increasingly parlous times, especially to a superior officer, was a chancy business. Trautloft solved the problem for me: "Hannig, you know me and I you. You can speak quite openly to me. I want your honest opinion of the situation there. The plain unvarnished truth. Is that understood?"

"Jawohl, Herr Oberst. You know of the bombing mission II/ZG 76 has just flown. They were jumped by Mustangs and all but wiped out. You have the casualty figures there. Converting the survivors on to single-engined fighters is out of the question at the present time. Psychologically they are simply not up to it."

There was silence at the other end. Then, after a while: "I can accept that fact. Your task is completed. Do you and Kabbe wish to return to your units immediately, or go back to Landsberg and finish your course?"

I explained that we only had our small packs with us and that we would have to return to Landsberg. Trautloft agreed to this and ended the conversation by wishing us both well.

Kabbe and I collected our travel warrants and returned by train to Landsberg in time to complete the course as scheduled on 21 December. After that we were all given six days Christmas leave. I managed to contact Gisela and invited her to spend Christmas with me and my family, to which she readily agreed. I had already studied the train timetables. If we met up at Küstrin on 22 December we could be home in Silesia the following morning.

All went according to plan. The train was on time arriving at Siegersdorf and soon we were treading the familiar path – familiar to me, that is – that I had taken to and from school as a boy. It had not yet snowed in this part of the world but the spirit of Christmas was in the air. As we had no telephone at home I had not been able to warn my parents of our coming; we were to be their surprise present. From the wooden bridge over the River Queis we could see the schoolhouse in Hermannsdorf that was our family home. Smoke was rising from the chimney, a sure sign that the fire was lit. I was looking forward to seeing my parents and sisters again, and had no doubts that Gisela would be welcomed with open arms. She, for her part, confessed to feeling more than a little nervous about meeting my family for the first time.

We went around to the back door as usual. As it was still closed I knocked and waited. Mother opened it and the moment she saw us her face lit up. Shouting for father and the girls she hugged and kissed first Gisela and then me. Our dachshund Hexe came bounding out of the kitchen, jumping up at both of us, howling out loud and almost turning somersaults in her excitement. The welcome extended by my father and sisters was equally warm and loving – although perhaps not quite so demonstrative as Hexe's – and my fiancée had immediately become part of the family. Father sat down at the piano and played the Triumphal March from Aida, which delighted Gisela, who is also very musical. After that we chatted, catching up on each other's news, while mother made up a bed so that Gisela could take a nap; we were both exhausted from the overnight train journey. Towards evening we all got together again, sitting around and talking animatedly. Gisela won father over completely by asking him to play something else on the piano or harmonium.

I had an officer's trunk at home, a metal-bound affair, in which I stored my extra uniforms, officer's dagger and other assorted valuables that I had no use for at the front. Now I added my personal documents – my pay-book, pilot's licence, chequebook and the like. I retained only my front-line identity card, which had to be carried on operations at all times and which was the official substitute for the other items.

This was a safety measure. The future was looking increasingly bleak and uncertain. What might it hold for us, living as we did in two of the Reich's easternmost provinces? If our families had to flee before the advancing Red Army it would be advisable to arrange a rendezvous point somewhere further to the west where we could all meet up again. Father said that the safest place he could think of was Uncle Mieke's. He was not really an uncle, but an old friend of father's from their teacher-training days together. He was now the manager of Count von Schulenberg's estate at Altenhausen near Magdeburg. Gisela's suggestion was her school friend who was working as a nurse in the hospital at Garmisch-Partenkirchen.

With these unpleasant matters settled, we put them to the back of our minds and concentrated on enjoying the festive holiday. Christmas Eve with its candle-lit tree, traditional biscuits, exchange of presents and the singing of carols – accompanied by father on the harmonium – was a deeply moving family celebration during which our thoughts naturally turned to my two brothers at the front and to Kurt, who was no longer with us. On Christmas Day mother prepared roast goose for dinner, a special treat as she was such an excellent cook.

On 26 December our neighbour, Farmer Göckel, kindly drove us back to Siegersdorf station in his coach and pair. Father was having heart problems and had to remain indoors. Mother was looking after him and the girls. Every leave taking from my loved ones at home was becoming harder. As we set off down the village street my three sisters continued waving until they were finally lost to sight.

Upon arrival at Heiligenbeil I found my movement orders already waiting for me. I was to proceed to Königsberg-Neuhausen airfield and there pick up six trainees who had just completed the Ergänzungsgruppe course and whom I was now to deliver to the Geschwader in the Courland. Gisela came with me to the station on the morning of 28 December to see me off. We were both rather quiet. There was not a lot to talk about. Everything had already been said. We wanted to get married on her birthday, 12 February 1945. This time I was leaving behind someone who had become more precious to me than life itself.

At Neuhausen I met up with the new pilots and introduced myself. We collected our machines from the depot and I went through the usual formalities. First there was a short pre-flight briefing to be given before I handed my flight plan in to control. Next it was out to the aircraft, get strapped in with the help of the mechanic, start her up, taxi out and check the R/T. Then line up ready for take-off. One last quick glance at the instruments, everything OK, look across to check that the others' engines are all running smoothly – and then start to roll. All routine so far, but what would we find at the end of our journey?

The weather was fine; hardly a cloud in the sky and good visibility. The further north we flew the more snow there was on the ground below until, finally, the whole landscape was covered in a white blanket. Winter had arrived. We landed at Schrunden (Cirava), where Geschwader HQ was now based. Here I handed over my charges. At the same time I took the opportunity to submit the necessary documents requesting the CO's permission to get married on 12 February. Then I took off again for II Gruppe at Libau-Grobin to rejoin my old 6 Staffel which I had left so abruptly a month earlier. My comrades were clearly pleased to have me back – Füchsle's reception I need hardly describe – and when flying was over for the day and we were relaxing in our quarters my return was duly celebrated with a few bottles of something wet.

As we sat around swapping news I was brought up to date with all that had been happening during my absence. I was told that the Red Army had launched a third major offensive against the Courland's defenders on 21 December. As in the first two, the enemy's ground troops had been strongly supported from the air. JG 54's two Gruppen were in action daily against large numbers of Soviet aircraft, mainly Il-2s and their fighter escorts. I also learned, to my sorrow, that my good friend Oberfeldwebel Hans-Joachim Kroschinski had been shot down in the opening hours of the offensive.

A member of I Gruppe, he had been at readiness on the morning of 21 December when his Rotte received the order to scramble at around 08.30 hours. A formation of twelve Pe-2s, escorted by six Yak-9s, had been reported approaching. Two against eighteen – six of which were Yak-9s, the best fighter the Soviets possessed and certainly the equal of our own Fw 190A-8s.

Kroschi and his wingman sighted the enemy machines and went straight for the bombers. They each claimed hits, but then the escorting fighters fell upon them. The wingman later reported seeing his leader's machine diving away with a small tongue of flame coming from it. But then he himself had his hands full as he tried to escape from the six angry Yaks. I Gruppe subsequently received information from a party of ground troops that the pilot of the burning Focke-Wulf had baled out badly injured and had been taken to the main dressing station of the 121st Infantry Division. After that all trace of Kroschi had been lost. With seventy victories already to his credit, he would have been in line for the Knight's Cross had fate not intervened.

On 21 January 1945 the Red Army crossed the border into Silesia. Forty-eight hours later the evacuation by sea of the civilian population of East Prussia began. The whole of the eastern front was collapsing. Only on the Courland Peninsula were German forces standing firm. A fourth enemy offensive was hurled against them on 24 January. The attackers were repulsed after ten days of bloody fighting.

At the end of January the Geschwader received orders from the RLM transferring several of its higher scoring Knight's Cross winners back to the Homeland. They were to be given conversion training on to the Me 262, the world's first operational jet fighter. Among those to leave was Leutnant Ulrich Wöhnert, the Kapitän of 5 Staffel. Early in February I was instructed to take his place as Staffelführer of 5/JG 54. So, together with Füchsle I moved across to 5 Staffel's dispersal area where we settled in quite happily. I knew everybody, of course, both pilots and ground crews. There were no problems at all. These only arose with the arrival of another order from Berlin.

This one decreed that the establishment of each of our two Courland-based Gruppen was to be raised from three Staffeln to four to bring us into line with most other Jagdgruppen. This meant that II/JG 54 was now to have a new 8 Staffel, which was to be made up from personnel and equipment drawn from the other three. It was quickly realized, however, that this enforced reorganization offered no advantages whatsoever and the order was soon rescinded. This left us with one Staffel too many. One would have to go. And as I was the junior Staffelführer of the four, it was my 5 Staffel which was broken up and dispersed between the others. II/JG 54 thus now consisted of 6, 7 and 8 Staffeln.

The time and effort expended in complying with this piece of bureaucratic irrelevance must have been considerable. At this stage of the war it could ill be afforded. It had not the slightest effect on the Gruppe's performance and efficiency. In fact, the only tangible result was the havoc it wrought on the reorganized Staffeln's records – not least their carefully compiled, and now considerable, collective scoreboards, which had to be restarted all over again from 1!

Deprived of my short-lived command, I was offered the choice as to which Staffel I wanted to join. I opted to return to my old 6 Staffel under Helmut Wettstein, where Füchsle and I were welcomed with open arms. It was good to be back among old friends for what looked like becoming a life-or-death struggle to the finish.

During one of the Pe-2 night raids on Grobin our quarters in the woods were so badly damaged that we were forced to move to the much smaller Libau-Nord, the field sandwiched between the two ship canals. Here we were billeted in the private houses lining the road along the edge of the airfield. Most of these were still occupied by their owners. I shared a cosy room on the top floor of one of these houses with Helmut Wettstein. I had a couch on which I could spread out my Russian sleeping bag. My personal items I kept in my flight bag on a chair standing at the foot of the couch. I was quite content. There was electric light and we even had a small desk where we could do our paperwork and write our letters.

The house itself was solidly constructed, but with wood cladding. It stood in a small garden through which ran a tiny stream, now frozen over. This made a perfect slide and kept us in trim during our off-duty hours. And there were plenty of those at this time of year; the combination of frequent snowstorms, poor visibility and the fading light of the short winter days saw to that. Short of a thick fog clamping down, the weather couldn't have been more qbi if it tried.

One evening as the two of us were sitting in our room together Helmut suddenly asked me out of the blue: "Norbert, when do you think the war will be lost?"

It was a simple enough question. But in those days to utter such words was nothing less than sedition. Even to mention the possibility of Germany being defeated was regarded as subversion of military discipline and morale. It was an automatic court-martial offence punishable by the firing squad. I therefore looked at Helmut in no little surprise. But he calmly returned my gaze as he patiently awaited my answer: "When they're in artillery range of the Ruhr and Upper Silesian industrial basins at the latest," I replied – and the way things were going that wouldn't be long. "And what are we going to do then?" he asked. "We'll stick by our men whatever happens," was both my response and my firm intention. "Good. That's all I wanted to hear you say." It was the only time the impending end of the war and all that would mean was mentioned between us.

Although cut off from the rest of the eastern front, the Courland defenders were not unaware of the growing chaos and turmoil elsewhere. But detailed information was hard to come by. The field post was no longer getting through. And for those of us whose families lived in the eastern provinces the uncertainty and lack of news was a constant worry. I had not heard from Gisela or my parents for some time, and my letters home remained unanswered.

At the beginning of February Major Erich Rudorffer was appointed Gruppenkommandeur of II/JG 7, the home defence fighter unit flying Me 262 jets. His place at the head of our Gruppe was taken by Hauptmann Findeisen, who had won the Knight's Cross while serving as a tactical reconnaissance pilot. The change of command ceremony was attended by the AOC Luftflotte 1, Generaloberst Pflugbeil, in person. Afterwards the General's adjutant, Oberst Bader, had me called over.

"Hannig," he said, "you've put in requests through channels for permission to marry and for home leave on 12 February. I've got the papers for you in my briefcase. Do you still want to travel – and if so, where to?"

"Herr Oberst, I'm afraid the situation is unclear at the moment. I have had no news as to the present whereabouts of either my family or my fiancée. I hope that they are all safe. But I shall remain here." Although hard, the decision was the correct and logical one to make. It would be up to the future to see what happened.

On 10 February the Red Army captured Liegnitz. But our Ergänzungsgruppe had vacated the town's airfield some three months earlier. Nearer to home, strong formations of enemy bombers attacked our Libau bases on 14 February as part of a day-long aerial assault on the Courland's ground positions. JG 54 suffered a heavy blow during one of these raids when Oberleutnant Otto Kittel, the Kapitän of 3 Staffel, was shot down and killed by return fire from an Il-2. With a score of 267 confirmed victories Kittel was the Geschwader's most successful pilot.

Six days later the Red Army launched its fifth offensive against the Courland. As usual, the enemy's infantry and armour were supported by hordes of low-flying ground-attack Il-2s and their escorting fighters. We did what we could to protect our own troops from this ever-present scourge. But our supply of aviation fuel was now running low. Missions could only be flown upon receipt of a specific order. The sole exception to this rule was the airfield's own defence Rotte which, as hitherto, consisted of two machines kept at readiness at the end of the runway waiting to scramble the moment the green flare went up.

We all took turns manning the two readiness fighters. On one occasion I was at the end of the runway with my wingman, Unteroffizier Schorsch Kohler. He had been one of our Liegnitz trainees and had already claimed three kills since arriving at the front, for which he had been awarded the Iron Cross, Second Class. A good half-hour must have passed without any air-raid alarms or warnings of any kind. Under such circumstances the boredom gets to you after a while and your concentration is not all it might be. The tedium of waiting is simply too much. But suddenly I heard a loud whistle and saw the green flare: emergency scramble!!! In just over two minutes we were in the air awaiting further instructions from Gruppe ops. They soon came on air: "Edelweiß 1 from Gartenzaun, Luzie Anton immediately, Luzie Anton immediately and report in, Frage Viktor?"

"Luzie Anton?" – land? – if they wanted me to land immediately why did they send us up in the first place? Not a little puzzled I acknowledged receipt of the message and signalled Schorsch to follow me in. After landing I rang through to Gruppe ops as instructed. The new Kommandeur, Hauptmann Findeisen, was on the line. His Saxon dialect was unmistakable. He ordered me to come to the ops room immediately. The next pair of pilots on the roster had already taken over duty as the airfield protection Rotte, and so I made my way to the HQ building wondering what on earth all the fuss was about. The Kommandeur didn't leave me in the dark for long.

"Hannig, you took off with your Rotte without an official order or any authorization being given and are therefore in breach of the regulations concerning the unnecessary wastage of fuel. I have had to report the matter to the judge advocate in Windau. He will be here in two hours. Until that time you will stand by here."

"But I don't quite understand, Herr Hauptmann," I said in some surprise. "I heard the whistle and saw the green flare signalling an emergency scramble."

"That may well be. But you should have looked more carefully at the flare's trajectory. It didn't come from us. Somebody out at 6 Staffel's dispersal fired it off for some reason. Anyway, the judge advocate is already on his way. But don't worry, he's hardly likely to tear your head off." So I stayed in the ops building awaiting developments.

The Ju 52 from Luftflotte HQ duly landed. The judge advocate went into the Kommandeur's office, no doubt to discuss the matter with him first. A few minutes later I was summoned. I was asked to describe the incident in my own words. Then came the question: "And why didn't you look to see from which direction the flare had been fired?"

"Until now a green flare with a siren or whistle has never been fired from anywhere but Gruppe ops. I heard the whistle, saw a green flare, and didn't wait to see in which direction it was going. I immediately prepared to take off, fully believing that the emergency scramble signal had been given. Once in the air I received orders to land again, which I duly did."

"And how much aviation fuel was wasted unnecessarily by your action?" The question shouldn't have been asked. I could feel myself getting hot under the collar.

"Herr Judge Advocate, we were two single-engined aircraft in the air for no more than five minutes. You have taken a good half-an-hour to fly here in a three-engined machine, and still have the return journey to make. I am responsible for using a fraction of the fuel your coming here has required. I fully admit not looking to see where the green flare had been fired from. The emergency scramble was therefore a mistake – but mistakes do happen, unfortunately."

Had I perhaps overstepped the mark? But such idiocy had made my blood boil. The Kommandeur and the judge advocate looked at each other in silence. Then they both looked at me. At last the judge spoke: "You're right, Leutnant Hannig. You are exonerated and dismissed."

I saluted using the so-called 'German greeting' – better known as the 'Heil Hitler' – which all personnel had been ordered to adopt in place of the normal military salute as an outward demonstration of loyalty after the attempt on the Führer's life back in July 1944, and made my escape.

With no let-up in the weather there was very little for us to do. Our days were spent at readiness but, apart from the odd moments of excitement, aerial activity was minimal. We were on duty from before first light until darkness fell. But the winter days were short and the long nights undisturbed now by enemy bombers. Compared to the troops in the front-line trenches we were living in the lap of luxury. We did have one thing in common with them, however: the complete lack of fresh food and the monotonous sameness of our military rations. Everything was dehydrated: dehydrated meat, dehydrated potatoes, dehydrated vegetables.

The cooks did what they could, of course. But that did not extend much beyond adding water, some vitamin powders, and stirring vigorously. We became quite expert at guessing what was on the day's menu by the colour of the gruel served up by the field kitchen: brown, green or yellow. To wash this down there was barley coffee – the taste of which is indescribable, and the name of which in German is unrepeatable in English!

Fortunately, there were still plentiful supplies of various alcoholic beverages and tobacco goods. And as the local civilian population was chronically short of these items, but possessed livestock and vegetable gardens, brisk bartering soon got underway. Before long regular trading was being carried out to everybody's satisfaction and benefit. Then some pilots came up with the idea of getting fresh fish from the naval canal or the open Baltic.

One of the local delicacies was eels. These could be caught in three ways: either in pots, on a line, or by special eel rakes. We didn't have any pots. Angling in winter was a waste of time. This left just the rakes, and these we could easily make ourselves. All it took was two pieces of wood in the shape of a cross with a line of nails like the teeth of a rake driven through all four arms. The trick was to alternate the length of the nails: one long, one short, one long, and so on. A handle was fixed through a hole in the centre of the cross and the whole lot attached to a line. Once we had borrowed a rowing boat from one of the locals, it was simply a matter of rowing backwards and forwards dragging the rake behind us through the mud of the canal bed. Our efforts were remarkably successful and our catches provided a tasty treat for all involved.

Fishing in the open Baltic was a slightly riskier business – mainly because we used 2-kg bombs left behind by the Russians four years earlier. The fuses of these devilish little weapons could still be removed without too much trouble. We replaced them with detonators from hand grenades to which we attached a 1^1/$_2$-metre long fuse cord before sealing everything with candle wax. Labour and materials were supplied by the armourers in exchange for a share of the catch. After rowing out to a suitable spot, the end of the fuse was lit and the bomb thrown overboard. Then everybody bent to the oars again, rowing furiously to escape the fountain of water thrown up by the explosion. After it had subsided the boat was turned round and we went back to collect the stunned fish floating on the surface of the water – another welcome change from our multi-hued gruel.

The continuing bad weather throughout February, with further snowstorms, severe frost – and now fog – meant that air operations, both ours as well as those of the enemy, were almost non-existent. The ground troops were offered no such respite as the Red Army kept up its attacks even in the intervals between the major offensives. But while the soldiers in the front lines were locked in almost continual combat under the most adverse conditions imaginable, we would spend the evenings sitting around the warmth of a tiled stove and escape into another world listening to the MO reading from the works of Wilhelm Busch, or reciting passages from Schiller and Goethe.

At the beginning of March the thaw set in. Now we could at least sit outside in the sun in front of Libau-North's massive concrete bunkers as operations gradually got going again and we awaited orders for each next mission. With the better weather came the Red Air Force. The enemy was flying his newest types: late-model La-5s and La-7s, Yak-3s and 9s. American Airacobras and Kingcobras were also active, but we encountered them less often. Dogfights became harder and more bitterly contested. We began to suffer losses again. Oberfeldwebel Bienecke, Feldwebel Tittel and Unteroffizier Handtke were all reported missing after clashes with the enemy.

But we had our successes too. The old hares – of whom, despite being just 21 years of age, I now numbered among the eldest – all managed to increase their scores. There were targets enough. It was a matter of knowing how best to tackle them. If possible, I always attacked from an advantage of height. In diving on the enemy this height was traded for speed. One quick pass at my opponent – either in close, or from a distance using the correct amount of lead – and away again before he knew what had hit him. It was a tactic which allowed me to down several Il-2s and escorting fighters.

In between those times when we were ordered into the air the subject of food was still very much on our minds. So when a pilot discovered that the met staff, who lived a few houses down the road from our billet, were breeding rabbits it conjured up all sorts of visions. Fresh meat in a cage! A reconnaissance party was despatched to spy out the land. A high wooden fence surrounded the property which the 'weather frogs' had occupied since the beginning of the campaign against the Soviet Union. Some five metres behind this fence were grouped a number of rabbit

hutches. We would have preferred to purchase some of the animals, but
doubted very much that their owners would be willing to sell. There was
nothing for it. We would have to 'organize' instead of buy, and hope that
the weathermen would have some understanding of the motives of those
responsible for the disappearance of their livestock.

We sent out an advance guard to ensure that we didn't bump into one
of the military police squads that now regularly patrolled the streets.
Then we crept out into the darkness, removed two of the fence boards
that were hanging loose and climbed through into the garden. For my
wingman Schorsch, a butcher by trade, it was the work of a moment to
despatch four of the animals with a swift chop from the side of his hand.

We left the garden as silently as we had entered it, replacing the two
loose boards, and made our way back to our billet where everything was
ready and waiting. Schorsch skinned and prepared the rabbits for the
pan. The cooks then took over while we buried the skins in the garden.
We had invited the MO to share our feast of roast rabbit, which he gladly
did, declaring himself pleased at our healthy appetites. The met men
said not a word about their missing animals.

On the afternoon of 6 April I was again on readiness when the
scramble flare went up. I took a moment to make sure that it had been
fired from Gruppe ops, but this time it was a real emergency. I was still
taking off when the voice of the radar controller sounded in my
headphones: "To all cyclists, to all cyclists – enemy formation of
furniture vans approaching garden fence from the south, flying parallel
to the coast, Hanni 1000. I repeat…"

"Blaufuchs (Blue fox) 1 to Amor 1, Viktor, Viktor," I acknowledged
as I turned in the direction indicated with my wingman tucked in beside
me. "Still no contact. Please continue reporting."

It was an overcast day. The cloud base was solid at about 1,000
metres, the height at which the enemy formation was reportedly flying.
I remained lower in order to be able to spot them against the clouds. We
flew southwards along the coast until: "From Amor 1, enemy furniture
vans now some 3 kilometres off the coast and 10 kilometres from garden
fence."

I looked up to my right out to sea and there they were: twenty Il-2s
in tight formation slipping in and out of sight as they hugged the uneven
cloud base for protection. It was a smart move, for it meant that they
were safe from attack from above.

"Amor 1 from Blaufuchs 1, I have contact. Am attacking." I opened
the throttle and climbed to the right to get under the Il-2s. There we were
safe from the enemy's rear gunners as I closed in on the leading
machine. We knew from experience that the formation leader was
usually the only pilot who would have been briefed about the target. If
he could be taken out the remainder were more often than not at a
complete loss as to what to do next. From a range of just 50 metres I put

a short burst of cannon fire into his radiator before immediately diving away to the right. A gout of flame had erupted from the enemy's belly. It quickly took hold. The Ilyushin tipped forward and went down blazing like a torch into the water below.

The rest of the formation scattered, seeking cover in the clouds. With my katschmarek I remained beneath the grey layer waiting for one of them to reappear. A green shape re-emerged not far away. I attacked again and he too caught fire. I watched as the Il-2 plummeted down out of control to join his leader at the bottom of the Baltic. It was my forty-second and final kill of the war.

By this time we were level with our field, which was visible between the two canals below us and to the right. The other Ilyushins appeared to be jettisoning their bombs at random from the shelter of the clouds. Not one hit its target. Although we remained in the air for another hour there was no further sign of the enemy. We returned to base. Before landing I waggled my wings twice to indicate my two victories, both of which had been witnessed by those on the ground.

That evening there were drinks all round. It was a double celebration, for Füchsle had just produced half-a-dozen gorgeous dachshund puppies. All were quickly spoken for by six of the more ardent dog-lovers in the Staffel and I knew they would be in good hands. There had not been much in the way of food to accompany the drinks. But before the party broke up we again warned the three pilots who were billeted next door to the met men not to raid the latter's rabbit hutches as they were now sure to be guarded.

Ignoring our advice, the trio promptly did so. They were caught in the act and held at pistol-point while the MPs were sent for. No amount of persuasion or pleading on our part could get them released. They were to face a court-martial in two days time.

On the morning of 7 April the telephone rang in our quarters and I answered it, giving my name. The Gruppe Adjutant, Leutnant Gerd Schmutterer, was on the other end of the line: "Norbert, pack your things. You've been transferred to Lager Lechfeld for conversion to the Me 262." "Go and pull somebody else's leg, Gerd," I laughed, replacing the receiver.

He rang back immediately, assuring me that it was no joke and suggesting that I should come across to Gruppe ops to see the orders for myself if I didn't believe him. So I did. And there it was in black and white: I was being transferred back to Germany for jet training. That altered the situation.

One of the first things I did was to ring my friend Hermann Schleinhege, Kapitän of 8 Staffel at Schrunden, to ask if he would look after my dog for me, to which he willingly agreed. My orders called for me to travel across to Schrunden myself by train and fly from there on the evening of 8 April by Ju 52 back to the Reich. Taking leave of my comrades in the Courland was almost as hard as my last goodbyes to my family had been. We had had so many shared experiences and been through so much together in good times and bad. But orders are orders and so come 21.00 hours on 8 April I was aboard the Ju 52 when it took off for the night flight out of the Courland pocket back to Germany. With me was Leutnant Ossi Unterlerchner, who was likewise to begin jet training.

That same day the three would-be rabbit poachers had faced their court-martial. Having been caught red-handed they admitted the act and also accepted responsibility for the first thefts. I heard later that all three had been found guilty of illegal entry and pilfering. They were demoted and transferred to a Luftwaffe field division. Captured by the Russians, they spent four long years in a Soviet prisoner-of-war camp. They were not released from captivity and returned to Germany until 1949... and all because of four rabbits.

In the early hours of 9 April the Ju 52 landed at Greifswald to refuel before continuing west along the Baltic coast to Wismar, where JG 54's rear-area detachment was now based.

CHAPTER 6

Training on the Me 262; Last Ops with JG 7

Upon arrival at Wismar Ossi and I reported to Hauptmann Lehmann, the CO of our depot company. He handed us our travel warrants and, after collecting our rations for the journey, we set off by train for Berlin. We were to stay in the capital overnight before catching our connection down into Bavaria. But as we emerged from Berlin's Lehrter Station we were confronted by a lunar landscape of nothing but ruins and rubble. The shells of burned-out buildings, streets blocked by fallen debris – not a trace remained of the bustling city I remembered from my days at Werder and Werneuchen. Where the children's home had once stood in the Alte Jakobsstraße there were now just bomb craters. The capital of the Reich had been laid waste by the many Allied bombing raids; thousands of its civilians killed, injured or made homeless. I was absolutely devastated.

In the Courland, despite the enemy's overwhelming weight of numbers, we had always felt ourselves militarily more than a match for our opponents. But here in Berlin there was no sense of superiority at all, military or otherwise. Instead, an almost palpable air of impending doom hung above the scenes of destruction that we, as fighter pilots, had been unable to prevent.

Still shocked, we boarded the Munich train the next day for the journey south. We were to change at Augsburg for the final leg out to Lager Lechfeld. Despite travelling for three days and two nights we never made it. The train was subjected to incessant low-level attacks by roving bands of American fighter-bombers. We spent hours stopped in wayside country stations or hiding in the middle of forests. Finally on 12 April, somewhere near Schwandorf to the north of Regensburg, we were strafed by a Schwarm of Lightnings. Throwing ourselves down behind the railway embankment for protection, we watched as the locomotive was sieved by the fighters' cannon and machine-gun fire. End of our train ride.

I persuaded Ossi that we should try to hitch-hike the rest of the way, which we managed to do. On 13 April we arrived at our destination: III/EJG 2 Lager Lechfeld, the training Gruppe engaged in converting pilots onto the Me 262 jet fighter. We reported to the Kommandeur, Oberstleutnant Heinz Bär, holder of the Knight's Cross with Oak Leaves and Swords. He was one of the foremost personalities of the Luftwaffe's fighter arm and already had 204 piston-engined victories to his credit. To this figure he was to add a further 16 kills, claimed while flying the Me 262 jet, before the war ended.

When we made our presence known Bär was standing in the middle of a group of several other Knight's Cross wearers outside the mess. His words of greeting were unconventional to say the least: "Well, you pair of heroes, still want to win the war? Go inside and get yourselves a decent meal and then we'll see."

This was another world for us. Here the reality of the situation was out in the open and freely discussed; the end of the war regarded as inevitable. But neither Ossi nor I were prepared to give up quite yet. If everything really was going down the pan we wanted to fly this new bird, the Me 262, at least once before it happened. But how to go about it?

First, though, it was time to look after the inner man. Following the Kommandeur's instructions we went into the mess where the waiters served us with what was, by Courland standards, an absolute feast, complete with a half-bottle of red wine. After that we were assigned a room in one of the accommodation blocks which we were to share. Having deposited our things we took a walk around the base to get our bearings. The airfield was located along the eastern side of the main road running from Augsburg down to Landsberg am Lech. Across the road were large open fields and meadows, beyond which was a village surrounded by woods.

We had not long settled down for the night when the sirens began to wail: air-raid warning! Ossi and I grabbed our kitbags and hurried down the stairs. Not trusting the building's air-raid shelter in the cellar, we stuffed our kitbags under the stairs where they would be safe and made our way outside, across the road, and into the open fields. We wanted to put as much distance as possible between ourselves and the airfield.

There was still no sign of any bombers. But we kept going and were soon right out in the fields, a good halfway to the distant village. Suddenly, all around us, rows of lights clicked on. Without realizing it, we had blundered into the middle of the dummy airfield laid out to lure enemy bombers away from the real base back across on the other side of the road. And to make matters worse, the hum of approaching aircraft engines could now be clearly heard.

We began to run towards the village. The noise overhead grew louder, and 'Christmas trees' – bright white clusters of marker flares – began to descend, lighting up the night sky. We were still running as fast as our legs could carry us. To the north red flares cascaded down. Then green ones almost directly above us. The deep throb of engines overhead gave way to the shrill whistle of falling bombs. They were some way away, but the pressure waves nearly knocked us off our feet.

The village was getting closer. Suddenly we heard a child screaming in the darkness. We ran towards the sound and saw a little blonde-haired boy in floods of tears wandering aimlessly across the field. We scooped him up and continued running. We were almost at the village when we heard other voices shouting: "Over here! Over here! Here's the shelter!"

We raced across, still carrying the child, whose parents had not noticed that he had left the shelter and gone out into the field. Our lungs were bursting from the mad dash to escape the bombs, but we were safe. The airfield remained undamaged, too. But when we returned and retrieved our kitbags from under the stairs we discovered that they had been opened and rifled. My camera, which I had kept by me all the time I was in Russia, had been stolen. It was the first possession I had lost throughout the whole of the war.

After breakfast next morning we set out to find the classrooms and instructors so that we could begin our training. No joy. There were no lessons; no more practical instruction. The course had been wound up. People were making preparations to retreat southwards into the Alps. But having come this far, Ossi and I were still determined to get our hands on an Me 262.

We found an engineering officer standing outside one of the hangars and asked him whether he would be willing to explain the cockpit layout to us. He was delighted to discover that somebody was still showing an interest in his charges and proudly ushered us into the hangar behind him. After two solid hours we knew all that a pilot needed to know to be able to fly one of these revolutionary birds. We thanked the engineer warmly and now cast our eyes covetously across to the other side of the field where Me 262s were still taking off and landing. Flagging down a passing vehicle, we got the driver to give us a lift across to the take-off area.

There we spotted an NCO flying instructor. Ossi poked me in the ribs. I approached the Feldwebel, ready with a big fat lie: "We have just been given orders to begin conversion here. Is that still possible?" I asked innocently.

"Jawohl, Herr Leutnant. Two machines will be coming in again any minute. They'll still have enough juice for a familiarization flight. You can take those."

No sooner said than done. The moment the first aircraft landed and the pilot climbed out I was up in the cockpit adjusting the parachute harness. Smiling at the unsuspecting instructor, I closed the canopy and taxied out to the start line. It was my first experience of a machine with a nosewheel undercarriage. I was astounded at the excellent forward visibility this afforded the pilot on the ground.

Getting the all-clear for take-off, I eased the throttle slowly forward as the engineering officer had just demonstrated and was at once pressed back into my seat by the force of the enormous acceleration. The airspeed indicator started to tick off the speed: 100 – 200 – 300 km/h. Stick gently back, the nose came up and the Me 262 began to climb. Undercarriage and flaps retracted; still climbing – 400 – 500 km/h. I was gaining height as rapidly as I was gathering speed: 1,000 metres – 2,000 – 3,000. At 7,000 metres I eased the bird on to an even keel, reduced power to 80%... and was still doing 720 km/h! I stared in fascination at the instruments, not believing what they were telling me.

Then I glanced down out of the cockpit – a brilliant white landscape stuffed full of mountains! I had been flying southwards along the line of the Lech where everything had been brown with not a trace of snow to be seen. Now I was high over the Alps and heading straight for Switzerland. Time to turn this thing around. I retraced my route at the same incredible speed and soon saw the field far below me. Throttle back towards idle and into a steep turn to reduce speed. Slowly lose height, get the speed below 400 km/h and lower undercarriage – that had an additional braking effect – compensate for nose-up trim, hold her, sidle into the landing pattern. Shallow, careful approach; speed sinking, 300 – 280 – 240. Cross the airfield boundary at 200 km/h and set her down very gently for a long landing run. Then taxi in. For a brief second I had a mental picture of Walter Heck driving his Me 109 back to dispersal at Siverskaya. In the Me 262 it really *was* like driving a car, just a trifle louder. I was waved in, shut down my engines and climbed out. Thus ended my conversion course from the Fw 190A-8 on to the Me 262 at Lager Lechfeld.

When Ossi and I reported to the Kommandeur that we were converted, Bär simply shook his head. But on the strength of it we were transferred to Munich-Riem to join JV 44. This was the special jet unit commanded by Generalleutnant Galland who, as the story went, had thrown his medals and decorations at Göring's feet in order to get back on ops. But we quickly decided that Munich-Riem was not the place for us. It was awash with high-ranking Experten, every one of whom seemed to be sporting the Knight's Cross. When it came to flying a mission we wouldn't get a look in.

We therefore requested and received permission to be posted to the replacement Gruppe attached to Major Weißenberger's JG 7. This was a motley collection of some 200 pilots who, like ourselves, had been selected for jet training but had not had the opportunity to become operational. On 17 April the Gruppe was transferred to the satellite landing ground at Untermeitlingen, east of Munich. We arrived at about midday and were quartered in barracks behind which were deep slit trenches. During the course of the afternoon a wide variety of aircraft of all types, and from a miscellany of units, flew in and were dispersed in the open around the edge of the field.

Early next morning we were woken by the howl of engines and the hammering of heavy machine-gun fire. A squadron of Thunderbolts had spotted the parked aircraft and were busily engaged in shooting them to pieces one by one. We dived into the trenches in our night attire – mostly track-suits – and watched the destruction. When there were no more machines worth shooting at, the American fighters turned their attention to the slit trenches. Luckily these were deep enough to give us full protection and nobody was killed or wounded. Shortly afterwards, at morning parade, two volunteers were called for to fly a couple of Me 262s from Fürstenfeldbruck in to Munich-Riem. The US Army was approaching fast and somebody had presumably decided that the two jets had to be got out of the way.

Ossi and I volunteered and got the job. We collected travel rations and were given a tracked motorcycle combination and driver for the journey to Fürstenfeldbruck on the far side of Munich. It was a nice warm and sunny spring day. Avenues of budding lime trees threw their shadows on the verges along either side of the country road. We were bowling along quite happily when suddenly, as we breasted a slight rise, a horrifying sight met our gaze. A long line of living corpses garbed in blue-and-white were shuffling along the road towards us in columns of four.

The driver swerved off the road between two lime trees and switched off his engine. As the column passed eyes stared at us out of dark sunken sockets and stick-like arms were held out in supplication. What sort of creatures were these? Human beings? Speechless with shock, we grabbed our ration bags and began handing out food. It was all gone by the time an old man in a dark blue coat and with a World War One-vintage rifle on his shoulder came up to us and said: "Herr Leutnant, you are not allowed to give them anything, they are prisoners from the camp at Dachau."

We were almost physically sick. We had had some pretty nasty experiences at the front, but nothing to match this. I had to pull myself together before I could speak, "Just get out of here," I managed to keep my voice emotionless, "get going before something happens – go!" He went. We waited in silence until the last of the emaciated figures had dragged itself past us. Was this what we had been fighting for?

Still shaken, we were relieved to get to Fürstenfeldbruck and back into the 'normality' of a world teetering on the brink of general collapse. Ground crews were waiting for us with starter trolleys. Wasting no time, we climbed into the two Me 262s standing ready in front of the hangars. But when Ossi pressed the fuel injection button to get ignition his four nose cannon blasted into life, sending bits of hangar door flying in all directions – a faulty connection. Fortunately nobody was hurt. Unperturbed, the mechanics completed their tasks and we took off safely for the short hop to JV 44's Munich-Riem base to deliver the two jets.

After returning to the replacement group Ossi and I soon decided that this was no place to be either. Everybody seemed to be simply killing time waiting for the war to end. We wanted to return to the Courland or, if that proved impossible, to join some other operational unit. So when JG 7 called for volunteers for one of its combat Gruppen in Czechoslovakia we were first in line. The job entailed going back to Munich-Riem to collect a couple of Me 262s that were to be flown to JG 7's main base at Prague-Ruzyn.

It was not quite so simple as it sounds. When we got to Munich we discovered that the jets had no radio equipment installed. This meant that there would be no contact with ground control – or between ourselves in the air – during the entire flight. Take-off was scheduled for the morning of 22 April. But during the night the heavens opened and Munich-Riem was a quagmire. Taking off from a waterlogged airfield would be critical. Then, in the morning, Thunderbolts appeared overhead. They did not come down to ground-strafe. Several of their number had fallen victim to Riem's formidable flak defences in the preceding days and weeks, and the Amis had developed a certain respect for the place. But their presence meant that we could not show ourselves.

Finally, towards midday, the skies were clear. But there were still large patches of standing water on the field's surface as I walked out to my machine. One of the ground crew asked: "Herr Leutnant, do you want to use take-off rockets? You'll have no trouble getting off then."

I had never heard of take-off rockets so he briefly explained what they were. The machine I was to fly was a fighter-bomber version of the Me 262. And instead of bombs a pair of rockets could be attached to the weapons pylons. Ignited by pressing the bomb-release switch, these rockets supplied additional thrust during take-off. Once they had burned out they were automatically jettisoned. It sounded a good idea to me, so I agreed. Ossi also opted to give them a go.

We settled into the cockpits and began to run through the start-up procedure. It was then that Ossi found that the starter motor of one of his turbines was unserviceable. He could not take off with me, so I taxied out on my own. Given the go ahead, I started to roll. When the needle of the ASI touched 100 km/hr I pressed the bomb-release. There was a tremendous jolt, I was pushed harder still into the back of my seat, and the windscreen was suddenly full of clear blue sky as I arrowed upwards even faster than before.

After a refuelling stop at Hörsching, near Linz in Austria, I took off again and set course almost due north for Prague. Upon landing at Ruzyn I reported to Oberleutnant Stehle, the Kommandeur of I/JG 7, who welcomed me to the Gruppe and assigned me to Oberleutnant Grünberg's 1 Staffel. I was back in an operational unit at last.

But here too in Prague-Ruzyn there was a general feeling in the air that it was all over. The war was lost and nobody believed for a moment in the promises of "final victory" still being trumpeted by the die-hards. The British and Americans had more or less given up their raids on Germany's towns and cities. There was nothing left to bomb. The only aerial activity was that in support of the enemy's armoured and infantry units now closing in for the kill from all sides.

As Prague was too far from the Russian advance through Silesia we were unable to take part in the fighting for my own home province. Where we were, in what was then called the Protectorate of Bohemia and Moravia, everything remained quiet until the end of April. Then, on 2 May, there was an uprising by the Czechs in Prague who tried to seize a number of key points in and around the capital, including the one-time civil airport on which we were based.

We were ordered to fly ground-attack missions in support of our troops fighting the insurgent forces. The effects of our 30-mm cannon fire were devastating. Trucks simply disintegrated or were tossed bodily into the air burning fiercely. Temporary street barricades thrown up by the Czechs were blasted apart by swathes of shells ploughing through them. The uprising was quickly crushed. Renegade Russian troops under General Vlasov, ex-Red Army prisoners of war who had volunteered to fight for the Germans, tried to change sides again by coming to the Czechs' aid. We also attacked their columns as they advanced on the capital.

On 6 May I/JG 7 transferred to Saaz (Zatec) closer to the German border. From here a few final missions were flown the following day against Czech insurgent forces and Vlasov troops. On the afternoon of 7 May the Kommandeur called the Gruppe together. He told us that Generaloberst Jodl had signed the unconditional terms of surrender at Rheims early that morning and that the war was over. The Gruppe was to prepare to set out by road for Germany immediately. Then he turned to the pilots: "Those of you who flew the last missions can keep your machines. Each of you is to fly back to Germany, to an airfield of your choice, and there surrender to the Allies."

It was a generous gesture in recognition of services performed and duty done – a guaranteed ticket out of Soviet captivity. The Me 262 in which I had just landed was standing at its dispersal point already refuelled for the next mission. I hurried over to my quarters to fetch the rucksack that I had drawn from stores in exchange for my kitbag and then made my way back out to my machine. But looky there, a pilot whom I hardly knew – an Oberleutnant – was already sitting in it. As I approached he said:

"Hannig, you can't fly home to Silesia any more. Why don't you let me have this crate and you take my BMW motorbike – it's standing over there – and travel back with the road column. I want to get to Hannover, my wife and children are waiting for me there."

I agreed to his proposal and found myself swapping an operational and fully-armed Me 262 jet fighter for a 500cc BMW motorbike. Astride my new possession I tacked myself on to the convoy which set off from Saaz at about 16.00 hours on the main road south towards Podersam (Podborany). It was slow going. A lot of other German units had chosen the same route to make their escape. I rode along beside one or our fuel tankers. Squeezed into the cab together with the driver sat our Staffel Chiefy and two of the ground crew. During one of our many interminable stops one of the ground crew called down to me: "Herr Leutnant, couldn't you please let me have the motorbike? My wife has been trying to make her way westwards with our two small children. They're being put up in a village not far from here. I'd like to go and look after them. You could have my place up here in the cab."

What was I supposed to do, turn him down? Once again I agreed to trade. The Unteroffizier jumped down from the tanker. Thanking me profusely he straddled the BMW and roared off. I climbed up into the cab to continue the journey towards Podersam. Chiefy asked me if I could use a new pay-book, saying we'd be sure to need some identity papers when we became prisoners of war. I agreed and he fished out a clean pay-book bearing all the necessary stamps and signatures. He spent the next few minutes filling in my personal and service details before handing it to me with a flourish. Armed with this I would hopefully be able to hang on to my front ID card, which was the only form of identity I was carrying with me.

Podersam is a small market town. Five roads enter its central square: four from the east and one from the west. The former were all choked with traffic waiting to get across the square and leave by the one road heading westwards which, after some 18 kilometres, joined up with the main Prague-Karlsbad highway. The traffic was being controlled by field police who were letting vehicles from each eastern road in turn into the market square to take their place in the queue heading west. The local inhabitants were standing around the edges of the square watching the organized chaos. Stopping and starting we slowly inched our way towards the town centre. One of the field police waved the head of our convoy into the square. We were about to follow when his baton went up – halt! Vehicles from the next road were ordered forward and our column was split in two.

After traffic from the other three roads had been filtered across the square it was our turn to move again. Beckoned forward by the field police the driver trod on the accelerator and jammed home first gear. The overloaded tanker – which was not only full of aviation fuel but also had a 200-litre drum of petrol strapped to the back – jerked forward. There was a loud crack and it came to a dead stop. The clutch had gone. We weren't going any further in this vehicle.

Urged on by the impatient police, who wanted the road cleared, the tanker was manhandled bodily out into the square and pushed to one side. While we were thus engaged the rest of our column had moved on. I managed to find a place on a truck from another unit that was carrying wounded. We finally got across the square and on to the road heading west. It was still slow going. There were open meadows to the right of the road; on the left a steep wooded hillside. We came to another stop. A truck ahead of us had caught fire and was blocking the road. I saw a private car bouncing across the field on the right trying to get round the obstacle. I grabbed my rucksack and dashed over to it. I quickly explained to the driver that I had been separated from my unit and was trying to get back to it – could he please give me a lift?

Although the two back seats of the DKW were empty he refused. I tried another tack: "Have you got enough petrol to reach Karlsbad?" I asked him. "Probably not," he admitted with some concern.

"If you take me with you, I can get you 200 litres," I offered, thinking of the drum on the back of the tanker. "If that's the case you can come along."

I climbed in and directed him the short distance back to the town square where, luckily, the drum had remained untouched. After filling the tank we threaded our way out of town through narrow side streets. Once in open country we followed winding minor roads through several small villages and hamlets before striking the main western artery to Karlsbad. When we reached our destination I asked the driver to take me out to the airfield which he did. I got out of the car and was on my own. A straggler among hundreds of thousands of other German troops. I could do what I liked, and so proceeded to explore my surroundings.

I went across to the flight control building. From there I could see the remains of aircraft of all types scattered around the edges of the field, abandoned and blown up. But a row of five apparently undamaged Fieseler Störche closer to hand caught my attention. More in hope than expectation I decided to give them a closer look. To my surprise they were fully tanked up. And when I tried the door handle of one of them it was not locked – the key was even in the ignition. I noticed a pile of weapons behind the seat, but there was no sign of the owner.

Looking around to make sure I wasn't being watched, I threw my rucksack aboard and quickly clambered in. I fastened the harness and turned the ignition. The motor sprang into life immediately. I did not dare let it warm up for too long, but taxied out and took off. This was more like it. Better than any motorbike, fuel bowser, car or my own two feet. I pointed her nose westwards. Even without a map Germany shouldn't be too hard to find.

I had been in the air for a good twenty minutes when an olive-brown engine cowling appeared outside the cockpit window next to me. It was attached to an Auster and the five-pointed white star on the machine's fuselage told me it belonged to the winning side. I looked over my shoulder and saw another one right behind me. I couldn't start a dogfight – what with? – so I waggled my wings.

The pilot alongside did the same and then waved across to me, indicating that I should follow him. I nodded my head. We continued to fly westwards before putting down on a landing ground near Eger (Cheb). We landed in perfect formation; me side-by-side with the leading Auster, the second one still sitting tightly on my tail. I was beckoned in to a dispersal area where – for the last time in my wartime career – I switched off an aircraft engine. Then I climbed to the ground.

I was immediately surrounded by several ground crew, rifles at the ready. One of them approached me and I addressed him in his mother tongue: "I would like to speak to an officer please."

He seemed a little taken aback, but shouted my request across to one of his comrades who went off somewhere to telephone. A little later a jeep arrived. A lieutenant got out and came over to me. I rose from the wheel of the Storch on which I had been sitting, came to attention and, when he was three paces in front of me, saluted with my hand to the peak of my cap saying, again in English: "Leutnant Hannig of 1 Staffel JG 7. I have been ordered to report here for internment."

I lowered my hand. The 'comrade from the other side' returned my salute with equal formality and introduced himself by name, rank and unit. I thus learned that I was not among Americans as I thought, but with a Canadian unit.

"May I have your pistol, please," the lieutenant requested. I undid my holster and gave him the weapon. "And may I have the holster as well – as a souvenir?"

This too I handed over, although him wanting it as a souvenir struck me as a little strange. But I was in no position to argue – other people, other customs.

"Have you any other weapons in your possession?"

I suddenly remembered the four Panzerfäuste – the German army's equivalent to the bazooka – and the box of hand grenades stuffed behind the pilot's seat of the Storch and so I answered in the affirmative. I climbed back into the machine and reappeared with a Panzerfaust under my arm. The onlookers took to their heels in a flash. Only the lieutenant stood his ground, asking calmly if there were any more such items inside the aircraft. Again I said yes, and brought the whole lot out. We had capitulated and there was no sense in being uncooperative. I defused the Panzerfäuste, something we had been taught to do at Libau-Grobin, and then the lieutenant took me in the jeep back to his HQ.

There we reported to a major, who was given the details of the circumstances behind my arrival. He greeted me in a friendly enough fashion and enquired whether I was hungry. For the third time I found myself replying yes to a question from my captors. This produced a plate piled high with steak, mashed potatoes and Brussels sprouts. For dessert I was even given a bowl of pineapple – something I had never tasted before in my life.

Stupidly, I had forgotten to take off my pilot's wristwatch and hide it in my pocket. A sergeant had spotted it. He approached me, expressing keen interest. You're a bit late, I thought, for a number of his comrades already had several watches apiece. But I agreed to swap the watch for 120 cigarettes – better than nothing.

Shortly afterwards I was taken by jeep to a factory yard where hundreds of German soldiers had already been collected together. It was here that my personal possessions were given their first real 'going over' by a large Negro soldier standing a good six feet tall. In his right hand he held a riding crop that he continually slapped against the palm of his left hand. I was first ordered to empty my pockets. I was promptly deprived of my pocket knife, which he threw on to a pile of other knives beside him. I noticed it slide to the floor and surreptitiously placed my foot over it.

Next came the contents of my rucksack. I took out each item individually, holding it up in front of him and turning it this way and that so that he could inspect it thoroughly before I neatly refolded it and placed it on the floor next to my rucksack. Slowly the rucksack emptied as the pile of clothing beside it grew higher. All the while a group of half a dozen or so of his comrades were standing in the background enjoying the performance and making loud comments. This put him off his stroke a little, but I wouldn't be hurried. Finally, with a curt nod, I was allowed to pack everything back into my rucksack, including my knife which I slipped in unnoticed.

The night was spent in the yard out in the open. The next morning the officers were called out. Three large, high-sided trucks had pulled up outside the factory gates. We were ordered to climb aboard them. I saw that the officers in the first truck were being squeezed in like sardines. Packed tightly together, their arms were pressed against their sides and they couldn't move. As one of the first to be loaded on to the second truck I braced myself against the back of the cab, arms outstretched in front of me. Others followed suit and despite the pushing from the tailgate end we were not jammed in quite so closely. After our luggage was thrown in on top of us the trucks set off.

The journey that followed was a nightmare. The trucks hurtled along the roads; the drivers taking bends and corners at suicidal speeds. The mass of humanity packed into the back was thrown about so much that the sides of the trucks were buckled. After two hours of this torture our vehicle slammed on its brakes and we were ordered down. We were at Eger airfield – about 300 metres from the factory where we had started from! During the journey one truck had overturned, killing a number of its occupants. Another arrived back with several officers severely injured. We were the only ones to escape with nothing more than bumps and bruises. This was our introduction to the Americans.

Among the prisoners at Eger was a group of generals. The most senior of them wore both the Knight's Cross and the Pour le Mérite from the First World War. He imposed strict discipline and order so that our hoped-for release could be carried out quickly and smoothly. To this end the prisoners were divided up into companies, battalions and sections. These were then assigned to specific areas of the airfield, each of which had been marked off in squares by laying lengths of gauze bandages. An officer was detailed to take charge of every group.

I was responsible for 200 men: a company of the Hermann Göring Division under their senior NCO and about 60 Hitler Youths who had been impressed into the Volkssturm. These latter were children aged 14 to 17 who still knew how to cry. My last wartime command rejoiced in the title of 6 Company, II Battalion in Section B of the Assembly Camp for Prisoners of War on the airfield of Eger! American tanks had drawn up all around the airfield perimeter to mount guard over us.

It was 8 May 1945 and I was a prisoner of war of the US Army.

CHAPTER 7

PoW of the Americans, Russians and British

The Americans were not prepared for what was to follow. They had expected the number of German prisoners of war to be in the region of 30,000. But it turned out to be ten times that number. There was no suitable accommodation, water, food, sanitary facilities or even any medical care for the wounded and sick among the prisoners. An exception was made for the female military personnel who were separated from the men and housed in buildings.

The situation was made worse by the onset of a heat wave which increased everybody's thirst. We were allowed to move freely within the camp. A small stream ran along its perimeter. This news immediately spread like wildfire. The water was drunk, as well as being used to wash our bodies and our clothes. It soon became polluted. This posed the very real danger of an epidemic and endangered everyone, including the Americans. As a first measure our captors therefore organized tankers to bring in drinking water which was strictly rationed.

Hunger drove many to go digging for potatoes out in the neighbouring fields, which had only just been planted. The Czechs shot at the prisoners and there were a number of casualties, killed and wounded. Some units had arrived with their supply trains intact. They had sufficient provisions, but refused to share them with the rest of us as demanded by the Americans. This aggravated the tension between the haves and the have-nots. My company possessed a few dozen army loaves. The senior NCO and I agreed that a hole should be dug into which the bread could be placed and kept under guard. Everyone received a slice each in the morning, at midday and in the evening to still the pangs of hunger until such time as the Americans began to provide food. This worked, for after four days a field bakery started up and began to supply us with fresh bread. Field kitchens were also brought in which served warm soup once a day. Slowly the situation was getting back to something like normal.

In the evenings, after dark, the white-washed wall of a house on the edge of the field was used as a screen to show German films. This helped to take our mind off things, for there was of course no mail and therefore no news from relatives.

The American guards around the camp fence had developed the habit of lighting up a cigarette and then throwing it into the camp. If one of us bent down to pick it up – for we were desperately short of cigarettes – he would find himself being photographed. As I could manage without a smoke I used to walk along the camp wire waiting for a cigarette to be thrown in front of me. I then derived huge pleasure from squashing it underfoot before the bemused gaze of the thrower.

Because of the continued danger of an epidemic, and the overcrowding in the assembly camp, the prisoners were being prepared for rapid release. Large tents were erected and questionnaires distributed throughout the camp. These had to be completed by everyone. The first to be discharged were the members of the Hitler Youth. Then came those whose homes were in the American sector. Prisoners with families residing in the British and French zones would follow later. Uncertainty surrounded the futures of those who had lived in what was now territory occupied by the Russians: East Prussia, Pomerania and Silesia. But as I naturally wanted to be released as soon as possible I gave Garmisch-Partenkirchen, Bahnhofstraße 8, as my discharge address, not realizing that there *was* no Bahnhofstraße in Garmisch. My first port-of-call was to be Gisela's friend, Eva, who worked as a nurse in the local hospital and might have some news of her.

On 23 May I joined the queue of those waiting to be released. In front of the discharge tent American GIs were busy relieving the German soldiers of their national insignia, badges of rank and decorations. Everybody had to run this gauntlet before they were permitted to enter the tent and be submitted to questioning. As I was wearing my leather flying jacket, which did not carry the national insignia, I took off my epaulettes and my Iron Cross, First Class for safe-keeping, entered the tent, answered the questions – particularly those concerning my past history as a National Socialist – and was duly issued with a discharge certificate. I was then transported by truck – this time sitting with the others on benches – to the Marienplatz in Munich. It was my first official release from captivity, complete with papers to prove it, and I can still remember the exact spot: in front of the third archway of the Munich town hall.

No regular train services were running yet. I therefore followed the railway tracks out of the devastated city on foot in the direction of Starnberg, from where I hoped to be able to hitchhike to Garmisch-Partenkirchen. I had got as far as Gauting when I was hailed by a man working in a garden who asked me where I came from and where I was heading for. He then kindly invited me to stay and rest for the night. I gratefully accepted his offer. His wife went to great lengths to make a fuss of me. I was one of the first released PoWs they had met and I had to recount all that had been happening to me. They let me take a bath –

I still had some clean underwear – I was given food and slept in a normal bed. They told me that the French were in Starnberg and were rounding up discharged German soldiers again and sending them off to France to work in the coalmines.

Extra care had therefore to be taken when, after a warm farewell from my hosts, I continued on my journey the next day. I by-passed Starnberg before regaining the road to Garmisch where I stopped a wood and gas-powered lorry, which was loaded high with potatoes. The driver agreed to give me a lift. Climbing up behind the cab I hid myself in the potatoes so that I could not be seen from the road. There was still one French control point on the far side of Starnberg which we managed to pass without any trouble. After that it was a clear road all the way down to Garmisch.

Eva had a flat in the town, but she wasn't in when I got there. She was working in the Hotel Sonnenbichl, which had been turned into a military hospital surrounded by barbed wire, and which she was not allowed to leave. There was neither news nor any trace of Gisela. I went to the Sonnenbichl and waited at the barbed wire fence. When a nurse appeared in the garden I asked if she would be kind enough to fetch Eva. She did so. We were delighted to see each other despite being separated by three rolls of barbed wire. Sadly she had not heard a word from Gisela. What was I to do next?

I decided to wait a few days before setting off for Altenhausen where I hoped to find my family at our agreed rendezvous point. I accepted a temporary job as a farm labourer in Garmisch. But as no news was forthcoming I was soon saying my goodbyes again and starting on my long trek to Altenhausen near Magdeburg. I first followed the scenic German Alpine Route via Vorderriß to Lenggries. Here I heard organ music being played in the village church. The glorious sound reminded me of my youth. In the village street a bored-looking policeman watched me as I went through the gate into the churchyard. I saw a large number of first class bicycles propped up in front of the house of God. I opened the church door, but couldn't enter because it was packed with people. A notice pinned to the door read: 'Service of thanksgiving for the happy return of our soldiers'.

The reference to a 'happy return' gave me the idea of borrowing one of the many bicycles. With a pair of wheels I would no longer be dependent on hitching a lift and would be able to reach my next destination much more quickly. I straddled the second-best machine and started pedalling. I greeted the dozing policeman as I passed him. Surprised by so much politeness, he returned my salutation with a friendly wave.

After my first discharge from prisoner-of-war camp I had only one thing on my mind: to find Gisela and my family, or at least discover their fate. Everything else was of secondary importance. Because of the war

I had lost touch with my loved ones. I was homeless, without a profession, and hence without income. All I had in the world at this moment was what I carried in my rucksack and my firm belief in God.

At the beginning of June I finally reached the farm in Niederbergkirchen where I had previously arranged for a job during the harvest. I was gladly welcomed by farmer Reiter as an additional farm hand. Two other discharged prisoners of war were already employed there. One of my fellow workers who came from Coburg gave me the address of his parents and asked me to pass on news of him on the next leg of my journey. I was to tell them that once the harvest was gathered in he was intending to return home. When I pedalled off my severance pay was half a loaf of bread and a piece of bacon – but not a Pfennig in hard cash.

In Coburg I managed to find the parents of my fellow farm labourer. They were both delighted and relieved to hear the news I brought them of their son. They pressed food and drink on me, insisted that I stayed the night with them and gave me ample provisions for the coming days. And so I continued on my way slowly northwards on my borrowed bike until the middle of June when I finally reached the estate manager's office of our Uncle Mieke in Altenhausen.

The little house was already bursting at the seams with nine people living in it. It had two rooms and a kitchen on the ground floor, two bedrooms on the first floor and a loft under the roof. The Miekes had been joined by their daughter, her husband and child, as well as Uncle Müller from Breslau, complete with wife and two daughters. I was now the tenth lodger. I was nevertheless warmly welcomed. They had no news of either Gisela or my family. But on my journey through Germany I had made a point at longer stopovers of always leaving details of my next destination so that it would be possible to trace my steps. First of all I was given emergency quarters in the utility building. On my arrival the Haldensleben district, in which Altenhausen was situated, still belonged to the American zone of occupation, which meant that my discharge certificate was valid here.

It was the Soviets who had captured Berlin. But as the western Allies still recognized the city as the capital of Germany they wanted sectors of this major prize too. The district of Haldensleben was therefore exchanged for the western half of Berlin. On 1 July the Americans withdrew their occupying troops from the area and the Red Army advanced across the River Elbe to take their place.

After the departure of the Americans a Russian billeting officer – in fact a sergeant – arrived with two men. He made his way through the village, inspecting the houses and their furnishings, before announcing to Uncle Mieke that the two ground floor rooms of his home were being commandeered for a general who would be arriving the next day. With this he saluted and left.

The next day the new 'guests' arrived. I was working in the large garden which bordered the approach road to the village. Towards midday a column of American trucks pulling 15-cm howitzers approached. The trucks were piled high with sofas, upholstered armchairs, iron stoves, plus assorted household goods and Russian soldiers. They drove into the village to one of the large farmsteads, where they parked their vehicles and artillery, fell in and were assigned to their quarters.

The general did not arrive until evening and was escorted to our home by the billeting officer. Right away the general demanded to meet all the occupants of the house and had us lined up in the hall. He looked at the ten of us, and then at the sergeant and asked him something. There followed a short dialogue between them, whereupon the general turned, saluted, and left. The interpreter explained that the general offered his apologies. He had not known how many people were living in the house already and had gone instead to one of the farms which had more rooms to offer. In his place a senior lieutenant, Sergei Urbanov, was billeted in our parlour as the local military commandant. He introduced himself, shook everybody by the hand and spoke almost fluent German. This was new behaviour coming from a Russian.

A few days later it transpired that the senior lieutenant, and new local military commandant, was an excellent pianist when, after asking Uncle Mieke's permission, he was allowed to play the cherished piano in the music room. Uncle Mieke was himself a gifted pianist, also an atheist and very particular.

A week later all the men of the village were again collected from the houses and fields by the Russians and brought to our courtyard. Their status as prisoners of war or otherwise was to be examined by a Russian commission. American release documents were not accepted as valid. Search parties of Russian troops were coming and going, reporting to our local commandant and appeared to be looking for someone. I myself was moving freely among the village population assembled in the courtyard without attracting attention. There were communists living in the village who must have heard that I had been a Luftwaffe officer and had flown the Me 262, which was of interest to the Soviets. If they were searching for me there was no point in my hiding, for I intended to remain here and wait for news of my family.

I therefore went directly to Sergei and asked openly whether they were searching for someone? He admitted they were: a Luftwaffe officer who had flown jet fighters and who was supposed to be living in the village. So it *was* me they were after. I hesitated only briefly before revealing the fact. He did not want to believe it at first, but then I fetched my American discharge papers to prove that I had been in the armed forces. He shook his head, called in the search parties and told me that I would have to accompany him. He advised me to bring a loaf of bread along, however – it could take a long time.

Once more I had to say farewell to dear friends. With my loaf under my arm, and flanked on either side by a Soviet soldier as a guard of honour, I fell in at the back of the column, which was marched off to a factory in Alleringersleben. Here, as at Eger, several thousand men were lying around on the bare ground waiting for whatever was to come. Rumours were rife. But nobody had any firm information. Time and again individuals were pulled out of the crowd. Some returned, others didn't. During the second night I was fetched by a guard who took me into a largish room in the factory where I was made to stand in the glare of two strong spotlights. Completely dazzled, I could hear the low murmur of voices in front of me. Then the interrogation started.

I was asked my name, first name and personal details, when had I entered the armed forces, when was I promoted, where did I fight and for how long? I stuck to the dates in my pay-book, which I had stowed away in my officer's trunk at home. Because the war was over I also told them all the units I had served with and that I had been a fighter pilot. There was only one question that I did not answer truthfully. They wanted to know whether I had dropped bombs on Russian soil. I replied in the negative, although I had flown some fighter-bomber missions in the Leningrad area. However, they had no way of knowing this and were in no position to check. But to have volunteered the fact would without doubt have got me into serious trouble. Then they interrogated me about my experiences on the Me 262 jet, its performance and technical data. Here too I willingly supplied the information they wanted. I was still in the beam of the spotlights and my reactions were being carefully observed. Then the interpreter asked, "Would you also fly the aircraft for us?"

"After I have found my family, why not?" I replied. Once again a low murmuring all around me. Then another question, "We would like to know your opinion of the Soviet Air Force?"

Without hesitation I answered in all honesty: "Not a lot. It was only your vast superiority in numbers, often 10:1 or more, which defeated us." This answer caused some hilarity all round. There followed a whispered conversation and a command in Russian. The spotlights were switched off and a chair was brought for me. I was permitted to sit down and found myself in the centre of several tables arranged in a 'U', at which some fourteen Russian officers were seated; directly in front of me was a general who had led the interrogation. A pad lay open before him and he began to write in it with a fountain pen. He tore off the written page and gave it to me. The interpreter translated: "Here is your release paper from Russian captivity. You are to report every month to the command post at Haldensleben and are to remain available to us. You can go now and look for your relatives."

And then something happened that I would never have dreamed possible. The general stood up, put on his cap, gave an order to the other officers, who also got to their feet, put on their caps and raised their hands in military salute, while the general spoke and the interpreter translated his words: "We Soviet officers know how to respect the courageous German soldiers. Keep yourself available to us. You may go."

I returned their salute and a guard brought me back to the others in the hall. There was no time for lengthy explanations as the soldier was waiting to accompany me to the gate. The guard on duty shouted his "Stoi" – whereupon I presented my written paper to him. He read it, came to attention, saluted and let me pass. I was free. Most of the others were transported to the Soviet Union and used as slave labour for many years.

To the surprise of all I returned to Altenhausen. Senior Lieutenant Sergei Urbanov looked at me incredulously. I gave him my release paper, which he read several times, particularly the name of the general and his seniority number which gave him the authority to release German officers from a prisoner-of-war camp prematurely. Somehow, because I had flown the Me 262, I had become a specialist in the eyes of the Soviets and was of value to them.

I resumed my job as a farm labourer. Another discharged soldier was also working on the farm and shared a room with me. I told him of my Russian release paper which I kept in my bedside table. Next morning the paper, plus the bicycle borrowed at Lenggries, and my room-mate had all disappeared. Once again I was an outlaw. Senior Lieutenant Sergei Urbanov had been recalled to the barracks in Haldensleben and the local command post shut down. But he knew all about my release paper and would help me. I went to the barracks and asked the guard to have him called, as there was something I needed to discuss with him. The duty sergeant at first tried to drive me away with a curt "Tawai". But I remained sitting on the steps in front of the guard house. Finally, the guard commander went to the telephone and then informed me that the senior lieutenant would come out to me during his lunch break. We were oddly pleased to see each other again. I recounted what had happened to me. He immediately sat down at a table in the guard house, demanded a sheet of paper and issued me with another release document, which confirmed in writing that I had been discharged by the said general. He wished me good luck for the future. I watched over this piece of paper like a mother hen. It was not going to be stolen again.

Will Hahnel, the Mieke's son-in-law, was an aircraft engineer. He had last worked in Görlitz (now Zgorzelc) and had left his flat there standing empty. In the meantime a few trains were running again, mainly goods trains, but without any kind of timetable of course. As there was still no news of my family only one option remained open to me: to go and see if anybody had returned to our home in Hermannsdorf. I possessed a valid Russian release paper, and Will wanted to accompany me at least as far as Görlitz. So, at the end of July,

taking a few supplies for the journey, we set off for Görlitz. There were
no train tickets to be had. You simply waited at the station for a train to
pull in, asked where it was heading and climbed into a goods wagon, the
driver's cab, between the carriages, or wherever there was space. People
hung like bunches of grapes from every train.

It took us three days to reach Görlitz. We went to Will's flat which
was as packed with refugees as the house in Altenhausen. I enquired
about the conditions further east and was told that from the station at
Horka goods trains were leaving for Silesia several times a day.
Although the region itself was now under Polish administration, the
trains were still controlled by Soviet troops. So off I went.

Horka was a marshalling yard which showed no signs of having been
bombed. Here again hundreds of refugees – women, children and
elderly men – were waiting with their worldly goods in the hope of
getting home. Several goods trains stood on the tracks, two locomotives
already under steam. Refugees were climbing into the empty wagons of
one train. Apparently it was soon about to leave via Kohlfurt, Bunzlau
and Haynau for Liegnitz. That would suit me nicely as far as Kohlfurt.
From there I could take to the familiar pine forests of my boyhood
home, walking through Siegersdorf to Hermannsdorf.

Every train was guarded and accompanied by Russian soldiers.
Alongside one box wagon a young Russian had propped his machine
pistol up against one of the wheels and, sweating profusely from his
exertions, was helping the refugees to clamber on board. I gave him a
hand with loading the human cargo. A long whistle from the engine.
Doors slid shut, we were ready to depart. The young Russian scrambled
up into the brake cabin, leaving his machine pistol behind. I picked it up
just as the train started to move and climbed in after him. Laughing, I
held the weapon out to him butt first. He looked quite startled, took the
gun from me and gestured to me to sit down next to him. He then
proceeded to open his knapsack, taking out bread, bacon and sausage,
which he shared with me. He spoke a little German. I explained to him
that I wanted to get off at Kohlfurt. He knew the stretch and the way the
Poles were behaving there. He said excitedly: "You no get off with
others. Poles with rifles – go zap, zap, zap! Take everything. You wait –
then go other side – off – run into wood."

I was as grateful for his advice as he was for the return of his gun.
Things happened exactly the way he had described them. The Poles,
some armed with rifles, immediately surrounded the refugees alighting
at Kohlfurt. I waited, climbed down from the brake cabin on the other
side of the wagon, jumped off and ducked into some high ferns. I
crawled along until I reached the pine forest and only then did I get to
my feet and start on my way through the trees, keeping parallel to the
rail tracks. It was midday. The sun was warm; perfect weather for a
country walk. The blueberry and cranberry bushes were full of fruit. The

berries were delicious. I must have been walking a good three hours when I heard a cow lowing miserably. I followed the sound and found the animal with a swollen udder and a rope round its neck standing alone in the forest. There was nobody to be seen. I approached the cow, stroked her gently, took my mess tin and began to milk her. I did not want to leave her on her own, so I took hold of the rope and started walking. But it was difficult to lead her through the forest. So I went back to the railway embankment and followed the path running beside it. Shortly before Siegersdorf station the path curved slightly into the wood. Thick bracken obscured the view of the fields ahead. I made my way through the thicket with the cow in tow – and found myself standing in the middle of a battery of Russian artillery.

The guns and trucks were lined up in neat rows across the meadow. To one side lines of tents had been erected, in front of which sat groups of soldiers. The path went right through the campsite to a wooden gate on the far side. This was guarded by a soldier with a machine pistol. The Russians were as surprised by my visit as I was by their presence. I hesitated a moment, then carried on walking. I approached the gate, went past the sentry and walked out on to the village road. The sentry had let me pass without challenge. But then a Pole came towards me along the road. He addressed me in Polish which I did not understand. He stopped me and asked whether I was German? I confirmed this, whereupon he tore the rope holding the cow out of my hands and screamed something at the Russian sentry who came running. The soldier held on to me until the guard commander arrived.

They took me before the local commandant who was billeted, of all places, in Burchard's inn, where I had always left my bike before catching the train to school. Our families were good friends. The Burchards had two children, a boy my age and a girl. I knew their house as well as my own. When I was led into the presence of the area commandant – a captain, accompanied by an interpreter – I claimed on the spur of the moment to be the son of the innkeeper who had returned to search for his parents. I was able to describe all the rooms in the house. But he demanded that I be identified by an old village resident who was now living in one of the houses on the brickworks estate. These workers' dwellings, each with a neat little garden, had been built in three rows along the bank of the River Queis. With a soldier either side of me, the interpreter took me to the old man's house. He was lying in bed upstairs. I realized at once that the old gentleman was mentally confused and was not aware of what was going on around him.

There was still a chance to bluff the Russians, but I nonetheless felt a pang of guilt when I went over to him and addressed him as Grandpa: "Grandpa, you know me, don't you?" was my first question. "Yes – yes", came the feeble answer. "You know that I am the son of the Burchards?"

"Yes – yes", he replied again. I was careful only to ask questions which he could confirm with "yes – yes" and thus convince the Russians of my identity.

The three of them had been listening and were apparently satisfied. They held an animated conversation between themselves and then went down the stairs ahead of me and out of the front door. They hadn't noticed the open backdoor through which I now dashed. I ran through the gardens of all three rows of houses before leaping down the bank of the Queis and hiding in the undergrowth. I listened intently. Everything was quiet. The Russians had lost me. I still had a walk of some three kilometres in front of me before I reached home. And somehow I had to cross the River Queis, which was in full spate. From my hiding place I watched a goods train slowly making its way along the 30-metre-high railway embankment towards the viaduct and realized that here was my way across the Queis. Cautiously I left my hiding place. Nobody was following me. I climbed up the embankment and was about to cross the viaduct, when a loud "Stoi" stopped me in my tracks.

A civilian wearing an armband slowly approached me, rifle held at the ready. It was an old man; a Polish military guard. I realized immediately how stupid I had been to contemplate the viaduct. Of course it would be guarded. But now it was too late. From up here on the rail track I could see our schoolhouse down in the valley of the Queis. I was home, but in front of me was a Pole pointing a rifle at me. He spoke a little German and asked what I was doing. I explained, pointing to the schoolhouse and saying: "That is my home. I want to go over there to find out whether my parents and three sisters have returned."

He looked me over before making up his mind, "Go across the old wooden bridge down there, that way you won't get your feet wet." He meant the bridge I used to cycle across on my way to Siegersdorf station. I had assumed it would have been destroyed in the fighting. For a long time the River Queis had formed the main front line between the Soviets on the Hermannsdorf side and the Germans defending Siegersdorf on the western bank.

I thanked the Pole and clambered slowly down the railway embankment. I went over the old wooden bridge and made my way straight across the meadows to the schoolhouse – only to find it deserted. It was filthy, the kitchen full of straw and manure. The piano and harmonium were standing in the open in front of the house. The furniture had been reduced to kindling and the windows broken. In the utility building outside, a firing slit for a machine gun had been knocked through the wall of the laundry room and a pit dug in its tiled floor. The trees in the orchard had been felled and trenches dug between the stumps. But the well and its pump were thankfully still intact and fresh water was available. Such was the state in which I found my home upon my return.

There was no trace of either Gisela, my parents or my three sisters. All I could do was wait. I made a bed for myself on a ripped-open settee and two blankets that I found in the attic. I slept like a log. The next day I explored the neighbourhood. Some farmers' wives had returned with their children. They told me something of what they had suffered, of rapes and murders committed by Russian soldiers fuelled by alcohol.

There was no food. We lived on potatoes that had been stored in a clump from last year's harvest and which the Russians had not found. They were small, shrivelled tubers which had already started to rot. We collected grain from the fields where stalks from the previous year had withstood the winter and had re-grown. We also collected mushrooms, blueberries and cranberries in the woods. One afternoon when I returned from the woods, the ten-year-old son of my neighbour came running out to me: "Norbert, Norbert, come quickly! The Russians want to loot."

I ran with him back to the farm and was faced by a young Russian soldier who was leading a gang of some fourteen Polish youths between 14 to 16 years of age. The Russian carried a machine pistol, the youngsters two bulging sacks. I went straight up to the Russian and demanded: "What do you think you are doing here? I... policeman appointed by Russian commandant. If you make zap – zap –zarrap... then my boys go to commandant and you...", here I made the sign for a rope round the neck, which was clear enough.

They had not expected to be confronted by a policeman. The Russian immediately assured me that they did not want to steal but only to find something to eat. I told him that we did not have any food ourselves. He went to the two sacks, opened them and pulled out a side of bacon and some meat, which he wanted us to cook. We shared both bacon and meat, which the farmer's wife prepared with some potatoes, while the gang of youths sat in the yard outside. Then the Russian asked me, "Do you have vodka?" I did not have any but remembered that amongst the broken glass in our larder I had found an unopened bottle of 'Herz-Punkt-Vier', a patent heart medicine, which I had kept. That tasted like alcohol, I thought.

I led him to the schoolhouse where I retrieved the medicine bottle and showed it to him. He did not want to steal anything but insisted on paying for it. But first I had to take a swig from the bottle. Then he sampled it and wanted to buy. He reached into his breast pocket and pulled out a bundle of newly printed 100-Mark notes and started counting them out in front of me on to the table. Every so often he asked, "Enough?"

I answered "Njet!" – one of the few Russian words I knew – waiting until he had only a few notes left in his hand before saying "Karascho" – OK. He had no idea of the value of the money. He went away satisfied. I wasn't too unhappy either: 3,500 Reichsmarks – approximately £300 – in cash, which I carefully hid in my room. Then the gang departed.

At the beginning of August I was blueberrying in the woods when I saw an old man in the forest pulling a handcart. He was looking around helplessly, but hadn't spotted me. I made my presence known and went over to him, asking if I could help in any way. He answered yes, saying that he came from Thomaswaldau, the neighbouring village to Hermannsdorf, but had now got lost trying to find his way home. I was able to put him back on the right track and chatted to him about the universal subject of interest between strangers in those days 'where to and where from'. The old man mentioned that he had spent the previous night in the house of a teacher's wife, who had three daughters with her and apparently hailed from this area.

I thought I must have misheard. With growing excitement I asked him to repeat what he had just said. He stuck to his story, insisting that he had stayed in Nieder-Seifersdorf, a village near Görlitz, with this woman and the girls in a small house which had been damaged by artillery fire. He could not recall their name. I had to investigate this lead at once. I thanked the old man and hurried back to pack a few things and say goodbye to the neighbours. Early next morning I set off back to Görlitz by train over the same route which had brought me here. Trains heading westward were ignored by the Poles in Kohlfurt. At Horka the train stopped. I got off, took to the road and asked the locals where Nieder-Seifersdorf was and the quickest way to get there. The shortest route was via Niesky; nearly 15 kilometres. A farmer gave me a lift on his cart and put me down in the village.

Here I enquired after a woman refugee with three children and was directed to a small house on an estate where I discovered my sister Maria in the garden. I whistled our family tune, a sign of recognition between all of us. Her head shot up. She saw me in the village street and a second later was in my arms in tears. I was howling too. But they were tears of joy at being reunited. I asked about father and mother and my other two sisters. She told me that mother was inside bedridden with serious concussion, while my sisters were still at work on a farm nearby. Father had been conscripted into the Volkssturm and had been declared missing after a battle involving Soviet tanks in Thomaswaldau. Gisela had arrived a few days before they had first fled from Hermannsdorf and had escaped with them, but had then travelled on to Luftwaffe area HQ in Dresden to report.

Mother had to be carefully prepared for the news of my arrival. She had been injured after driving a pregnant woman to hospital in Görlitz. On the return journey the horse had shied and thrown her off the carriage on to the road where she had lain unconscious until found some time afterwards. She was brought back three days later, her head heavily bandaged. She was now being looked after and tended by a local nurse, but could not be moved.

Two days after my arrival in Nieder-Seifersdorf the village was searched by green-capped NKVD soldiers and all the men were taken away. I put my faith in my release paper and reported voluntarily. They took us to some old air-raid shelters in Niesky which the NKVD had converted into a prison. Here, during my first interrogation, I produced my release paper. The interrogating officer took it and read it. He then called for a guard, who kept a large-calibre pistol pressed against the back of my neck as he escorted me into a pitch-black room in the cellars. The next day I was brought before the interrogating officer again. He now had my file in front of him. My release paper was returned to me and I was allowed to leave. After I got back to the house the family discussed the next course of action. We agreed that I should travel with my three sisters to Uncle Mieke's at Altenhausen, leaving mother in the care of the nurse until she was able to travel. We would then come back and collect her in three weeks time. I gave the nurse 300 RM for her trouble. The next day we four set off on our journey.

In Altenhausen I had managed, with Uncle Mieke's help, to change my job as a labourer and now worked on a larger farm where my sisters and mother could also be accommodated. I took over the running of the cow shed with fourteen cows. The three girls also pitched in; Barbara worked in the household, Maria drove a cart pulled by draught-oxen and my youngest sister, Elisabeth, was a nanny. It was Bärbel – Barbara – who drove back to collect mother three weeks later in order not to risk my being arrested again. In the first week of every month I had to report to the commandant's office in Haldensleben.

In the meantime autumn had arrived and the fields were being tilled. I was busy ploughing with the draught-oxen one afternoon when Maria, who knew where I was working, suddenly appeared with Gisela! I left the oxen standing where they were and rushed to take her in my arms. She too was to stay at the farm and look after the running of the kitchen at Elly Müller's, whose husband was still missing.

Gisela later told us of her odyssey. She had escaped from Heiligenbeil by plane and made her way by train to Silesia. She had even visited my father while he was in Bunzlau with his Volkssturm unit. She had then got to Hermannsdorf just in time to flee with mother and the girls, before going on to Dresden. She had been in the city on the night of the now infamous raid but managed to escape alive from the inferno. From there she travelled to relatives in Berlin, where she learned that her mother was in Holstein. Having gone up there and found her mother safe, she then journeyed the length of Germany down to Eva in Garmisch to search for me. She had been tracing my carefully signposted route northwards ever since.

Next Günter and Jochen sent word. They had found each other up in Holstein on the farm of an acquaintance and had been waiting for news from Uncle Mieke in Altenhausen. As soon as the first message from them arrived, we immediately sent word in reply and they turned up shortly thereafter. With Günter driving one of the horse-drawn wagons and Jochen looking after the pigsty, the whole family was now together and working on the farm.

Gisela and I had decided to marry at Christmas. We wanted now more than ever to build a future together. And when in November it was announced that trainee teachers were needed, we applied for places because we could not all work on the farm indefinitely. We chose Christmas Day as our wedding day, because we could only be spared for one day from cow-shed and kitchen duties. The farmer's wife was agreeable and happy to help with the wedding reception.

On the floor of the 'parlour' lay a large carpet – a good 4 x 5 metres – which the farmer's wife refused to hide, despite our warnings. Nobody could have prevented its confiscation if the Russians clapped eyes on it. On Christmas Eve 'Mama', Gisela's mother, arrived by train to attend the wedding celebrations. We had just seated ourselves at the large table to celebrate in the candlelight of the Christmas tree, when we heard the knocking of rifle butts outside on the farm gate – Russians! Mama was completely unsuspecting: "Who is knocking so loudly on the door, my dear?"

"Those are Russians, dear Mama. We must all go upstairs quickly," Gisela replied, hurriedly helping to gather the tablecloth with all the pastries and little presents together. Günter and I meanwhile made our way slowly to the front door calling loudly. When we opened it we were faced by sixteen Soviet soldiers who demanded to be let in to stay overnight. They simply barged in and would not be put off. Their leader, a sergeant, demanded to see all the rooms. We showed them to him. He decided to spend the night with all the soldiers in the parlour, as the carpet was large enough to provide a bed for all of them. We were helpless to prevent this. They moved in and stayed the night stretched out on the carpet.

On Christmas Day morning they were up and about by 9 o'clock but showed no signs of leaving. I went to the sergeant and explained that we needed the room ourselves at lunchtime. He asked why. I told him that there was to be a wedding and that otherwise there wouldn't be enough space for everyone. He then said that he wanted to celebrate with us, which was the last thing we needed. After much persuasion we got him to line up his men and march them off. We breathed a sigh of relief. But – surprise, surprise – in the corner of the room someone had left their gun behind. Nothing could be worse, it would give them a perfect excuse to return. So I grabbed it and ran after the column which had already reached the end of the village street. I shouted and hollered, until the sergeant noticed me and looked back. I showed him the machine gun, holding it by the barrel. He halted his men, searched for the miscreant, took the gun and ordered them to march on again. I don't know whether this had been a deliberate ploy of his, or simply negligence on the part of one of his soldiers; either way, we had got rid of them and could now start the wedding preparations.

From the village policeman, a former waiter, we three brothers had hired black suits including a dinner jacket and a top hat for myself. Gisela wore a dress fashioned from white parachute silk. Our mothers, my sisters, Uncle Müller and his family and a few friends all dug out their best clothes. At 1.45 pm precisely, to the sound of bells, the bridal procession made its way on foot from the farm to the village church. And at 2 o'clock Father Brützel began the solemn service. Gisela looked lovely and I looked like an extra out of a Fred Astaire film. The organ played, after which Erna Müller, the gifted violinist of the family, and Egon Maul – who under a different name was to become a famous singer on the Berlin radio – gave a rendition. A laurel garland in the form of a heart had been placed in front of the altar into which bride and groom had to step before the ceremony. This elicited from my brother Günter the clearly audible aside, "Stepped in it already."

Uncle Mieke, the atheist, explained in simple terms to my mother the special features of the church's interior, while we listened to the priest and both loudly answered the all-important question in the customary way. We exchanged rings and were now married. Afterwards it was back to the farm. There a veritable banquet had been laid on. Laughter and lively conversation filled the whole room. There was so much to talk about and so many experiences to relate.

When it started to get dark Günter ordered, "Outside for the honeymoon!!!" We wondered what was going on as we made our way out into the yard. There, in front of the landau, stood the two dappled draught-oxen, named after a pair of local Nazi leaders, held by my sister Maria. The landau's two lanterns had been turned inwards to illuminate the married couple in the open carriage. In the centre of the village the road circled the village pond. This was our honeymoon route. The guests had armed themselves with saucepan lids and with much loud banging and crashing we started off. People in the village, fearing the Russians had returned, bolted their doors and gates. It was a truly splendid trip to round off a wonderful day. The next morning I was back – minus the topper – milking our cows in the barn.

At the beginning of January 1946 I once again had to report to the local commandant in Haldensleben. There were the usual questions by the interrogating officer, who compared my answers with entries in a file. During the questioning, when he had been called outside for a moment, the German secretary – whose son had attended the air college at Werder with me – quickly whispered: "Herr Hannig, your file has been requested. Need I say more?" Then the interrogating officer returned and let me go.

If my file had been requested then my departure to the Soviet Union as a 'specialist' was imminent. I was not prepared to suffer another, possibly even longer, separation from Gisela and my family. I hurried home, packed a rucksack and went to the station where I asked the station master to stop the next refugee train passing through from Berlin to Marienborn so that I could climb aboard unseen on the other side. He duly obliged. This time nobody had accompanied me to the station to avoid attracting attention. After an hour I crossed the border into the British zone. Shortly before Marienborn the train happened to stop in an open stretch of country. I jumped off, as I had no desire to be taken to a refugee camp.

Gisela had given me the address of her Aunt Mieze, who had been in charge of the officers' mess in Heiligenbeil and whom I knew very well. She had since found a home in Rendsburg in the far north of Germany and that was my next destination. I was made welcome and put up on the couch while I looked for work and food.

At the post office I chanced to bump into Fritz Harder, the courier pilot of the Weihe runabout aircraft of our old Geschwader, JG 54. Our chat centred around the usual and because I had not yet found work, he came up with a suggestion: "I'm still officially a prisoner of war in a British camp in Nortorf. That's where they put together working parties of prisoners to work for the British armed forces. The man in charge of this is an Oberst Treskow. I am sure he'll take you on. You'll get paid, plus clothing, a place to sleep and good food. I'll take you along if you wish." That was exactly what I needed. I thanked Aunt Mieze for her hospitality and, leaving my new address with her, went along to the camp at Nortorf.

For a third time I voluntarily became a prisoner of war. I was now about to get a taste of British captivity, having already experienced what the Americans and the Russians had had to offer. I was accepted and assigned to a working party as team leader. I received pay, wore British Army battledress, lived in a small room in a camp of Nissen huts behind Castle Gottorp in Schleswig, and for the moment my most urgent daily worries were over. I immediately sent for Gisela, as she would be allowed to live with me in my room.

As team leader I did not have to work myself, but was responsible for overseeing the work and keeping discipline. The first job involved clearing out the barracks at the Schleswig-See naval aviation base. All the wooden furniture was carried out of the rooms into the barracks yard, where a British soldier rendered it unusable by putting his foot through a back panel, or a door, or in some other way. Pictures and frames ended up on the bonfire. Then the whole lot was doused in petrol and set alight, despite there being thousands of German refugees nearby who would have been delighted to have just one stick of this furniture.

The iron bedsteads were taken away by lorry, as were the mattresses. Gisela and I could do with one of the latter. So I told one of the working party to feign illness and lie down on a good horse-hair mattress. This was then used as a stretcher to put him in the ambulance for transport back to the barracks at Gottorp. The British guard on the gate at Schleswig-See allowed the vehicle to leave without question. It then pulled up in town so that the 'patient' could get out and have a day off. And we ended up with a very good mattress.

Our second assignment was to dismantle a landing strip made of perforated steel plates. This had been laid out in the grounds of a magnificent farm estate near Lindaunis for the use of an RAF air vice-marshal. A British company was still billeted in the main building. Their mess was in a barracks block close by. Although our soldiers were supplied with cold rations, they had got into the habit of collecting and eating the leftovers from the plates of the British troops placed in the open windows of their mess. When I discovered this I at once had my party fall in and declared that as of now nobody was to collect and consume half-eaten food. If they did, they would face dismissal and thus lose all the privileges they otherwise enjoyed by working for the British. This had the desired effect and was understood by all.

When the British personnel noticed that nobody was coming to eat the leftover food in their mess tins any more, a master sergeant approached me and asked the reason why. I replied quite reasonably that if they wanted to let us have additional food, it would be most appreciated – but only if it was done in a proper manner. From then on the men were given a supplementary meal from the field kitchen. I politely refused a kind invitation to eat in the mess and continued to eat with my party.

I established closer contacts with some of the liaison corporals. They were all straight, likeable and intelligent people. They visited Gisela and me in our barracks block. When they noticed that our cooking pot consisted of a large tin, and that our plates were made of flattened tins too, they smuggled crockery out of their own kitchens and brought it to our room hidden inside their battledress. Gisela was pregnant, a fact which could no longer be disguised. Because we had neither nappies nor a pram, they brought us items such as cigarettes and coffee which we could exchange on the black market for all the baby essentials. They helped us entirely of their own accord, for which we were extremely grateful. But at the end of July our work was completed, much to the regret of all – including our employers – and the working party was dissolved. Everyone was to be officially released from their prisoner-of-war status. For our discharge we were driven to Neustadt, where I received my British release documents on 9 August 1946.

My third period of captivity was at an end, and for me the war was finally over.

Postscript

Phoenix from the Ashes

It was ten years before I sat in an aircraft cockpit again.

Those who had said, only half-jokingly, before Germany's surrender, "Enjoy the war, the peace will be terrible," were not that far wrong. By the spring of 1945 Germany's towns and cities, her industries and infrastructure, lay in ruins. The country itself was divided, the vast majority of the eastern population driven from their homes. But for all her citizens, whether in the east or west, the one overriding concern was one of survival. People left with nothing had to begin rebuilding their lives all over again.

With a young wife, and soon a baby son, to feed, my path in the immediate post-war years was little different from many thousands of others. We started at the bottom and slowly worked our way upwards step by step. In my case this entailed exchanging my job on a farm for that of heavy labour in an iron foundry. I then secured a position as a representative for a small oil company before becoming a messenger with the US-run High Commission of Germany (HICOG).

During this time the relationship between the USA and the USSR had frozen into the Cold War. It was decided that West Germany was to take its place within NATO and that a new Bundesluftwaffe should be formed to help defend Western Europe.

In 1955 I was invited to be part of that process. It was a tempting offer: re-entry one rank higher than that at the time of surrender in 1945, a four-month trial period which, if successful, would mean immediate promotion one rank higher still upon acceptance as a regular officer. Above all, there was the prospect of being able to fly again.

But like all tempting offers it had to be carefully weighed. I was now well established in the commercial world. Since the birth of our son Lutz in 1946, Gisela had presented me with two beautiful daughters, Roswitha and Jutta. We were now five. The decision to rejoin the ranks of the military could only be taken with Gisela's blessing. She gave it and supported me wholeheartedly throughout my second Luftwaffe 'tour'.

This began in January 1956 when I became a member of the first refresher course for ex-wartime pilots, CR-1, at Landsberg am Lech. The field and its surroundings conjured up memories of the Me 262. But I was not exactly being 'pressed back into my seat' as I chugged around the area in a North American T-6 trainer!

I subsequently trained and served as a flying instructor before being selected to attend an international officers' course at the Air University of the USA in Maxwell, Alabama. Pilots from over thirty countries took part. It was an unforgettable experience: not just the flying over Alabama and Florida, but the chance to meet and get to know so many different cultures and backgrounds.

Returning to Germany I served on a special staff tasked with setting up the Bundesluftwaffe's new Air Academy in Hamburg. But as there was a shortage of trained pilots for the force's newly-forming operational units, I volunteered for flying duties. Converting on to the F-86 Sabre Mk VI, I first instructed and was then appointed as a Staffelkapitän to Jagdgeschwader 73 in Oldenburg.

Among the initial plans for the Bundesluftwaffe was one for the establishment of six light Kampfgeschwadern to be equipped with the Fiat G-91. I was to take command of the fifth of these units and was schooled on the Fiat at Waffenschule 50 in Erding for the purpose. But when a shortage of personnel prevented the plan from being fully implemented, I landed instead on the staff of the Department of the Luftwaffe in Cologne/Wahn. This was followed by a posting to the staff of the 4th Allied Tactical Air Force (4 ATAF) at Ramstein.

After several years serving with American, French and Canadian officers in 4 ATAF, I was transferred to the General Staff of the Luftwaffe in Bonn. Here I was introduced to ministerial work and experienced the traumas and crises involved in the introduction of the F-104G Starfighter into German service.

While still on the active flying list I opted for early retirement and spent the next eleven years employed in the aviation industry. Since 1981 I have worked from home as a freelance consultant. Now, sitting on our balcony with the 'girl in the blue hat' beside me, I am content to enjoy the view across Lake Constance to the Swiss Alps beyond.

Or am I? Spectacular as the mountains are, my eyes often travel upwards to the blue skies and billowing clouds above – one last yo-yo, perhaps?

Appendix

10 Commandments Governing the Conduct in War of the German Soldier

(Original text taken from the inside cover of the Luftwaffe pay-book)

1. The German soldier fights fairly to win victory for his people. Acts of cruelty and unnecessary destruction are unworthy of him.
2. The combatant must be in uniform or be identified by a specially introduced, clearly visible emblem. Fighting in civilian clothes without such a marking is forbidden.
3. No opponent who surrenders may be killed, not even irregulars or spies. These will be suitably punished by the courts.
4. Prisoners of war may not be mistreated or abused. Weapons, maps and diagrams are to be confiscated. No other possessions may be taken.
5. Dum-dum bullets are prohibited. It is also forbidden to make such ammunition by adapting normal rounds.
6. The Red Cross is protected. Injured opponents are to be treated humanely. Doctors and field chaplains may not be hindered in their medical or pastoral work.
7. The civil population is inviolable. A soldier is not permitted to plunder or deliberately to destroy. Historic monuments and buildings used for religious services, the arts, sciences or charitable purposes are to be particularly respected. Goods or services provided by the population may only be used when so ordered by a superior and only against recompense.
8. Neutral territory may not be included in acts of warfare either by trespassing, overflying or shelling.
9. If a German soldier is captured he must give his name and rank when asked. He may not, under any circumstances, divulge information about his unit, or about the military, political and economic conditions in Germany. He must not be persuaded by either promises or threats so to do.
10. Contravention of the above orders in official matters is punishable. Violation of principles 1-8 above by the enemy should be reported. Acts of retaliation are permissible only if ordered by a higher military authority.

GERMAN OVERVIEW OF THE EASTERN FRONT, SUMMER/AUTUMN 1944

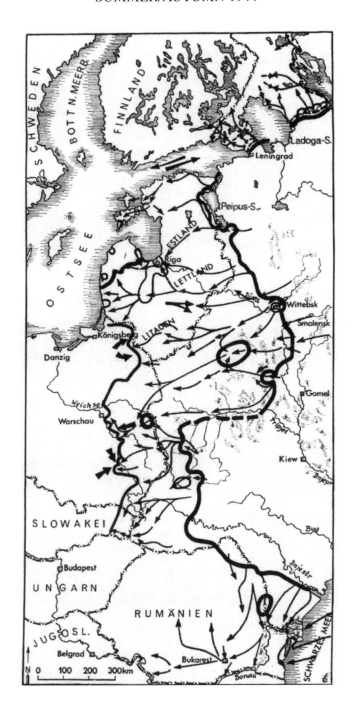

Index

Stackpole Military History Series

Real battles. Real soldiers. Real stories.

Stackpole Military History Series

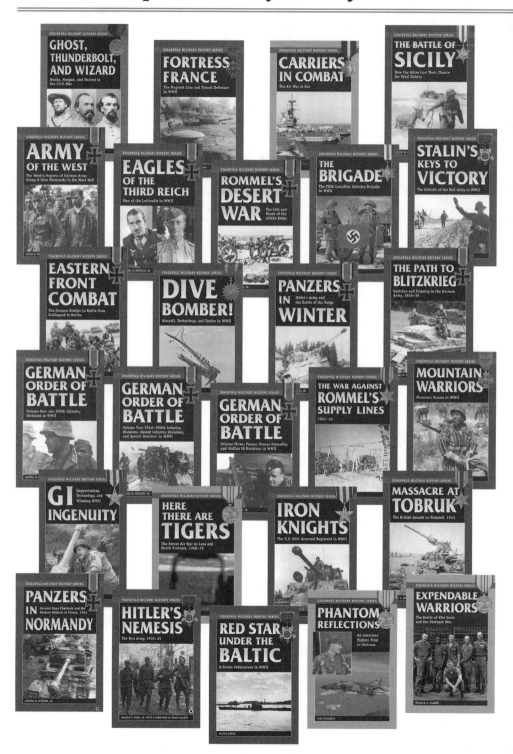

Real battles. Real soldiers. Real stories.

Stackpole Military History Series

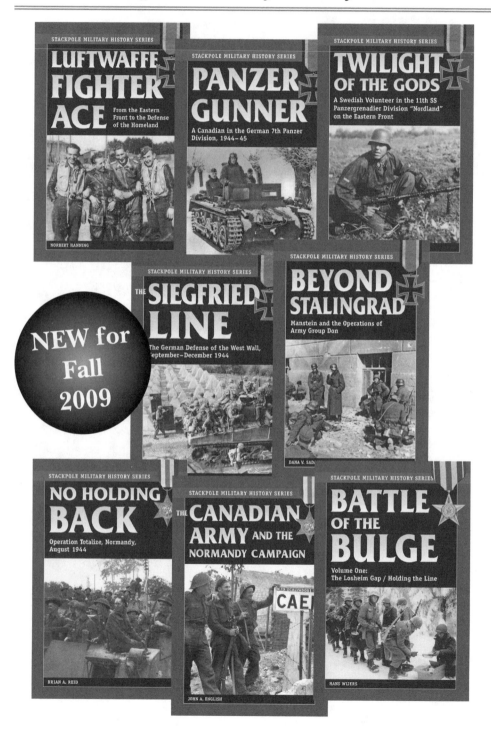

Real battles. Real soldiers. Real stories.

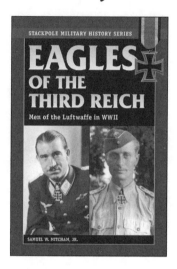

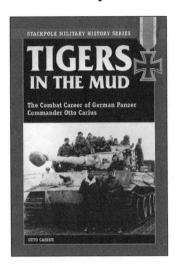

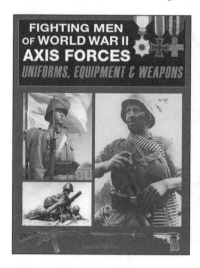 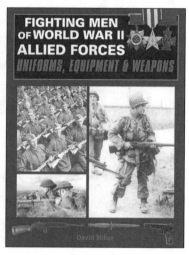